TOXIC RAGE

A Tale of Murder in Tucson

A.J. Flick

WILDBLUE
PRESS

WildBluePress.com

TOXIC RAGE published by:

WILDBLUE PRESS
P.O. Box 102440
Denver, Colorado 80250

WILDBLUE PRESS is registered at the U.S. Patent and Trademark Offices.

ISBN 978-1-947290-85-3 Trade Paperback
ISBN 978-1-947290-84-6 eBook

Interior Formatting/Book Cover Design by Elijah Toten
www.totencreative.com

TOXIC RAGE

INTRODUCTION

Oct. 5, 2004, became a day I will never forget – for two big reasons.

It was a Tuesday, and it began much like many other workdays for me. I had been with the now defunct *Tucson Citizen* since October 1993 and was the reporter assigned to cover the courts. Most mornings I spent at Pima County Superior Court sitting in on trials, hearings, sentencings and—my favorite part—combing through court files. On that particular Tuesday, after spending the morning at Superior Court, I decided to take a side trip on my way back to the newspaper by visiting Pima County Juvenile Court to look up some records.

So it was about a quarter past 2 when I finally headed south on Park Avenue on my way to the paper. About a block away from the newspaper plant, a car pulled out in front of mine, and we collided.

It took just a couple of minutes for police to arrive, since there was a substation two blocks away. Nobody was seriously hurt, although the other driver, a young woman (driving without insurance and having caused a similar accident months earlier) was so hysterical that officers called for an ambulance. I went back to the paper to write a couple of stories. Afterward, I called a couple of friends and told them what happened. They proposed meeting at a sports bar at North First Avenue and East Prince Road that was our favorite hangout. A cold beer never sounded so good to me.

It was about 6:30 p.m. when I arrived. Over the course of the next several hours, more friends came in as they heard about my accident. I don't think I bought one drink that night.

I know my friends sure made me feel better about being in my first car crash. We stayed until midnight or so, and then my friend drove me home, heading up North First Avenue a few blocks. We saw some big spotlights up ahead but assumed it was nighttime construction or perhaps an accident. We dismissed the sight as we turned east to the apartment complex where I lived at the time. It'd been an eventful day, and I was glad to call it a night.

The next day, one of the biggest crime stories of recent years broke loose. Around 10:30 the night before, a young doctor was found slain at a medical complex on North First Avenue just south of River Road. This was about a mile from where I was the previous night. Wow. That was kind of spooky. And it explained the spotlights, because the cops would have used them to investigate the scene. But who hasn't heard about something bad happening when you can say, "Oh my gosh! I was just there (fill in the time lapse) before that happened!"

At that point, I didn't have anything to do with covering the murder of Dr. David Brian Stidham. It was still a story being followed by our cop beat reporters. However, I—like most Tucsonans—followed the updates over the next two weeks with great interest. I was not only interested because I knew this would be a big story that I would be following once a suspect was arrested and indicted, but because it was so unusual for someone of Dr. Stidham's station and character to be killed. Ten days after Dr. Stidham's death, two suspects were arrested. The suspects' identities were a shock, especially since another doctor, Brad Schwartz, was one of the suspects. Shortly after the arrests, the *Citizen*'s then city editor, Ann Eve Pedersen, suggested that I start compiling any background information I could find on Dr. Stidham, Dr. Schwartz and the alleged killer, Bruce Bigger. She proposed a magazine-style article that took the three lives up to the point where their paths merged, which turned out to be one of my favorite articles and a popular read.

Over the next three years, the Stidham murder case became the primary focus of my beat. It wasn't the biggest murder case I had ever covered—that distinction came to me in the spring of my senior year in high school, believe it or not, and has yet to be eclipsed. It was a case in which I saw—for the first time—how emotion and politics irreparably warp the criminal justice system. In the summer of 1978, three Casa Grande brothers broke their father, Gary Tison, and another inmate, Randy Greenawalt, out of the Florence state prison. Over a two-week span, Gary Tison and Greenawalt killed a young Yuma family and Colorado newlyweds. The state launched its biggest manhunt to date, ending in a roadblock shootout in which the oldest brother was killed and his father escaped, later to be found dead in the desert. The surviving brothers and Greenawalt were tried in Yuma, which I covered for the TV station I worked for. They were each sentenced to death. Greenawalt was eventually executed. The brothers were resentenced to life years after the publicity died down and two judges from another county weighed what the brothers actually did compared to what they were accused of. Even then, one of the judges said the only thing holding the brothers in prison was politics.

The Tison case taught me that there is always another side to the story—even if most people don't want to see it. Would the Stidham murder case fall victim to the frailties of the American criminal justice system? We would see.

Even today, you can't talk to too many people in Tucson before you find someone who had known either Brian Stidham, Brad Schwartz or both. Many Tucson parents had taken their children to either or both doctors. Their stories run the gamut between revelation and revilement.

"Dr. Schwartz saved my child's eyesight!" a bowling alley employee told me one Sunday when she heard I was writing this book. "He's a great man!"

Many of my co-workers had meet Schwartz. One couple came away with bad feelings when Schwartz told them their child needed surgery. "There are only two who can save your child: God and me," Schwartz told them. "And God's busy." Another co-worker said she never got any negative vibes from Schwartz. He was extremely professional when she took her children there, she said. And, though this woman is attractive, he never came on to her, contrary to the womanizing behavior otherwise reported.

Brad Schwartz has never granted any interviews. After he was sent to prison, though, he did answer letters from me, always stressing his innocence, questioning the integrity of the judge and the prosecutors, wondering why no one bothered to investigate whether the victim's widow who seemed to know about his murder before she was told about it or a career criminal committing armed robberies and carjackings in the same area where Dr. Stidham was killed could have been involved in the murder.

Schwartz has many explanations for things that came up during the trial. A huge knife that a woman claimed to have seen on the alleged hit man's bike was a BBQ set. When he spoke to a man about getting something "taken care of," it was referring to his offer to examine the man's children. Most often, he blames the victim's widow for Brian Stidham's death.

"I am innocent!" Schwartz claimed.

The case still continues to attract national attention, too. It's been the focus of several true crime shows, and, not too long ago, my former editor told me that a true crime TV show was looking for me. When I made contact, I was surprised that it was this case that the show was interested in. After all this time, I asked a producer, why this case? "The cast of characters," he told me. "You can't make this up."

In 2018, yet another true-crime show is re-examining the case: "Missing Time" on the Discovery ID network.

At the same time, this case continues to surprise me with its twists and turns. Recent court filings have presented yet another accusation of a conspiracy to commit murder, from one of Schwartz's main accusers.

The information in this book was gleaned from law enforcement reports, transcripts and other documents within the public domain from related criminal and civil court cases, trial testimony, newspaper accounts of the case and independent research.

Some of this information has never been presented outside of court documents. Some of this information jurors didn't hear. Some of this information people involved in the case don't want you to know.

CHAPTER 1

On the morning of Oct. 6, 2004, in Tucson, Arizona, Lourdes Lopez was getting ready for work and listening to the news on the radio when she heard about a murder that occurred overnight. Her heart skipped a beat. Throughout her law career as a prosecutor and now criminal defense attorney, she wasn't unfamiliar with the situation of hearing about a heinous crime on the news and then having the case land in her lap. But this was different. What few details were being related over the radio concerned Lourdes. They, too, were all too familiar. A man was found dead in a medical complex at First Avenue and River Road the night before. His Lexus was missing. While the report didn't mention the victim's name, Lourdes knew in her now deeply troubled heart that she might have known him.

"Please God," she whispered to herself. "Don't let it be Brian. Just let it be some other poor person."

Lourdes's fears weren't just sympathy for someone who had just been killed, but terror that she knew the killer—a man she almost married. He had spoken often of wanting to have his rival killed ... could he possibly have carried out his evil wish? Lourdes remembered countless times over the past two years that the threats had been made and the countless times that Lourdes dismissed them as ranting of a man pushed to his limits. Brad Schwartz, the man Lourdes had broken off her engagement to just months ago, couldn't have had Brian Stidham killed, she reasoned. But the more she told herself that, the more she remembered his lies, lies that led to the doom of their relationship and, perhaps, Brian Stidham's life.

Tucson, for all of its worldliness as a metropolitan center pushing a million residents, still thinks of itself as a small town. There may be drive-by shootings in certain parts of town that don't garner much attention, but this murder was different. It was at a midtown medical complex off a busy street where thousands drive each day. This murder topped all of the newscasts that day and was a front-page story in the afternoon daily, the *Tucson Citizen*. Lourdes couldn't shake the fear that she thought the murder victim was Brian and that Brad had ordered his death somehow. Lourdes tried to go about her normal business that day. She was working as a criminal defense attorney, but she'd spent years at the Pima County Attorney's Office as a criminal prosecutor. That's what she was doing when she met Brad Schwartz, who saved her foster daughter's eyesight, and began an on-and-off affair with him. Lourdes spent the morning of Oct. 6 in depositions downtown, but as she was heading back to her office that afternoon, she got the idea to call Brian's office. Maybe Brian wasn't killed, she thought. Maybe she's just overreacting. It was just an eerie coincidence that Brian had an office in that medical complex and drove a Lexus, right? Lourdes dialed Brian's office, pretending to be a parent who needed to make an appointment to see Dr. Stidham and hoping against all odds that the person who answered the phone would happily make that appointment. Instead, Lourdes heard a glum voice at the other end of the line.

"There's been a tragedy. Dr. Stidham has been killed."

Lourdes froze. This couldn't be happening. This doesn't happen in Tucson. To her. To people she knows. There have been many twisted turns in Lourdes's life, but this was just too bizarre to be true, right? How could someone she had loved so much that she wanted to convert to Judaism and marry have someone killed? If the victim had been anybody but Brian, Lourdes would never have thought Brad had anything to do with it. Her mind raced. If Brad did do it, and her gut told her he had, would he remember all the times he threatened to kill Brian in front of her?

"I'm gonna fucking get him," Brad had said to her earlier that year. "That fucking guy's gonna die. He's gonna fucking die."

Brad, a talented eye surgeon with a once-thriving practice, had brought Brian to Tucson from Texas to take over the children's eye surgery while Brad focused on the adults and other pursuits, such as plastic surgery. But the deal went bad when Brad was caught writing illegal prescriptions for Vicodin, a growing addiction to soothe his own shoulder injury (Lourdes had filled some of the prescriptions and was asked to leave the prosecutors' office when she was charged along with Brad in federal court). While Brad was in court-ordered rehab, he turned the entire practice over to Brian. Instead of maintaining Brad's lucrative practice, Brian decided to go off on his own. That infuriated Brad, and in the two years since, it had become his obsession to seek revenge. Sometimes, Brad had said he wanted Brian humiliated— perhaps by someone finding child pornography in his office. But other times, the threats were intimately sinister, including talk of having Brian killed at his new office and have it look like a break-in or fatal carjacking. By the time Lourdes and Brad broke up in May, his threats against Brian occurred almost nightly.

The more Lourdes thought about it, the more she convinced herself that Brad had somehow ordered Brian's death. She wondered if he was crazed enough to have Brian killed, would he want people eliminated who had heard him talk about it? Lourdes's name had to be on top of that list. Lourdes called her brother-in-law and asked him to stay at her house that night, just in case Brad came over and threatened her or the kids.

Lourdes, who knew Brad Schwartz better than anybody, knew it was just a matter of time before he made contact with her. The night after Brian Stidham's murder, he called and asked to come over.

"I need to show you something," Brad said. "I need to come over."

Despite her misgivings, Lourdes allowed him into her home, where he called up news reports about the murder on her computer.

"I didn't have anything to do with that, Lourdes," he said.

"I need you to leave my house," Lourdes said, trying to hold her ground.

"OK, OK," Brad said. "But please, Lourdes, come outside with me. Please."

Lourdes followed Brad out, but kept within eyeshot of her brother-in-law, in case she needed his help.

"Lourdes," Brad said. "I had nothing to do with it. Look me in the eyes. Lourdes, I didn't do anything."

"Please," Lourdes begged. "Please, Brad, just go."

Lourdes *knew* that Brad had Brian killed. She didn't know exactly how, but what really scared her was what she should do now. To have Brad hounding her for sympathy, for support, was only confusing her and adding to her agony. Typically for Brad, he called her constantly from that night on.

"I need a friend to talk to," he pleaded with her. "You are my friend. I need you. This is such a hard time for me."

Lourdes knew that she was Brad's only friend. He trusted her. But did she trust him? Their relationship began with a lie—Brad told her he was divorced, but he wasn't. Their affair—one of many Brad had throughout his marriage—led to his divorce. Lourdes knew that Brad wasn't faithful to her, too. So Brad lied to her. Brad dragged her down into the rapidly spinning decline of his personal and professional life, thus forever altering hers. Does this mean he's capable of having someone killed? As much as Lourdes didn't want to believe it, she was certain he did have Brian Stidham killed. But she also still loved Brad Schwartz. She couldn't trust him, and she wouldn't marry him, but could she hurt the man she loved by accusing him of cold-blooded murder? Brian Stidham, the talented eye surgeon and young husband and father of two, was dead and didn't deserve to die by someone else's hand. What would she do? What could she do? Lourdes just didn't want to believe that his threats were true—because had she taken them seriously, would Brian Stidham still be alive? Lourdes spent her days defending criminals accused of horrible crimes. Could she have let a killer get so close to her without knowing what his intentions were? Should she call the police? Brad denied anything having to do with Brian's death. But Lourdes knew he did. She just wasn't sure what she should do. So, for now, she did nothing.

CHAPTER 2

There's an inside joke in Tucson that nobody here is a native. Of course, that's not true, but you can talk to hundreds of people before you find someone who was actually born and raised in the Old Pueblo. In the 1940s and 1950s, swarms of Easterners descended upon Arizona for health reasons. The dry desert air was considered much better for those plagued by lung problems. That no longer was true in the last half of the 20th century as those transplanted Easterners often brought with them all the non-native plants that caused allergic reactions in the first place. Still, Arizona keeps attracting its share of visitors who prefer the "dry heat" and—most prominently—its mild winters to the humid summers and snowy winters of other regions. Winter visitors—snowbirds, Arizona residents call them, sometimes not in an endearing way—often set up houses in the desert as well as their hometown. Many visitors fall in love with the desert so much that they end up moving there. Tucson is no exception. Bounded by the Catalina Mountains on the north, the Rincons on the east and south and the Tucson Mountains on the west, it's a growing community bordering on a 1 million population mark, but still considers itself a small town.

Brad Schwartz probably never dreamed that he'd live in a place so different than New York. Staten Island, N.Y., has had a small, but thriving, Jewish community since the turn of the 20th century. Adding to that, many Jewish families moved from other New York boroughs to Staten Island in the mid-1960s as the island's farms gave way to developments, thanks in large part to the opening of the Verrazano-Narrows Bridge in 1964 that linked the island and Brooklyn. Henry and Lois

Schwartz were one such couple. Bradley Alan Schwartz was born on Jan. 14, 1965, in Brooklyn, but spent his youth on Staten Island.

The Schwartzes kept Kosher, meaning that they adhered to the dietary restrictions of the Jewish faith. The Schwartz kitchen had different sets of dishes, cooking utensils and pans and silverware for meat and dairy products. This is a tradition that Brad Schwartz maintained through his adult life, at least as far as his family life went. Those who dined with Schwartz and his family found that innocently mixing the dishes would arouse Brad's anger.

Henry Schwartz taught social studies, geography, economics and political science to high school students in the New York City public school system for 35 years until he retired in July 1996. His wife, Lois, worked in the administration at a large brokerage firm for 10 years until she retired. Henry and Lois Schwartz were determined to put their children through college, which Henry admits wasn't easy on a teacher's salary. Henry and Lois Schwartz eventually moved to Florida near their daughter, who became a nurse and had two children, one with autistic tendencies. The retired Schwartzes became very active in the lives of their two Florida grandchildren and their three Arizona grandchildren as much as they could, they say.

Later, Brad Schwartz would say that there was no type of abuse or neglect during his childhood and no one in the family had ever been involved in the criminal justice system. As a boy, Brad showed interest in baseball and basketball and the Boy Scouts. Eventually, he achieved the rank of Eagle Scout.

Brad attended public schools until he was enrolled in a private religious high school in New Jersey. After graduating from high school in 1983, Brad enrolled in the State University of New York at Binghamton, where he studied history and math and graduated at the top of his class in 1987.

He was accepted into the University of Rochester's School of Medicine, where he graduated in 1991.

While at Rochester, Brad met and married Joan Samuels, who graduated from the private university's prestigious Institute of Optics. The couple was married on May 3, 1991, in Cedarhurst, N.Y. The young Schwartzes set off for Norwalk, Conn., where Brad accepted an internship in internal medicine at Norwalk Hospital. After that, Brad became a resident in ophthalmology at the Medical College of Virginia in Richmond, where the couple's first two children were born, Ariel in August 1992 and Rayna in June 1995. In Brad's last year in Richmond, he was chief resident of the ophthalmology department. While in Richmond, Brad began suffering tremendous dental pain that required a total of eight root canal surgeries, two extractions and surgery on his jaw and sinuses. Despite the medical treatments that included prescription painkillers, his pain wouldn't go away.

Once Brad was given a fellowship in pediatric ophthalmology at the Wills Eye Hospital in 1995 in Philadelphia, Joan was free to abandon her optical engineering career for full-time motherhood. A year later in July 1996, Brad accepted a second fellowship in neuro-ophthalmology at Allegheny General Hospital in Pittsburgh, where he remained in the ophthalmology department until the middle of 1998.

Perhaps in part lured by warmer climes and the fact that Tucson is the hub of the optics industry, Brad and Joan Schwartz then moved to Arizona, where he accepted a position from a Phoenix-based ophthalmology group to open a southern Arizona office. Brad planned to take the town by storm—and he did. But in the process, some say, he rattled a few too many cages. The stage was then set for the crest of Brad's professional life and the resounding crash of his personal life.

CHAPTER 3

Far from the urban clatter of New York City's boroughs sits the sleepy East Texas town of Longview. Like many Southwestern cities, Longview owes its life to the railroad.

Brian Stidham and his friends, who grew up in the 1970s thinking they lived in Dullsville, might have been shocked to know that Longview once was a rowdy railroad town with about half the early town comprised of saloons and gambling dens. The notorious bank-robbing Dalton Gang once visited Longview in its early days—and was subsequently run out of town on horseback by gun-toting residents. The public school system that Brian, born Aug. 13, 1967, attended experienced a growth spurt in the 1950s, but his high school wasn't integrated until the fall of 1970. When Brian was a toddler in 1969, optimistic city leaders hoped Longview's population would crest to 116,000 by 1985. But when Brian and his friends became Longview High School's Class of 1985, the town numbered around 75,000.

"It's 75,000 and holding," says Porter Howell, a musician who grew up in Longview and later met Brian through a mutual Longview friend. "Nothing changes."

Many of the kids who attend Longview's public schools keep their friends for a lifetime. For Brian, his closest circle of friends merged in the eighth grade. Brian grew up in a supportive but ambitious family. He was named after his Uncle David, but never called David. Whatever Brian put his mind to he accomplished. For instance, Brian was not a natural musician. But he wanted to play the drums and by the time he was in middle school, intimidated rival drummers including Duane Propes. Propes was in the eighth grade at

Judson Middle School when he first encountered Brian, who was playing drums for the Forest Park Middle School band.

"He used to whip my butt," Duane told the *Tucson Citizen*.

When the two boys were sent to Longview High School, they called a truce.

"It took us by complete surprise that we got to be buddies," said Duane, who later co-founded the hit country band Little Texas along with Porter Howell.

"We had a common bond," Duane said. "But he was so nice about it. We just hit it off."

Music came naturally to Duane, not Brian.

"They called me the wonder drummer," said Duane. "But he had to fight tooth and nail to compete.

"But he worked his tail off to be perfect, and by our senior year he was all-state, and I was the alternate second chair," Duane recalled. "I had to go sit in the audience and watch him with his mom and dad."

Any jealousy Duane might have felt was overpowered by friendship for the shy doctor-to-be.

"We became best friends and every day, we'd hang out together," Duane said.

With their mutual friend, Joe Little, Brian and Duane enjoyed the small delights of their small East Texas hometown.

"We washed his truck, hung out, spent a lot of time doing homework, running around," Duane recalled. (So far as anyone knows, the only time Brian got into trouble with the law was when he was caught with liquor at age 20 in Georgia. His prosecution was deferred, according to the Texas State Board of Medical Examiners, which licenses physicians.)

Hanging out together included sharing big dreams of their futures.

"When we were probably freshmen, everybody knew that Brian was going to be a doctor, Joe Little was going to be a lawyer, and I was going to be a musician," Duane said. "It was in the cards, and it was exactly what happened."

Coming of age in Longview in the 1980s wasn't always as boring as Brian and his friends imagined it to be.

"Longview High School could be a dangerous place," Duane recalled. "There were fights all the time. We grew up in that time where somebody would say, 'I'm gonna kick your ass,' you say, 'Well, all right, where do you want to do this?'"

Brian wasn't the kind of person who went around looking for fights, his friend said.

"Neither one of us were fighters," Duane said. "I think the last fight Brian was in was in the seventh grade."

By pursuing a career in medicine, Brian was following a family tradition. His namesake uncle was a physician as was his grandfather.

"It was just what he wanted to do," Duane said. "He had a calling.

"But he was a genius at that. He could do it easy," Duane added.

After Brian and Duane graduated from high school in 1985, they headed to Nashville together, where Brian enrolled in Vanderbilt University and Duane signed up at neighboring Belmont University. The two friends saw each other often during those early college years. Their college graduation would change all that, though, as Brian left Nashville to attend Harvard University's medical school. While Brian was fast-tracking through Harvard—graduating in three years—Duane and Porter Howell formed Little Texas with other Lone Star state refugees. Just as Little Texas was beginning to hit the charts, Brian was working in the residency program for internal medicine at Texas Southwestern Medical School in Dallas.

One year after arriving in Dallas, Brian switched from internal medicine to ophthalmology.

"Brian could have been a brilliant cancer research scientist," Duane said, adding that his friend spent a summer at the prestigious Johns Hopkins University.

Internal medicine meant too many emergencies, Brian figured.

"He told me he went into pediatric ophthalmology because he didn't want the phone to be ringing in the middle of the night," Duane said. "And he just loved kids so much."

Soon, Brian was ready to make a lifetime commitment of another sort: Marriage. He had noticed a pretty neighbor— "Brian never hung out with ugly women, I'll give him that!" Duane said—named Daphne Herding.

"His heart, his sincerity was so appealing, so approachable," Daphne Stidham told the *Tucson Citizen*. "He was easy to talk to and made me feel so good inside. I felt safe with him."

Brian and Daphne became early-morning running partners, spending many evenings sipping Japanese sake and sharing conversation.

Two years after they met, Brian and Daphne became engaged.

"He was engaged to another girl at one point," Duane said. "And we (his friends) didn't like her. It was, like, two weeks before the wedding and he bailed. It was a big Georgia society wedding, too. He said, 'I'm making a mistake. I can't do this.' So he got out, and we all said, 'Yay!'

"Daphne was different. Daphne is kind of like him: quiet, very reserved. She's a woman of few words. She chooses her words carefully. She just has a very sweet soul and is just a dear. She's hard to describe. She's ... just cool, you know," Duane said.

"And, she's gorgeous!" Duane added, grinning. "But you could tell that they fit. They meshed. They read each other's mind, that type of thing."

Duane was proud to serve as the best man at the couple's May 31, 1997, garden wedding ceremony at the Crescent Hotel in Dallas.

After a Hawaiian honeymoon, the newlyweds moved to Indianapolis, where Brian took a fellowship in pediatric ophthalmology and adult strabismus—eye misalignment—which would become Brian's specialty. After a year in Indiana, the couple returned to Texas, where Brian joined the faculty of the University of Texas in Houston. There, he reunited with his friend, Joe, who had indeed become an attorney, and eventually, his musical pal Duane, who was nursing a broken heart from a divorce.

Fatherhood came for Brian in the year 2000, when Daphne gave birth to their son, Alexandre Brian. Daughter Catherine Elizabeth would join the family in 2003.

Ever ambitious, though, Brian was constantly looking ahead. An ad in a trade journal caught his eye regarding a position in Tucson, Arizona, to help a fellow eye surgeon's pediatric practice. Brian couldn't wait to check it out.

CHAPTER 4

Brad Schwartz arrived in Tucson in September 1998 with the intention of establishing an office for a large Phoenix eye clinic chain as well as his own private practice. Tucson was a growing metropolitan community with only a couple of pediatric ophthalmologists at that time. What Brad might not have known when he signed on with the Arizona Pediatric Eye Specialists group is that Tucson ophthalmologists didn't want to have any part in a Phoenix operation opening within their city limits. That was strike one against Brad Schwartz, and that came before he even stepped foot in Tucson.

Kerri Delorme was assigned by APES' founder, Dr. Michael Pachtman, to help Brad establish the Tucson office.

"APES is a powerhouse of physicians, great surgeons, subspecialized surgeons," Delorme told the *Tucson Citizen*. "So here is a semi-small community of doctors and eye surgeons (in Tucson) being invaded by the big, bad APES. They weren't very receptive, but Dr. Pachtman handled it very well and went forward with the office.

"In the meantime," Delorme said, "we had Dr. Schwartz out there in the community ruffling feathers left and right. Very, very aggressive, wanting to meet and talk to them all. Why? To make his presence known. He was staying—no matter what. And with the financial backing of APES, it was easy. Now, if he had come on his own and behaved in that manner, he would have been bankrupt, if you know what I mean."

Part of Kerri's duties in setting up the office was to set up credentials with insurance plans, which she admits can try the patience of the most even-tempered people. Brad was not one of them. And he was not alone. Many physicians resort to temper outbursts when dealing with insurance companies. "I had become accustomed to Dr. Schwartz calling, screaming about something, and then he had gotten my voicemail at one point and left a vulgar message, cursing left and right. I do believe a medical director from an insurance company had denied a surgical procedure for a patient due to medical necessity. Well, *no* doctor, as you know, wants someone sitting behind a desk telling a surgeon what he can and cannot do. In this voicemail, he indicated that he could kill him, he was so angry."

Kerri reported the phone call to APES, which lodged a harassment claim against Brad on her behalf, though she was not offended.

Perhaps it was just the impetus APES needed to rid itself of Brad Schwartz. After his contract expired in a year, Dr. Pachtman chose not to extend it. That seemed to be fine with Brad as he planned to open his own practice, Arizona Specialty Eye Care. The problem was, his contract with APES had a clause in it that he wouldn't open an office within a certain distance of where APES had opened its office. Brad Schwartz not only defied that clause, he brashly opened his office in August 1999, a month before his contract expired, in the same neighborhood. APES sued Schwartz in Pima County Superior Court and eventually both sides settled.

With the patient load he'd built up with APES, plus being the only local ophthalmologist who works with ear, nose and throat surgeons and neurosurgeons to remove tumors of the brain, sinuses and eye socket, Brad had no trouble setting up his own practice. He also agreed to treat some patients without insurance for free. His pro bono work also extended across the border when he became involved with a group called *Manos de Ayuda*, which means "helping hands" in Spanish. The all-volunteer group set up a monthly clinic in Nogales, just across the U.S./Mexico border, and Puerto Penasco, Mexico—a seaside community popularly known in Tucson as Rocky Point—to bring modern medicine to children in the Third World. Brad was glad to be able to use his abilities to help the children he saw through *Manos de Ayuda*. Some of the Mexican women wove a beautiful tapestry for him, which Brad proudly displayed in his office. Locally, Brad also became the official ophthalmologist for the Arizona State Schools for the Deaf and the Blind and volunteered his services at the VA Medical Center. His community involvement also extended into his family life. The former Eagle Scout got his son into Cub Scouts and became active in his children's school lives as well.

Brad's dental woes also intensified around this time. Because he couldn't chew properly, he lost a lot of weight. In addition to managing a busy schedule at work, Brad also had to juggle his own medical appointments, which was challenging. In desperation, he turned to illegal prescriptions of Vicodin for the pain and Ritalin, for his attention deficit order, a poorly conceived solution that would soon enough come back to haunt him. Within a year, Brad also would experience sharp pains in his right shoulders and numbness in his fingers that would cause him to undergo spinal surgery.

In 2000, the Schwartzes' third child, Danielle, was born. By then, Brad and Joan's marriage was noticeably crumbling. Though some would say that the union was doomed from the start because of Brad's wandering eye, the marriage deteriorated rapidly after the couple moved to Tucson. In 2001, Joan filed for divorce after she reportedly caught him in the arms of another woman: Lourdes Salomon Lopez, who was a prosecutor with the Pima County Attorney's Office. Lourdes met Brad after she brought her foster daughter to him to treat her crossed eyes in December 2000. The attraction was immediate, she said.

"He had called me to see how (my daughter) was doing," Lourdes said. "We started talking on the phone and became friends and then we started dating."

Brad seemed to have a curiosity about the law, she said.

"We would talk about our professions," she said. "He would ask me how I would try a case. I guess (we'd talk about) the things you do when people are close. They talk about their professional lives."

During this time, Brad's practice was flourishing. Despite whatever the local medical community thought about Brad as a person, his specialty was greatly in demand, and other physicians referred many patients to Arizona Specialty Eye Care. By the summer of 2001, Brad had more patients, almost, than he could handle, and he was making more than $2 million a year. He was featured in an article in the *Tucson Citizen* for his part in treating a toddler whose parents took him to see Brad thinking he had a lazy eye. Brad saw something much worse, a cancerous tumor covering the boy's right eye. Once removed, the boy was fitted with a prosthetic eye and declared cancer-free. Brad even found the strength during this time to quit taking the Vicodin. His own doctor suggested prescribing painkillers stronger and more addictive than Vicodin, but Brad refused. When he had spinal surgery in November 2001, he took as few prescription pills as he needed and stopped taking them entirely two days after surgery.

With a clear head, Brad soon began to think about how he could expand his business, including, perhaps, doing some plastic surgery. The first step, he decided, was to find someone to take over the pediatric practice, so he could concentrate on adults. So Brad took an ad out in a trade journal for a pediatric ophthalmologist.

Brian Stidham saw that ad as an opportunity to move his career forward. His friend, Duane, wasn't so sure. Duane tried his best to talk Brian out of moving to Tucson, which the musician had visited with his band.

"Dude, I've been there," Duane told Brian. "Weird things happen there. I swear, there's an aura of evil to it. I wish you would think about this."

But Brian could not be dissuaded, especially after he visited Tucson.

"It's a beautiful place," Brian said. "I can live right there by the mountains and go hiking. It's a great deal for me there. The partner I'll be working with is ultracool. He's giving me the keys to the kingdom. It's going to be great. I'm going to be doing exactly what I've always wanted to do."

Daphne was also reluctant to move away from her family and home state. But she couldn't help noticing how instantly enamored Brian was with Tucson, from the minute he set foot there.

"He had never seen anything like the West, the cacti, the vibrant sunrises and sunsets," she told the *Tucson Citizen*.

"Honey, we've got to come here," Brian told Daphne. "We've got to stay here."

Brian gushed about Tucson's proximity to mountain parks, where he could go hiking. He especially loved a popular area called Sabino Canyon in the foothills of the Catalinas.

"The most beautiful things in life are free—love and family and nature," Brian said.

Daphne agreed to move their young family to Tucson.

"Our mission was to die there," Daphne said.

Brian wasted no time in becoming a vital part of Brad's practice. While Brad still saw some young patients because of his specialty in neuro-ophthalmology, Brian had no trouble filling up his schedule. Brian's love for children endeared him to anxious parents. He set the children at ease with colorful hats. Brian's casual demeanor often clashed with Brad's more formal style. On more than one occasion, Brad chastised Brian for his preference of wearing surgical scrubs even when he wasn't in surgery. Brad preferred a dress shirt and tie, believing it projected a more professional appearance, and told Brian he should adopt the dress code. Still, Brian preferred the more comfortable and casual blue scrubs.

Brian also was an instant hit in the medical community.

"Brian is a very nice, soft-spoken guy who most people liked very much," said Dr. Kevin Concannon, a pediatrician who also socialized with Brian and Daphne, said in a deposition. "I mean, you wouldn't—it didn't take very much to like Brian. You just as soon as you started talking to him, you go, 'He's a nice guy.'"

Brian didn't know that in coming to Tucson, circumstances had already been set into motion that eventually would cause his demise.

***

Some people say that doctors make the worst patients. When Brad was in the throes of his Vicodin addiction, he decided to take his own care into his hands. It didn't take much to convince Lourdes to help Brad out. Lourdes had migraine headaches sometimes and Vicodin helped her. So in agreeing to fill some prescriptions, Lourdes got to keep some of the pills. Brad also talked his office manager, Laurie Espinoza, into helping him out. He also obtained the names and birthdates of some of her relatives to fill more prescriptions, some for Ritalin, which Brad used to counter the effects of his attention deficit disorder.

When Brad called in a prescription for Vicodin in Lourdes's name in August 2001, red flags were raised. The pharmacist thought it was odd that this doctor was picking up a prescription for his patient.

"She's at a wedding on that side of town," Brad said. "So I'll just pick it up and deliver it to her."

When Brad arrived for the pills, the pharmacist demanded to see identification.

"I left it in the car," Brad said. "Be right back."

The pharmacist watched Brad leave the store and then, minutes later, drive away.

It didn't take long for the Drug Enforcement Administration to get wind of Brad's illegal prescriptions.

DEA Agent Marcus Brown called Lourdes at home on Oct. 22, 2001, in hopes of arranging an interview regarding prescriptions she filled for Vicodin on June 24 and July 10. There was no answer, so he left a message for her, saying that he needed an interview with her regarding "an important matter," but didn't leave details.

The next day, Lourdes left a response on Agent Brown's voice mail, identifying herself as an assistant Pima County prosecutor and consenting to an interview. The two eventually agreed to meet the following day at noon on the 10th floor of the Pima County Legal Services building, where Lourdes' office was.

Dave Wickey, another DEA agent, accompanied Agent Brown to the interview.

"Are you a patient of Dr. Schwartz's?" Agent Brown asked Lourdes.

"I see him informally," Lourdes replied.

"What do you mean?" Agent Brown asked.

"Dr. Schwartz treated my foster daughter, Veronica Rodriguez," Lourdes explained. "He gave her some eye drops."

"When was this?"

"I guess around December?" she said.

"Did Dr. Schwartz ever give you any prescriptions?" Agent Brown asked.

"No," Lourdes said.

However, she added, she had been seeing Brad "socially."

"Did Dr. Schwartz ever prescribe Vicodin for you?" Agent Brown asked.

"No," Lourdes said. "I've never had a prescription for a strong medicine like that. He may have given me some medicine for migraines, but I can't remember what the name of it is."

"How many times did you get that medicine?" Agent Brown asked.

"I can't remember," she answered.

"Did you get any Vicodin on June 24?" Agent Brown asked.

"I don't remember if I did."

"There are records from Walgreens that you did pick up some Vicodin on that day, and it was paid for by insurance," Agent Brown said.

"I probably did pick it up, then," Lourdes said.

Agent Brown told Lourdes that there was evidence that a similar situation happened on July 10, where a prescription of 150 pills of Vicodin was called in by Brad in her name and picked up by a man matching Brad's description.

"Did you get the pills?" Agent Brown asked.

"I don't recall," Lourdes said. "Sorry. I may have gotten Vicodin on a couple of occasions, but I can't remember when."

"Does Dr. Schwartz pick up the Vicodin for you?" Agent Brown asked.

"I don't recall."

"Did anything special happen to you around August 25th?" Agent Brown asked.

Lourdes said that she was a bridesmaid at the wedding of Kim Hunley, another prosecutor, around that time, but that she couldn't remember the specific date.

"On August 25th, Dr. Schwartz called in a prescription for 150 hydrocodone tablets in your name and told the pharmacist that you were attending a wedding on that side of town, and he would come in to pick it up for you," Agent Brown said. "When he arrived, the pharmacist asked him for ID. Dr. Schwartz said he left it in his car. The pharmacist watched him leave the store, get in a vehicle and drive off."

Both agents noticed that Lourdes wasn't surprised to hear about the Aug. 25 incident, including Brad's strange behavior.

"Did you ask Dr. Schwartz to call in a prescription for you?" Agent Brown asked.

"I don't remember," she said.

"On July 10th, a prescription was paid for in cash, $75.29. Would you have paid cash if you had insurance?" Agent Brown asked.

"I don't remember."

"You should be able to remember whether you got Vicodin, since, as you said earlier, that you didn't get that kind of medication for your migraines," Agent Brown said.

Lourdes looked down at her desk.

"You should ask Dr. Schwartz about this," she said.

"The Vicodin was called in to the pharmacies by Dr. Schwartz, but he was using your name," Agent Brown said. "You should be able to remember something like that. I could remember an oddity like that."

"That's you," Lourdes replied.

"Did Dr. Schwartz attend your friend's wedding?" Agent Brown asked.

"No."

"Do you remember asking Dr. Schwartz to pick up Vicodin for you on August 25th?" Agent Brown asked.

"The wedding day, it was very stressful," Lourdes said.

"Did you have a migraine that day?" Agent Wickey asked.

"Yes, I did."

"Did you see Dr. Schwartz the day of the wedding?" Agent Brown asked.

"Yes."

"Was it at his office?" Agent Brown asked.

"Near the office."

"You said you had been seeing Dr. Schwartz socially," Agent Brown said. "How many times a week do you see him? Once? Twice? Three times a week?"

Lourdes again dropped her head.

"There are certain aspects of my life that I would like to be left private," she said softly. "I do see Dr. Schwartz socially. Just leave it at that."

"Why can't you remember anything about Vicodin prescriptions?" the agents asked her.

"I can't remember," she said. "Talk to Dr. Schwartz. I'm not trying to be an obstructionist, but you should talk to Dr. Schwartz about this."

"I have to inform you," Agent Brown said, "that this is a federal inquiry, an investigation, and you shouldn't discuss this meeting with Dr. Schwartz."

Lourdes looked puzzled.

"I can't talk to Dr. Schwartz about this?" she asked.

"No," Agent Brown said sternly. "This is a federal inquiry, an investigation,

and Dr. Schwartz doesn't have to be informed about our meeting."

"If you are giving me a directive," Lourdes said, smiling, "I won't discuss this meeting with Dr. Schwartz."

"The only exception," Agent Wickey said, "is if you tell your supervisor, or whoever's above you in the chain of command here."

"OK," Lourdes said.

"And I would urge you to look for that Vicodin bottle from June 24," Agent Wickey added.

"OK, I will," she said. "And I'll tell my supervisor immediately about our meeting."

The agents thanked her and left the office, suspicious of Lourdes' lapses in memory about the Vicodin prescriptions.

***

In December 2001, agents burst into Brad's office. Brad was out of the office, but Brian was there, and clearly startled.

"What's going on?" he asked as agents began seizing records and charts. Whatever problems Brad had been having, Brian said later to Laurie Espinoza, he had no clue that the DEA was involved until the raid.

Brian had been seeing patients, but the DEA agents demanded that every activity halt while they searched the office. Not only did that upset Brian and the patients, but the medical office staff as well.

Unbeknownst to anyone in the office at that point, Brian had been having some serious concerns about working with Brad.

"The raid scared the hell out of me," Brian confided to his friend, Kevin Concannon, a pediatrician. "I mean, I haven't been here for that long, and these guys come in, grabbing everything, taking all the charts, disrupting the patients and the staff. What the hell is going on here? Sometimes I think it's not worth it. I should just go back to Texas."

"Don't give up," Kevin urged. "This isn't the end of the world. Brian, you're a very good surgeon. Tucson needs a pediatric surgeon like you. Don't leave Tucson just because Brad Schwartz is an odd fish."

Brian definitely didn't want to leave Tucson. With Kevin's advice, Brian explored thoughts of setting up his own practice in Tucson. Kevin set Brian up with a practice manager, who could help him transition into his own office. He'd even found a suitable space, a vacant office in a medical complex on North First Avenue near East River Road.

***

The DEA investigation added to the strain of Brad's marriage. In April 2002, Brad and Joan decided to separate, and he moved out of the home. They agreed that he would pay $2,000 in alimony and $4,000 in child support at first, which eventually would increase to $6,500 in monthly alimony.

During this time, another legal matter arose. Joan filed a lawsuit on behalf of Brad's practice against Laurie Espinoza, saying that she had embezzled money from the business by cashing a check without authorization. Laurie, in turn, filed a countersuit, saying that Brad mistreated his staff. Eventually, both sides settled when Laurie agreed to pay the money back.

With Laurie gone, Brad called Kerri and asked her to drive down to Tucson from Phoenix because he was looking for someone to manage his office. On her way back to Brad's office, he introduced her to Brian Stidham. Kerri observed that baby-faced Brian seemed very polite and reserved, but there was a caution about him. Kerri also was bothered with Brad's admission that he was separated from Joan. Something was just not right about this, Kerri thought to herself. Things weren't stable in Brad Schwartz's life. She turned the job offer down.

***

The DEA made formal contact with Brad in May 2002, and he agreed to talk to them. He admitted writing the illegal prescriptions, but tried to lessen the involvement of Lourdes and Laurie Espinoza.

On May 17, Brad was arrested for shoplifting at the Tucson Mall. Other than a string of citations for running red lights, it was his only criminal infraction thus far. He passed it off as a case of absent-mindedness. The case was eventually dismissed.

***

Lourdes, meantime, took steps to protect her interests legally in the DEA case and hired Rafael Gallego, a well-liked defense attorney and friend. Gallego called prosecutor Russell Marsh with the U.S. Attorney's Office to arrange a meeting regarding Lourdes' statements to DEA agents Brown and Wickey the previous year.

"Miss Lopez wishes to cooperate in this investigation," Gallego told Marsh.

Brown and Wickey were summoned to Marsh's office on July 18, 2002, to meet with Lourdes and Gallego.

"I picked up 150 tablets of Vicodin that Brad called in on June 24th, 2001," Lourdes told the agents. "I paid for it with my insurance. But I only used some of the pills."

"How many?"

"A handful, I guess, maybe 10 to 20 tablets," she said. "Dr. Schwartz took the rest."

Lourdes told the agents that she knew she was going to "share" the pills with Brad before she went to pick them up.

"He was the one who suggesting that I take the Vicodin," she said.

"Did you pick up 150 tablets of hydrocodone on July 10th, 2001, that were called in by Dr. Schwartz and paid for in cash?" Agent Brown asked.

"I didn't pick up those pills," Lourdes said.

"Did you know that Dr. Schwartz was going to pick up those tablets?"

"Yes," she said. "I had to have known. I know that Dr. Schwartz picked up the pills, but I never saw them."

"Don't you think it's strange that he would call in prescriptions in your name and pick up the medication for his personal use?" Agent Brown asked.

"No," she said. "He said he was going to get it in my name."

"But don't you think that's strange?" he asked again.

"No," she said. "It's nice to have Vicodin around."

"Do you know that Dr. Schwartz tried to pick up 100 tablets of hydrocodone in your name on August 25th, 2001?" he asked.

"Yes," Lourdes replied.

"Why did you lie to us back in October?" Agent Brown asked. "You're not a very good liar."

"I know," Lourdes said. "I was caught off guard."

"What do you mean, you were caught off guard?" Agent Wickey asked. "The purpose of our meeting was explained to you in detail."

"You knew Dr. Schwartz was doing something wrong," Agent Brown said. "You knew it, because you kept asking us to ask him about it."

"Your answers aren't making any sense," Agent Wickey said.

Lourdes began to cry uncontrollably.

"Mr. Gallego," Agent Brown said, "does your client need some time to compose herself?"

"Yes, please," Gallego said, whisking Lourdes away for a 15-minute break.

Lourdes composed herself and faced the agents again.

"I lied," Lourdes said, "to protect Dr. Schwartz."

"Did you also lie because of the predicament he created for you?" Agent Brown asked.

"Yes," Lourdes admitted. "I really care about him. I really do. And I don't want to, you know, 'rat' him out. That's ... that's why I lied. That's why I told you to ask him, so that he could say what was going on, and I didn't have to."

Lourdes began to cry again, but quickly pulled herself together.

Russell Marsh asked Lourdes if she had told Brad about the meeting with the DEA agents, although she had been ordered not to.

"I did," Lourdes admitted. "But I don't want to go into any specifics about that."

Lourdes also told them Brad discussed his talk with the DEA with her.

"He said he'd told the investigators about my involvement," she said. "But ... I don't remember the rest. I blocked out the rest of the conversation."

"Don't you think it's strange," Agent Brown said, "that he implicated you to the authorities and that you blocked out what he said?"

"Can I have a five-minute break to think about the conversation?" Lourdes asked.

After the break, Lourdes told the agents that Brad had told the DEA that he wrote or called in prescriptions for her and that he got and used the medication and that she knew about it.

"He also told me," she said, "that he didn't want to tell the authorities about my involvement."

"Has Dr. Schwartz discussed the investigation with you?" Marsh asked.

"Yes, we've had a lot of conversations about this case," Lourdes said, the last being the night before.

"Do you realize," Agent Brown said, "that you've violated the directive that was given to you during the October 2001 meeting by telling Dr. Schwartz that you've met with investigators?"

Lourdes nodded.

"Yes."

"It's true, then, that you lied to us when we talked to you in October," he said.

"Yes," she replied.

"Don't you know that it's wrong to lie to investigators?" Agent Brown asked.

"Yes, I do," she answered.

"Did you know it was wrong and, in fact, illegal to allow Dr. Schwartz to call or write in prescriptions in your name and use the medication for himself?" Agent Brown asked.

"No," Lourdes replied, startling the investigators. "Even if it's in my name, I'd give it to him.

"I stand by that," she said.

Though Lourdes had promised to tell her supervisor at the Pima County Attorney's Office about her contact with the DEA, it wasn't until mid-July, after coming clean with the agents, that she notified the office. An indictment in federal court was likely to come, so Lourdes couldn't avoid hiding her secret any longer. The reaction from County Attorney Barbara LaWall was swift: Either resign or be fired. On Aug. 2, 2002, Lourdes resigned as a deputy county attorney. On

Sept. 26, 2002, she was indicted in federal court on four counts of helping Brad obtain illegal prescriptions.

Laurie was indicted on 36 counts.

Brad was indicted on 77 counts.

***

Kerri Delorme, who had worked with Brad setting up the APES office in Tucson, heard about his indictment through her mother, who lived in Tucson. Kerri decided to call Brad up to see how he was doing.

"I'm being set up by everybody," Brad complained. "I had nothing to do with all this."

Kerri shook her head, knowing that he had once asked her to fill a prescription for him under her name, but she had refused. She figured that if he had been taking the pills when he first got to Tucson, it must have been a long-festering problem. Why did it take so long for him to get caught? Kerri wondered.

On Oct. 12, 2002, Brad voluntarily enrolled in a 30-day treatment program at the Cottonwood de Tucson rehabilitation complex, where he met Dr. Mark Austein, a specialist in addiction medicine. After Brad left Cottonwood, the two physicians stayed in touch and became friends. Mark thought Brad to be a competent doctor and was so confident about his relationship with Brad that in December 2003, he loaned him $40,000, to be repaid with interest, with the final payment due in February 2006.

"A friend of mine had a drug problem that's been resolved," Brad told Mark when he asked for the loan. "But he has a cash flow problem."

In January 2004, Mark loaned Brad another $20,000 that Brad said he needed while he was divorcing Joan. As collateral, Brad put up his office building.

Brad never missed a payment up to October 2004. Mark also sold his white Cadillac Escalade to Brad for $38,000, to be repaid in regular payments. Mark thought the loans were the safest he could make because Brad was a successful surgeon whose income was rising rapidly, despite the setbacks to his personal and professional lives.

***

Two days after leaving Cottonwood, Brad left Tucson for the Chicago-area Rush University Behavioral Health treatment program for doctors with addictions. Brad was embarrassed by his addictions and lied to his staff and patients about the reason that he was going to be away for so long. For whatever reason, Brad told them that he had a brain tumor and needed to get surgery in Florida.

Because he anticipated being away for several months, Brad turned to his parents and Joan to help keep his office running while Brian was given the task of handling all the patients. Lois Schwartz also helped her daughter and grandchildren in Florida, so Brad's parents made arrangements for Henry to stay for a month while Lois would join him for about a week, then return to Florida.

Each morning, Henry Schwartz went to Brad's office to check the mail and find out anything important that had to be passed along to his son in daily phone chats. One day, Henry was shocked to hear that Brian intended to open his own practice and was handing out business cards to patients. Brian even was trying to recruit some of the staff members to come with him.

"It really rankles me," Henry told Lois, when she arrived. "I feel he should be terminated because of this."

Lois, who had experience in human resources, agreed. The Schwartzes decided to break the news to Brad, who called them that night at his bachelor apartment.

"He should be fired," Lois told Brad point-blank. "It's unethical what he's doing, and he should be fired."

"This is intolerable," Henry added.

"Watch out that he doesn't take more than his things," Lois warned. "I think you should just kick him out! Who knows what he could do with the computers?"

"All right," Brad said, "call Brian into the office and let's talk about this tomorrow."

The next day, Henry and Lois consulted with Laurie, who showed them the business cards that Brian was handing out. Brian was summoned when Brad called in the afternoon.

Brian admitted he was starting his own practice and didn't fight the dismissal.

"What about the patients?" Brian asked. "There are patients waiting to be seen in the lobby?"

"Don't worry," Brad said. "If there's a problem, we'll tell the staff to send them to the hospital. But you need to pack up and leave. Just leave, now. Don't take anything. We'll have everything that's yours sent to you."

By the time Brad returned to Tucson, on Valentine's Day, 2003, he was seething mad at Brian for leaving the practice just when Brad needed him the most. Not only did Brad have to contend with the fallout from the DEA case, but he had to salvage what was left of his practice.

In addition to his professional woes, Brad's relationship with Lourdes, which had always been topsy-turvy, was becoming more and more contentious. Both their tempers exploded on June 24, 2003. Brad was driving the Escalade while they were arguing and pulled over into the parking lot of a convenience store, where he tried to push her out of the SUV. Alarmed bystanders called police, who cited both on misdemeanor domestic violence charges.

Even after the police came, Lourdes was still hysterical. She had no way to get home, so she called on her good friend, Brad Roach, a prosecutor she had met at the Pima County Attorney's Office. Notwithstanding the disapproval of his wife, Brad Roach drove out to rescue and comfort Lourdes. Lourdes had no sooner taken a seat in Brad Roach's car when her phone rang. Lourdes cried even more when she saw Brad Schwartz's name flash on her cell phone.

"Don't answer it," Brad Roach told her. "Lourdes, just be done with it. It's not worth it. He's dragged you by your hair, hauled you out of his car, what more do you want? Do you want him to beat you to death? Let it go, Lourdes. I'm tellin' ya, he's not worth it! You deserve better than that!"

But the more Lourdes ignored the calls, the more persistent Brad Schwartz was.

"Just leave me alone," she told Brad Schwartz in a quivering voice. "Go away, Brad. Leave me alone. No, it's over, Brad. It's over. I don't want to see you. I don't want you to come to the house."

Brad Roach could tell that the message wasn't getting through so he grabbed the phone from Lourdes.

"Listen, you son of a bitch," Brad Roach snarled into the phone. "Stay away from Lourdes. She doesn't want to be near you. She doesn't want to have anything to do with you. Stay the fuck away."

"Brad," the voice on the other end said calmly, "this has got nothing to do with you. This is between Lourdes and me."

Brad Roach was shocked at how unemotional Brad Schwartz sounded, especially since Lourdes sounded like she was on the verge of a nervous breakdown.

Lourdes did notify her pretrial services officer at the federal court about the fight with Brad and the citations, which eventually were dismissed. As a result, the officer suggested that Lourdes stay away from Brad Schwartz, which Judge Bernardo Velasco later made formal.

Two days after the incident at the convenience store, Brad's attorney in the DEA case, renowned Tucson defense attorney Mike Piccarreta, asked Brad to write a letter detailing everything that had happened to him. Piccarreta thought the letter could be useful to explain Brad's actions if a trial should come about. On his home computer, Brad wrote up this memo:

6/26/03

Here is a partial list of the adverse consequences of my crime:

Indictment on 10/8/03 brought crime to public attention. I had not used any medication illegally in over a year before indictment—as documented with clean urine tests

I was immediately and summarily suspended by every hospital in Tucson without investigation

I was dropped by almost every health care plan in Arizona.

I was ordered by the Board to go for an inpatient stay for substance abuse problems. First, I was sent to Cottonwood de Tucson for 1 month followed by a 3 month stay at Rush University Behavioral Health professionals program even though no substance abuse issue was current.

My former business associate (Dr. Stidham) started his own practice while I was hospitalized and took four of my full time employees with him. He has badmouthed me to the physician community while he openly advertised the grand opening of his practice and placed his business cards and announcements while I was in Chicago at Rush.

Dr. Stidham plotted with Laurie Espinoza to get him credentialed on all health care plans behind my back while I was hospitalized. She also gave him all of my forms that I have designed and utilize in my office and have copyrighted.

Laurie Espinoza embezzled over $10,000.00 from my office while I was hospitalized and is currently being investigated by the Tucson Police Dept. Fraud Unit.

My patient population (which totaled over 15,000 patients is now dissipated. They have gone for care to other doctors/competitors.

I have paid over $175,000.00 in legal expenses, health (care) costs related to my inpatient stays in rehab.

My monthly income prior to my indictment was over $100,000 monthly. Because I have not worked since October 8, 2002, I have lose over $900,000 in pay (not including the above mentioned legal and health care costs.

I have gone through a painful divorce.

I have 3 small children who were kept from seeing me for the 4 months I was in rehab.

I have suffered shame, humiliation, and essentially excommunication from the medical community in Tucson.

My career in Tucson is likely done. I will have to relocate to another city if I am to practice. This will be all but impossible to do because it will require getting licensed in another state.

I have suffered a career threatening injury that resulted in herniation of another disk in my neck and has left me with potentially permanent numbness in my left hand.

I am close to filing for bankruptcy and have over $100,000.00 in credit card debt.

I have suffered the guilt of knowing that I involved friends and loved ones in my crime that has impacted negatively upon them as well.

I have previously had 10 full time employees who have since had to seek work elsewhere. My practice provided income for their respective families and loved one. This is also a small part of the guilt I bear.

Inability to work at the job that I love more than anything.

Two frivolous lawsuits have been filed against me immediately after the indictment in cases that did not involve any medical wrongdoing. The respective plaintiffs attorneys are hoping to capitalize on my negative public image of reaching settlements.

When Piccarreta put Brad's list into a final version, he omitted the part about Brian Stidham.

***

Brad was ordered to appear before the Arizona Medical Board to account for the prescription drug charges on Aug. 14, 2003. He admitted that he used some patients to prescribe medicine for his own use. In one case, he ordered 1,200 Ritalin tablets for a mother and daughter who were patients and kept most of them for his use. And he admitted getting Vicodin fraudulently.

"It's been a long road," Brad told the board. "I haven't seen any patients since October 2002. I don't blame anyone else but me for my problems. No one forced me to take any pills. I've got a big problem, and I'm truly sorry."

Brad discussed his treatment and assured the board that he was fully committed to his recovery, including submitting to regular drug testing.

On Sept. 11, 2003, the attorney Brad hired to help with his medical license proceedings, Kraig Marton, told the board that Brad had been sober two full years.

In October, the Medical Board released its findings, noting that Brad's conduct could have harmed patients who put their trust in him. The board ordered a decree of censure, placing Brad on five years of probation. While on probation, Brad was ordered to submit a statement under oath four times a year that he is complying with its orders, had a year to complete the board's Physician Assessment and Clinical Education Program in narcotics and medical records, was banned from prescribing or storing strong medications and had to enroll in the Monitored Aftercare Program for physicians impaired by alcohol or drug use.

Other conditions included going to group therapy once a week, attending 90 12-step meetings in 90 days followed by a minimum of three 12-step or other self-help group meetings a week as recommended by his group therapist.

Brad could apply to prescribe medicines after a year, the board ruled.

Of course, the board ordered that Brad not drink any alcohol or eat anything with poppy seeds as well as submit to regular urine tests for drugs.

Around the same time, Brian gave a deposition in a lawsuit involving one of Brad's former patients.

"I thought I should have you look over some of my deposition," Brian wrote to his lawyer after the deposition. "Better late than never, perhaps. The case involves a patient that I saw initially and referred to Brad for surgery. I joined Brad in October of 2001, saw the patient in November of 2001 and the DEA raided the office sometime around December of 2001. I don't know what ultimately went wrong but I assume that the patient had a poor outcome. As I said, I (naively) was not expecting the 'what did you know and when did you know it' interrogation, so I have subsequently thought of things I wish I had said or had said differently. My basic thought is that at no time up to and including the present has Brad ever confided anything in me. I suspect that to this day if I asked him if he has ever had a drug problem, he would deny it. In many places in the deposition ... I state that he and I never had any discussions regarding his substance abuse or the drug charges beyond his initial explanation to me. I should have said that he never told me anything whenever I asked about it. Sometime around summer of 2002 someone told me that they thought his brain tumor was a ruse and that he had been in rehab. I asked Brad about it and he promptly denied it and nothing more was said. Also, some time the week before the indictments were made I asked him about it again and all he said was 'it's no big deal' and there was no further explanation given. Is that something I should have said in the deposition? I didn't think about it until afterwards, but you could say we 'talked about it' despite the fact that he never told me anything. In any event, I don't want it to look like I am withholding information. There have been so many rumors (mostly confirmed now) for so long, that I find it hard to remember when I heard something, versus when I confirmed it was true.

"Lastly, FYI, Brad just sued one of my employees (his former employee) for back vacation pay. I take it that times must be tough around the old office, but I guess if you can't collect from patients you might as well collect from the old employees. I find it hard to believe that he hasn't sued me yet for something. I also saw as a patient one of Piccarreta's employee's children and later operated on one of his employee's parents. They love to tell me where they work. I suppose just to see what my reaction will be. What a mess! When exactly is all this going to go away?"

Brian's lawyer, John Escher, soon contacted Kraig Marton, Brad's attorney before the medical board, with news that Brad had been badmouthing Brian.

"Did you say anything bad about Brian when you were at Rush?" Marton asked Brad. "Or did you say anything when you got back?"

"No, of course not," Brad said.

"Well, if you did, don't do it anymore," Marton advised.

***

Brad agreed in December 2003 to plead guilty to 74 of the 77 charges. He could have faced up to four years in prison and a fine of $250,000, but instead, Judge Velasco decided to delay sentencing for a year. Lourdes and Laurie got similar deals. If all three defendants can stay out of trouble for a year, Velasco said, then the charges will be dismissed.

Brad was ordered to pay a $7,500 fine, surrender his DEA registration to prescribe drugs, comply with all the conditions imposed by the Arizona Medical Board and give the government $40,000 as reimbursement for the costs of prosecuting him.

Though Brad confidently pursued plans to rebuild his career, he still harbored a festering anger over what could have been, had Brian Stidham not stabbed him in the back, so to speak, when Brad went into rehab.

"Brad," Lourdes said to Brad, "if the shoe was on the other foot, you would be doin' the same thing. You would be worrying about how you're gonna feed your family. So don't be so upset about it. Let the guy live his life. Show him up. You are a better doctor."

"Well how can I do that if nobody gives me patients?" Brad asked.

"Prove to these people you deserve a second chance," Lourdes cajoled. "Have some compassion."

CHAPTER 5

Brad knew he'd have to push his anger aside long enough while his practice returned. It would take some time, since his license was suspended, but he had to get things up and running and prepare for the time when he could practice again. He thought about Kerri Delorme, and how well she'd set up the APES office when he first arrived. Kerri was surprised to hear from him.

"You know, I had to go to Rush Behavioral in Chicago after spending a month in treatment here," Brad said, seething. "Remember Brian Stidham? Well, I come back from rehab and there are no patients. Brian's gone and took them."

Kerri had seen Brad blow his temper before, but she was disarmed by his attitude toward Brian. Eventually, Brad got back on track with his request to offer her a job setting up and managing his new office, as empty as it was at the time. Kerri turned him down as politely as she could, not wanting to burn any bridges. She told Brad that she had already made plans to move to New York state.

Though a handful of Brad's employees had gone to work for Brian, there were still a few loyal staffers who remained with him when Brad was ready. One of those was his physician's assistant, Nader Shami. Nader began working for Brad in 1999. By the time Brian came on board, the practice was incredibly busy. Twelve people were working in the office on Farness Drive. It was Nader's job to talk to a patient first to find out what the complaint was, do some visual testing, try to figure out the problem and help Brad with a diagnosis. He also prepared charts, got the patient's history and conducted eye exams.

Before Brian arrived, Brad was seeing at least 60 patients a day. The years 2001 and 2002 saw about 60 to 80 patients a day coming in to see both doctors.

In late 2002, after Brian left and Brad went into rehab, Nader got another job and occasionally worked with Brian. A year later, when Brad's practice was up and running, Nader returned to Brad because he liked his position and enjoyed working with Brad. He never saw Brad improperly prescribe medications or saw him scream, yell or throw tantrums. He would get mad if he saw sloppy work, though.

"He wanted things done right," Nader said.

In September 2003, Brad's practice was noticeably slower than it was before. But by mid-2004, business was picking up. Nader had joined at the same pay that he'd had before Brad left for rehab, and now got a good raise, along with the other employees. Brad was seeing about 25 to 30 patients a day.

Nader spent more time with Brad than any of the other employees and though he was aware that there was a split between Brad and Brian, never heard anything derogatory spoken about Brian.

Brad's plans were to expand his practice to include some type of cosmetic surgery. He agreed to have a cosmetician, Julie Herrington, come into the office to offer Botox and other facial treatments, which would bring in more profits to his practice. Brad set aside an area of the office for Julie's needs and began buying the equipment she needed.

Once Brad began seeing patients again, he called Lucia Sanchez. She had been let go in late 2002 when Brad went into rehab as the receptionist. Lucia, who never saw any tension between Brad and Brian, gladly went back to work for him at the front desk. He was a demanding boss, sometimes calling in anonymously to see how her people skills were in setting appointments and checking patients in and out, but he also was kind in many other ways, such as giving her advances on her paycheck when she needed it. Lucia was glad that he was back in business and that the numbers of patients grew each week.

Brad also relied heavily on Claudia Jane Huerta, who did medical billing at the old office. Claudia's daughter, Sharon Payne, started working for Brad in August 2000 handling eligibility referrals. Both women returned to work for Brad when he called them.

***

Lourdes was shopping at a grocery store on the South Side of Tucson when she spotted an old friend, Rosalia Humo. Lourdes's sister, Linda Salomon, worked with Rosalia at the Pascua Yaqui casino years ago, and Brad had performed eye surgery on Rosalia a few years ago.

"How are you?" Lourdes greeted Rosalia.

"OK, how are you?" Rosalia said rather glumly.

"Just great! What have you been up to lately?"

"Nothing," Rosalia said.

"Are you working now?" Lourdes asked.

"No," Rosalia said. "I don't have a job anymore."

"You know what," Lourdes said, "Brad's back in town, and he's starting his practice up again. I think he might be able to use you, like doing billing and so forth."

"Yeah, that could work," Rosalia said.

"Sure, give him a call," Lourdes said. "I'll tell him you'll call."

But Rosalia didn't call. Truth be told, she wasn't putting any effort into getting another job. But in late November 2003, Brad tracked Rosalia down at her grandmother's house. Rosalia didn't want to talk to him and tried avoiding his calls, but he persisted and after Rosalia's grandmother complained about his constant calls, Rosalia returned the call in January 2004.

"Come to the office," Brad said. "I'd really like to see you and talk to you about this job."

"All right," Rosalia agreed, reluctantly.

Rosalia enlisted her friend, Margaret, to tag along with her as they headed for Brad's office in the late afternoon. Brad greeted the women in the lobby and asked Rosalia to step back with him in the examination room because Rosalia asked him to check her eyes.

"It's good to see you again," he told her. "How are things?"

"OK."

"Have you been having any problems with your eyes?" he asked.

"Um, sometimes," she said. "Sometimes they bother me."

Brad proceeded with the eye exam.

"I can't help but notice your tattoos," Brad said.

Rosalia wished Brad weren't so chatty.

"Yeah," she said.

"Are those gang tattoos?" he asked.

"Yeah."

"When did you get them?" he asked.

"I don't know, when I was 14, 15. When I was young and dumb," she said.

"Wow," Brad said. "You know, it's been a long time since I saw you. Things have been going on that are just too weird, you know?"

Rosalia nodded, not wanting to ask the question to find out what exactly was going on. She just wanted to get out of there. But Brad didn't need prompting.

"I've got this huge, huge problem," Brad continued. "And I need someone to help me get rid of this problem."

"What's the problem?" Rosalia reluctantly asked.

"You remember that doctor I was working with? Dr. Stidham? He's the problem," Brad said. "He's practically ruined my life. It's been hell just getting back to where I am. Do you think you could help me?"

"Like, do what?" she asked.

"Well, I was thinking that if someone planted pornography in his office, because he's a pediatric ophthalmologist, it would land him in real hot water. Lourdes has told me that something like that could ruin someone for life. And it would get out into the community, into the papers, that this children's eye surgeon was caught with pornography in his office. It'd humiliate him, just the way I was humiliated when he turned me in over the drug thing."

"How would you do it?" Rosalia asked, her curiosity piqued.

"I could take a picture of my son, naked, and then we could plant it in Brian's office. Then call the cops," Brad said. "Maybe you could put it there, or you could get somebody else to do it. Obviously, I can't be the one to do it. And then we could maybe plant some illegal drugs in his office. Maybe you know where you could get some drugs and we could put them there, too."

"Yeah," she said. "Why are you so mad at him to do that?"

"He stole my patients," Brad said. "When I was in rehab, I lost half my patients and half my staff to Brian. You know, I pulled him out of Longview, Texas, to come here. I paid a hundred and twenty grand to relocate him. All I asked for was a little loyalty, and at the first sign of trouble, he splits and takes half of everything with him. He doesn't know how much harm I can cause him. I know where he works. He has an office at First and River. This little complex where it's dark when he gets off late at night. Do you think you could find somebody, one of your gang members, to kill him?"

"What?" Rosalia said, shocked.

"I want him fucking dead," Brad said. "Can you find someone? I need someone who can make it look like a carjacking. He drives a white Lexus, and he always parks it in the same place. Leaves late at night. It'd be nothing for someone to knock him off and take the car. The cops would think it's just another random killing. I'm sure you know people who do this sort of thing. I'd pay them, too. Half up front, half after. Do you think you can help me, Rosalia?"

"Um, I can see about it," she said, unsure whether he was serious or not. Rosalia thought the sooner she agreed with him, the sooner she'd be able to leave and hope never to run into him or Lourdes again.

"That's great," he said. "I'm sorry that the job that Lourdes told you about isn't open anymore. But we might be able to get you in here part-time. And I might be opening an office in Nogales."

"Yeah," she said.

"If that goes forward, I could give you a job," he said.

"OK," she said, grabbing her purse and heading for the door to the lobby, where Margaret was waiting.

"Did you get the job?" Margaret asked, seeing that Rosalia looked upset.

"No, they freakin' hired someone else," Rosalia muttered.

Rosalia decided that Brad couldn't have been serious, so she made no attempt to find anyone who might actually follow through with his scheme. She hoped that Brad would forget about the conversation, too, but after a few days, the calls started coming in again to her grandmother's house. Brad wanted to know if she found someone to plant the pornography or ambush Brian at his office. Rosalia put him off as much as possible, saying that she was still trying to find someone. Eventually, he stopped calling, much to her relief.

The first month of 2004 would prove to be a rough one for Brad. His divorce was being finalized, and he was stretched to the limit. He turned to his parents for help.

"Dad, I'm just pinned down, financially speaking," Brad said. "I've got to pay Joan alimony and even though a friend of mine, Mark, another doctor, loaned me money, I still need about $40,000 to consolidate some debts. My credit cards are maxed out."

"It's incredible what they charge these days," Henry said. "Makes it almost impossible to pay back those credit cards. Those interest rates are egregious."

"Can you help?" Brad asked.

"I'll talk to your mother and call you back," Henry said.

"The divorce, it's all his fault," Lois said.

"But he acted like such a gentleman through it," Henry added. "He didn't fight Joan at all."

"No, he didn't," she agreed.

Henry called Brad back with the good news that they would loan him the money.

***

As part of his road to recovery, Brad had to submit to urine testing, not only for the federal court, but also for the state medical board. There was a LabCorp testing facility near his office on Wyatt Drive, near Tucson Medical Center. One of the first people Brad met there was Carlos Ogas, a hulking yet nonthreatening man who had been a phlebotomist there for about three years. In the process of getting all the paperwork straight, Carlos and Brad would chat. Carlos confided how he'd been having trouble with his eyes.

"Come to my office," Brad said. "I'll see you, no problem."

Carlos did go and get a free eye exam at Brad's office. Brad prescribed some glasses, which Carlos never did get because his truck got stolen with the prescription inside it. Carlos also asked Brad for a loan once, for $2,000 with his truck as collateral, but was turned down.

One day in the summer of 2004, Brad came into LabCorp and asked to talk to Carlos in private, in the back of the office. Carlos complied.

"Carlos," Brad said, "do you know anybody who can take care of somebody for me? I'll pay them."

"No," Carlos told him bluntly.

CHAPTER 6

Lourdes Salomon Lopez is a first-generation Arizonan, her parents having immigrated to the border town of Nogales, Arizona, and subsequently became citizens of the United States. After high school, Lourdes married her sweetheart, Danny Lopez, then enrolled at the University of Arizona in Tucson. In 1992, the young mother of two became the first member of her family to graduate from college when she earned her Bachelor of Arts degree. That year, Lourdes and Danny also separated. Their divorce became final in 1995, while Lourdes was attending the UA's law school, where she earned a law degree and became a practicing attorney after passing the bar exam in 1997. Lourdes's first job as a prosecutor with the Pascua Yaqui tribe ended with her firing in 1999. But it didn't keep Lourdes down as she found a job as a low-level prosecutor with the Pima County Attorney's Office. There, she forged strong friendships with other young prosecutors who were working their way up the ladder.

The working mom also explored expanding her family by taking on foster children. In the winter of 2000, Lourdes was caring for a girl, Veronica, who had one crossed eye. The girl's pediatrician suggested Lourdes take her foster daughter to Dr. Bradley Schwartz, so Lourdes set up an appointment.

The attraction between Lourdes and Brad was instantaneous and intense. Brad's gentle and professional treatment of Veronica impressed Lourdes, who took note also of Brad's extensive medical background. Lourdes was also taken aback by Brad's charm. On first impression, Brad looked more nerdy than sexy. Slim, pale and red-haired with small spectacles over his green eyes, Brad didn't immediately evoke any images of a ladies' man. Lourdes, on the other hand, didn't waste any time flaunting her sexuality. Even in the courthouse, she strode around on stiletto heels, wore skirts as short as she could get away with and made ample use of her cleavage.

The day after Veronica's surgery, Brad called to ask how she was doing, which warmed Lourdes's heart. So, when he boldly asked Lourdes if she would consider going out with him, it didn't take much for her to say yes. They had barely met, but Lourdes was flattered by how open Brad was to her about his life. He told her he had just gone through a separation with his wife and was now getting a divorce. Lourdes was hooked. She was in love.

Several months after they began dating, Brad asked Lourdes for a favor. She had seen how much pain he suffered from torn rotator cuffs in his shoulder as well as pain in his jaw.

"My doctor doesn't understand," Brad said, "it's too much pain, and the Vicodin prescription he gave me isn't enough. I've run out and I need some more."

"What can I do?" Lourdes asked.

"I'll write the prescription, in your name, and you give me the pills," Brad said.

"You can do that?" she asked.

Lourdes knew that what he was asking of her was not right. But he was in so much pain, pain that she could relate to because she suffered from migraines on occasion.

"Come on, Lourdes," he pleaded. "You're the only one I trust to help me."

Lourdes agreed, as she always did when Brad asked for her help. Lourdes liked being the one her man depended on for advice. During times when the couple was the closest to each other, Lourdes was surprised with the thoughts that churned in Brad's head. Whenever Brian Stidham's name came up, Lourdes knew that Brad would say evocative statements, even going so far as to say he wanted to have Brian killed.

"Brad, morally, you can't do that," Lourdes implored. "You're not God. You don't get to decide who dies."

Lourdes saw that her argument was having no effect on Brad in easing his temper.

"Well, Brad, you know what happens in the movies when people get hired to kill? They always want more money. They always have something over you. There's always gonna be somebody pressing you when you least expect it. The police always have an angle you never think of."

"No, they don't," Brad said. "The police aren't that smart."

"Yeah, Brad, they are!" Lourdes said.

She could see that everything she said to counter this crazy notion wasn't sinking in to Brad. But then Lourdes shooed the threats away.

"This is not gonna happen," she told herself. "He's just blowing off steam. He wouldn't really do something like that. I know he wouldn't."

Another time, Lourdes asked Brad just who he thought he would get to kill Brian, as if Brad knew any hit men.

"What do you call those guys, Lourdes?" Brad asked. "What's the word? You know, the slackers, the guys who don't give a shit."

"Um, *huachos*?" Lourdes said.

"Yeah, that's it!" Brad exclaimed. "*Huachos!*"

"Brad, that's stupid!" Lourdes said. "Those are the worst kinds of people! If you're gonna have a drug addict do it, a drug addict's gonna want more money later."

Lourdes was grateful that Brad had gotten help for his addictions. She might have missed having the occasional Vicodin herself to put a harried day to rest, but she didn't like seeing him in pain and then masking his pain with the drugs. Plus, she was more than glad to put the federal drug case behind them both, so they could get on with their lives. Lourdes hoped that, having gotten through this ordeal of being arrested, indicted, etc., Brad's court- and medical board-ordered substance abuse rehabilitation would draw them closer.

She was wrong.

Lourdes felt like she was being pushed aside. Suddenly, Brad, who was required to go into group counseling, had other people to confide in, people who knew more about what he was going through as far as the addiction went than Lourdes did.

"What are you doing to us?" Lourdes would ask him. "I helped you, all this time while you were gone in rehab. I paid all your bills. I kept part of your practice going. I kept everything here for you. I made sure everything got paid, and I helped Joan with the kids, and I did as much as I could. And now that you're back, it's like your substituting me for all of these other people that were in recovery. I think that's good that you have these people to talk to, Brad, I do. In some ways, it's very good. But I want to meet them. I want to be a part of this, too."

But Brad brushed aside her entreaties. Of course, he was spending time with some of those people. And the brutal truth was, whether Lourdes chose to acknowledge it or not, he was seeing other women, too.

***

As part of his agreement with the DEA and Medical Board, Brad checked into Cottonwood de Tucson, a rehab facility on Tucson's far West side. Brad knew what to expect, having gone through the program at Sierra Tucson previously. In between classes, he struck up friendships with a few of his fellow rehabbers, among them, a 35-year-old housewife named Aisha Henry who also was being treated for an addiction to painkillers as well as depression. Aisha gravitated toward Brad often, enjoying his company and the fact that a near-stranger could confide so easily in her.

"I can't believe you're in here," Aisha said. "I mean, you being a doctor and all."

"I don't think I would be here," Brad said, "if it weren't for Brian Stidham."

"Who's that?" Aisha asked.

"The man who ruined my life," Brad said, his anger rising.

Brad explained how he had brought Brian in from Texas, and while Brad was in rehab, he was counting on Brian to take care of the practice. Instead, Brian walked out on him, stealing not only his patients, but his staff as well. Aisha would come to learn that the topic of Brian Stidham and how Brad perceived him as ruining his life would come up frequently in conversations.

"If something happened to him," Brad told her, "I wouldn't be upset. You know, if he got into an accident or got killed. It wouldn't bother me."

To Aisha, Brad appeared obsessed with Brian Stidham and seeking some type of revenge for the harm he thought that Brian caused him. These thoughts also would be aired during group counseling sessions.

After Aisha's five weeks at Cottonwood were up, she went to live in a group home for additional counseling while Brad, she knew, was headed for Illinois and a specialized treatment center. She hadn't seen him for several months, when, by accident, they ran into each other in Tucson. Aisha was with her mother-in-law, and Brad was with a beautiful woman Aisha assumed was his girlfriend, Lourdes. The two friends were happy to see each other and exchanged phone numbers, so they could keep in contact. Brad remembered that Aisha had told him she suffered from migraines and he offered to examine her eyes for free. Before long, Brad was calling Aisha, and they spent hours on the phone, chatting. Brad asked her to visit him at his apartment, which she did. Aisha was trying to reconcile with her husband, but the chats with Brad were becoming intimate, and Brad's apartment offered them both some privacy to explore their relationship. In Brad, Aisha found someone she could talk to about what she was going through with her husband. Aisha had found out that her husband had cheated on her and she told Brad every detail of their troubled marriage. Brad caressed Aisha as she poured her heart out to him. Soon enough, the snuggling led to lovemaking. Aisha figured since Dallas had cheated on her, it was her to turn to cheat on him.

Sometimes, they would cuddle together and watch TV— Brad was a devoted fan of the *Godfather* movies as well as the HBO series about mobsters, *The Sopranos*. Sometimes, Brad seemed to get caught up in the imaginary Mafioso world. And, she noticed with great chagrin, he still seemed obsessed with exacting revenge on Brian Stidham.

"You know what you could do?" Brad asked her once. "What if you took your son to his office and then accused him of fondling your son? Would you do that?"

"What are you talking about?" she asked. "That's crazy!"

"But would you do that?" he asked. "Would you do that for me?"

"Do what, exactly?"

"Take your son to Brian's office, for a regular visit," Brad said. "Then, when you get home, say that your son told you that Brian molested him and call the police."

"You want me to call the police and say that?" she said, not sure if he was just kidding or really serious.

"Yeah," Brad said. "Just think about how much trouble he'd be in. He'd be ruined."

"No," Aisha said. "No, I can't do that, Brad. That's wrong. That's just wrong."

"Come on," he said, caressing her. "Do it for me. You know how much he's done to me. Do it for me. Help me, please, Aisha. Help me. Do it for me."

As much as Brad pleaded with her, Aisha refused to carry out such a plan.

"Just think about it, OK?" he begged her. "Consider it. Do it for me, Aisha."

Aisha hoped that Brad was just testing her. She agreed to consider the plan, just to get him to lay off. But he persisted. Three weeks later, he brought the subject up again.

"OK, I know how protective you are of your son," he said this time. "You don't want him involved. But you could go in there and say that he touched you. You could run out of the office, get hysterical, whatever, and make it look like something happened."

"What?" she said. "No, I couldn't."

"Yes, Aisha," he said. "Yes, you could. Come on, do it, Aisha. Do it for me. You can make it look good. Then all you have to do is report it to the police. He'd be so embarrassed."

Aisha still wouldn't agree to such a horrible plot against Dr. Stidham, no matter how far-fetched it was.

***

In the summer of 2003, Lourdes and Brad were going through yet another break-up when she called a friend, a firefighter she sometimes dated, to her house. Lourdes told Jeff Fairbanks that Brad sometimes said he wanted Brian Stidham killed.

"Do you think I should call Brian and warn him?" Lourdes asked.

"I can't believe that you're still talking to this person, Lourdes!" Jeff said. "What the hell is wrong with you? He's frickin' evil and he's a bad guy! He fucked around on you. He steals shit and he's crazy."

"Yeah," Lourdes said sheepishly. "But, you know, he needs somebody who'll just love him."

"You're crazy for talking to him, Lourdes," Jeff said. "I'll call if you want me to, but you better make damn sure you know what you're doing and what might come out of this."

Lourdes never did call Brian, nor did Jeff. Within weeks, Lourdes and Brad were back together and talking about getting married. Lourdes went so far as to tell Brad that she would convert to Judaism for him. Brad happily signed them up for classes at the Jewish Community Center, so Lourdes could learn about Judaism. Their relationship was energized by the lessons. As many questions as Brad had about Lourdes' professional life, she had about Judaism and its customs. She especially liked learning about the various holidays, especially Yom Kippur.

"It's about letting go of the anger that you have in your heart," Brad told her. "To let God allow you to have peace."

That night, as they were leaving class at the JCC, Lourdes took his hand as they walked to the parking lot and gently said, "What a great class!"

Brad agreed.

"You know," Lourdes said, "Yom Kippur, and what it stands for. That's exactly what I'm talking about Brad."

"What? What the fuck are you talking about?" Brad said, his temper beginning to flare.

"About Brian. About letting go of the anger."

"Fuck that!" Brad said, yanking his arm away from her. "You don't understand, Lourdes! You just don't understand! I have to piss for pretrial services! I have to fuckin' meet with them! I have to do what the fuckin' medical board tells me! I fuckin' hate my mom and dad! I have to go to rehab! My practice went to shit, and I'm going through a divorce!"

***

The occasional argument aside, by the fall of 2003, Brad was settling into a routine that included his new practice, his relationship with Lourdes, his children and meeting the demands set down by the federal court as well as the Arizona Medical Board. Brad had to submit to weekly drug tests at the federal courthouse and at a private facility, where he ran into a wide variety of people. One of the people he ran into frequently at the courthouse, Stephanie Nagel, who was facing charges for stealing mail that could land her in a federal prison for several years, thought Brad was friendly and didn't mind chatting with him. He flattered her and tried charming his way into her life.

"No," she said when he repeatedly asked her out. "Look, you're a nice guy, but you're not my type."

"Oh, come on," he'd prod. "Just think about it, OK? Just think about it."

"OK," she relented, "I'll think about it."

But Stephanie had no intention of going out with him. Stephanie thought after a while, Brad would lose interest, especially since she turned him down. But he kept engaging her in conversation each time they met. She noticed that his previous flirtatious, light-hearted approach had now become someone more macho, more tough and streetwise. He talked like one of the characters out of the TV show he liked so much, *The Sopranos*.

"Why are you here?" Brad asked.

"I'm waiting for my trial," she said, adding that she had recently just gotten out of prison on an attempted forgery charge.

Brad was curious what prison was like, so Stephanie obliged him by relating her experiences.

"Stephanie, did you ever meet anybody who can take someone out?" Brad asked.

"What do you mean?" she asked, hoping she was misunderstanding him. "Beat someone up or something?"

"You know, take someone out, rub 'em out, that sort of thing," he said. "There's this guy I know, a guy I used to work with, and he really did me wrong. I can't tell you what all he did to me, but he ruined my life, Stephanie. And I was just wondering if maybe you knew someone who could take care of this person for me."

"Just kill someone? For you?" she said.

"Well, I'd pay 'em," Brad said. "I don't know what they'd ask for, 500 bucks, maybe? It'd be easy. The guy works where it's real dark at night. His office can't be seen from the street. They could make it look like a robbery, like the guy was just robbed and got killed. Nobody would see."

"I don't know about that, Brad," Stephanie said.

"I'll give you my number," Brad offered. "And you can call me."

"OK, I'll see what I can do," she said, with no intention of actually going forward with the plot.

Stephanie tucked the slip of paper with Brad's number away, wondering how this conversation ever took place—in a federal courthouse, of all places—about a hit on someone, like it was an episode of *The Sopranos* or something. He couldn't be serious, Stephanie told herself. People don't just do these things, walk up to someone who's almost a perfect stranger and ask them to kill someone for money. Brad brought up the subject several times, asking if she'd found anyone, but each time, Stephanie put him off. When Brad got her number and kept calling, Stephanie eventually stopped answering. Eventually, she changed her schedule, so that she could avoid him at the courthouse, too.

***

Brad's relationship with Aisha Henry continued into early 2004, though it had cooled somewhat. Aisha noticed that he no longer talked about her wanting to humiliate Brian, and she told him that she was glad he had accepted his fate.

"Oh, yeah," Brad told her. "Everything's under control."

"Brad, that's great," she told him.

But then her heart sank when Brad explained why he was so calm. She knew that he'd been involved with an attorney, Lourdes. Brad told Aisha that Lourdes' husband was a criminal, involved in the drug trade, and he'd agreed to kill Brian for him. Aisha didn't ask Brad any more questions about this new plot, mostly because she was relieved that she was no longer part of the scheme. She wondered whether she should tell anyone, like the police or something, about Brad's evil thoughts. But in the end, Aisha kept silent.

***

Carmen Fernandez was a phlebotomist in her third year at LabCorp in April 2003 as well as a student at Pima Community College studying criminal justice. She had been married for six years, though separated, with one child. She met Brad Schwartz when he came into the office to give urine samples as part of his drug-screening agreement with the state medical board. Carmen's co-worker, Carlos Ogas, saw that Brad was instantly infatuated with Carmen and wanted to date her from the moment he stepped into the office. For her part, Carmen enjoyed seeing Brad. He was always glad to see her and seemed interested in what was going on in her life. At first, she demurred when he asked her out, but in less than a month, she caved in and said yes. Carmen and Brad spoke to or saw each other often, almost daily. Often, when she got off work, she would make arrangements to see him. Even though they had just met, Carmen felt she could tell Brad anything. In turn, she believed, he poured his heart out to her about his painful divorce and the events that led up to him having to submit to weekly drug tests—though he neglected to tell Carmen that he had gotten engaged to Lourdes Lopez in January. Sometimes, she had to admit, the pillow talk got a bit odd. At least, that's what she thought when he brought up the subject of wanting to hire a hit man.

"You see lots of people at LabCorp," he said to her. "Do you know anyone I could hire to take care of a person for me?"

"Um, I don't know," she stammered. "Can't you get in big trouble for that?"

"Nobody would find out," he assured her. "What about your brother? Can he help?"

Carmen had told Brad that her brother was in trouble with the law.

"I don't know," she said tentatively. "I doubt it. He's in Mexico now."

Carmen didn't know what to make of the conversation. She didn't want to ask any details, not sure if Brad was serious or not about it and not wanting to encourage this dangerous fantasy of his. But he kept bringing the subject up, sometimes when she was at his apartment and sometimes when he stopped in for his drug test. Each time, he would add more details. Brad gave her a photocopy of Brian's picture, on a piece of paper with his name, address, phone number and car license plate number on it. That the man he hated was another doctor. That the other doctor had taken Brad's patients. That the other doctor embezzled from him. That the other doctor worked where it was very dark at night with no security cameras. Carmen saw Brad's anger when he spoke about this other doctor and what he'd done to his life. He was obsessed with revenge.

Once, Brad was frustrated after not being able to rent a car. He told Carmen he'd been banned from renting cars because he rented one for a Danny Lopez, and something happened to the car that made Brad liable. Danny, Brad said, was going to be the one who killed Brian Stidham. In fact, Brad said he'd already paid Danny Lopez to kill Dr. Stidham, but before the deed could be done, Danny was killed.

Carmen was riding in his car on Miracle Mile Road near Interstate 10 on the first leg of a trip to Phoenix when he pointed out an enormous auto salvage yard.

"That's the perfect place to get rid of a body, don't you think?" he asked.

***

Rachel Atkinson took her infant son to see Brad Schwartz on Feb. 19, 2004, after her pediatrician noticed that the baby didn't have any bright reflexes in his right eye. Brad diagnosed a tumor that engulfed the boy's entire left eye. Rachel was more than pleased with Brad's surgical skills, crediting him for saving her young son's life. After the boy was fitted with a prosthetic eye, Rachel emailed a photo of him to Brad to show him how well he was doing. Brad responded, asking more specific questions about the boy and also initiating an electronic conversation with Rachel, as well. Rachel, who was recovering emotionally from breaking off an engagement, was receptive to Brad's advances and agreed to go out with him.

In April, the pair saw each other at least three nights a week. Most often, Rachel would go to Brad's apartment, where they would watch movies and make love. She was flattered to be dating a doctor. And she had no reason to suspect he was seeing anyone else. Whenever she became aware there were other women in his life, Brad passed them off as "just friends."

Brad often spoke of someone he was displeased with, a doctor named Brian who once worked with him but after they split, took all the patients. Brian, Rachel was told, was causing a lot of trouble at the hospitals, badmouthing Brad and preventing him from practicing surgery.

"I hate him," Brad said on more than one occasion.

"I can't take this guy anymore!" Brad said. "I wish he wasn't around anymore."

One evening, Brad told Rachel an outrageous story she refused to believe.

"OK, listen to this," he said. "I set up a deal once. I had somebody staking out Brian's office. It was all set up. This was going to be 'the night.' That was the night I was going to get rid of Brian. But I chickened out. I couldn't do it. It turns out later, though, that the guy I had hired to kill him had already died."

"Brad, I don't believe you," Rachel said. "You're not serious."

"I am serious, Rachel," he said. "It really happened."

"Brad, you're scaring me," she said.

Then Brad laughed.

"Ah, I was just tryin' to get a rise out of you!" he said.

"I knew you weren't serious!" she said, relieved.

One evening, Brad was in a particularly foul mood after a meeting in which he learned he wouldn't be able to practice at certain hospitals. Whenever these things happened to Brad, Rachel noticed, he seemed to funnel his anger in the direction of Brian Stidham. Rachel just brushed off Brad's rants, figuring that he was just being macho or get a rise out of her.

One time, Brad asked Rachel to get involved in his scheme to exact revenge on Brian.

"All you have to do is make an appointment to take your son in there, say it's for a second operation or whatever. Then accuse him of touching you inappropriately. Leave the office in a hurry, call the police, go home and tell them that he groped you."

"No, Brad, I don't want to do that," she said.

"Come on," he cajoled. "Do it."

Rachel did make an appointment to see Dr. Stidham. At that point, she figured, Brad couldn't care about her if he was going to ask her to do something so outlandish, so she would need a new doctor for her son. Of course, Rachel never intended she would make false accusations about Dr. Stidham touching her. In fact, she didn't intend at all to carry through with the appointment. She would call the morning of the appointment to cancel. The morning of Oct. 6, 2004.

***

Brad's relationship with Lourdes wasn't only complex because of their on-again-off-again status and legal issues, but also because loving Lourdes meant dealing with her complicated past. In November 2003, Lourdes' ex-husband, Danny, called and begged her to help when he was busted for drug possession. Lourdes dutifully bailed him out. The next month, Brad slipped Danny $5,000, knowing that Lourdes' ex needed some cash.

"Say that it's for your new kid," Brad said.

In February, a month after Brad and Lourdes became engaged, Danny came to Tucson to see his children with Lourdes. He also took a friend in to see Brad about his eyes. While he was in Tucson, Danny promised to take his and Lourdes' children back with him to Nebraska to see his new baby for the first time. But, at the last minute, he told Lourdes he was not going to take the children to Nebraska. Lourdes was angry with Danny for building up the kids' hopes and then leaving without them.

A month later, when Lourdes and Brad heard that Danny was killed in a gun battle with police, Lourdes thanked God that he had backed down on this one promise and hadn't taken her children with him to Nebraska.

Danny's death seemed to have an odd effect on Brad, Lourdes noticed.

"Now that Danny has been killed," Brad said to Lourdes, "and I see how much his children miss him, you know, I just have to let my anger go."

Lourdes couldn't have been happier to hear Brad say those words. She knew that it would be hard for a man like Brad to swallow his pride and let that deep-seated anger go, but just the fact that he acknowledged it and promised to ease up gave her great comfort.

In April 2004, Brad and Lourdes decided to rent a house, to prepare for their married life. Domestic bliss, though, didn't follow. They actually only lived together for two days after which a fight sent Brad back to his apartment. Bound by the lease, Lourdes remained in the house.

***

Breaking up with Lourdes didn't mean that Brad would be alone. As usual, he had hedged his bets and continued to see other women. He had personal ads in several online dating sites and frequently cruised through the hordes of available women. In April 2004, he noticed a Lisa Goldberg from Phoenix. Her name was Jewish, but she was actually raised Catholic. Nevertheless, Brad sent her an email to get a sense of her and see if she was worth pursuing. Unfortunately for him, Lisa emailed back that she was in a relationship.

"Well," Brad told her, "if that changes, let me know."

Lourdes had no doubts that Brad had quickly rebounded. She had suspected for some time that he was seeing a woman named Kristen Pedersen again. It wasn't beyond Lourdes to call one of his lovers up and demand they not see him.

Kristen picked up the phone one day to hear Lourdes proclaim, "Bradley and I are engaged!"

It took all Kristen had to not say what was on her mind: "Oh, really, dumbass! That was my parents' truck he used to move out of your home, you stupid twit! And this is Kristen, not Karina!" But Kristen held her tongue.

"Why did you *ever* in a million years have an attraction to Lourdes?" she later asked Brad. I feel like your instincts should've kicked in and warned you that she was *not* sincere. I cannot believe she is an educated, professional woman. All I can think about are the two times she called me. The first, to warn and threaten me, the second she thought I was someone else. She took me back to being a high schooler."

Unlike Lourdes, Kristen was reconciled to withstanding Brad's affections toward other women.

"Dammit, Bradley, *I love you!*" she told him. "You have literally had my heart from day one. There was just something about you. Even knowing that you had 10 girlfriends at once, including me. I still somehow thought it was me that you loved the most."

***

Though Lourdes harbored some hopes that she and Brad would eventually make up, the final split came in May 2004. The absolute proof came a month later. Lourdes drove to her office, parking the car in her usual space behind the building. Inside, she heard the sound of an engine starting and looked out the window in time to see Brad driving off in her car.

"That's low!" Lourdes said to her law partner. "Brad gave me that car, and now he just drove off in it."

"I can't believe he took your car!" he said.

"It's creepy, too," Lourdes said. "Because he must have been watching me to know when I'd be here, so he could take it."

"You're better off without him," he said.

"Yeah, I know," Lourdes said.

"You don't talk to him anymore do you?" he asked. "I mean, is it like, you guys run into each other, and it's awkward, or do you still stay in touch?"

"Well, we do talk sometimes," she allowed.

"Lourdes, you should just make a clean break."

"Yeah, I know," she said. "I know."

***

Any hopes that Aisha Henry had about Brad reconciling his feelings about Brian were dashed in the summer of 2004 when, during one of their tête-à-têtes, Brad asked Aisha if she would get her husband, Dallas, to do a favor for him. Brad had met Dallas when he and Alisha were both in Cottonwood. Dallas Henry was a stocky man, about 5-foot-7 weighing about 200 pounds.

"I'll pay him," Brad said.

"For what?" she asked.

"To hurt Brian," Brad said.

"No, Brad, no!" Aisha said.

"Come on, Aisha," he said. "I know you guys need the money. It'll solve all our problems. I'll give you $1,500 before and $1,500 after. All he has to do is beat Brian up, I don't know, crush his hands in some way so he wouldn't be able to operate anymore. Or, he could throw acid in his eyes, put him out of his career."

Brad told Aisha that Brian worked in a complex where there weren't any security cameras. Dallas could jump him after he got off work. Brad even offered to give Dallas latex gloves, so no fingerprints could be left behind. He had some acid, too, if that's what Dallas wanted to do. He'd even supply Dallas with some medical scrubs.

"I have scrubs at my office," he said, adding that he'd have to get some to fit Dallas.

Aisha didn't ask any questions, not believing for one instant that this would actually be carried out.

"Brad," she said, "I can't ask Dallas to do that. What would happen if he got caught? What would happen to me? To my son?"

Brad pulled Aisha toward him and gently caressed her.

"But you won't get caught," Brad cooed. "I promise."

Over the next two weeks, Brad continued to bring up the subject of Dallas hurting Dr. Stidham.

"OK, OK!" she finally relented. "I'll do it. I'll ask Dallas."

Brad was ecstatic. He was certain that he'd finally get the redemption he had long sought. Aisha took the $1,500 from Brad with trepidation. She and Dallas really needed the money. They were behind on their rent and had other bills piling up. Dallas also wanted to buy a gun because the store he was working in got robbed, and he feared for his safety. But she had no intention of asking Dallas to hurt Dr. Stidham. She looked upon the $1,500 as a loan that she intended to pay back as soon as she was able. She wasn't sure how she was going to explain to Dallas how she'd gotten the money and hoped that he would just be happy to have it and not ask any questions. Fat chance. Dallas was immediately suspicious about the money. When Aisha told him how she'd gotten it, he exploded into a rage. Aisha told Dallas that she would repay the "loan" to Brad somehow.

The next day, she called Brad with the bad news.

"It's not going to happen," she said. "We changed our minds. It's not something that we want to get involved with. But I'll pay you back soon, I promise. Dallas is just about to start another job, and we'll get the money back to you soon."

It was Brad's turn to fly into a rage.

"You don't know what you are doing to me," Brad growled. "He's ruined my life! I can't, I just can't go on like this. I'm suffering, and he's getting away with it, and you're helping him! Aisha, you know what I'm going through. You've seen how much he's hurt me!"

Some part of Aisha felt sorry for Brad and wanted to comfort him any way she could. But another part wondered if this was just one of his manipulations, that he really didn't care for her and was just keeping her around until he got his way. Aisha spent the next few weeks avoiding Brad's persistent calls. He always asked for the money back, and she knew that they wouldn't be able to repay him anytime soon. Again, she wondered if she should tell the police about his threats against Brian. And, time and time again, she decided not to. Not only was Aisha scared about going to the police, especially since she'd agreed to help Brad, but she had no proof of anything. It would be her word against his. And on top of everything, she wanted to believe that Brad wasn't the kind of person who could harm anyone. She saw that there was good in him; she knew it was there, even if he tried to suppress it with evil intentions. Aisha talked herself into believing that it would do no good to tell the police or warn Brian about Brad's tales because he wasn't really serious about it. So she kept her silence.

***

In late June 2004, Liliana Bibb was perusing the listings at the Internet dating site Match.com, when she came across Brad Schwartz's. She was intrigued and sent a message that she was interested in seeing him. Brad responded quickly, and the two arranged to meet at a Coffee Exchange café. The initial meeting went so well that Liliana felt comfortable asking Brad to attend a Fourth of July party at her house the following week. Before long, the two became lovers. They often met for lunch, and Brad sent roses to Liliana every week. Sometimes, he invited her children along on their dinner dates, which warmed her heart. Still, she wasn't expecting it when Brad proposed within only a few weeks of their first meeting. Liliana didn't seriously consider the proposal, but she continued to see Brad.

One evening, Liliana was spending the evening at Brad's apartment watching TV when he exploded into a rage while taking a phone call. Brad slammed the phone down.

"What's wrong?" she asked.

"A deal I had went bad," he replied. "I just lost $1,500."

"What happened?" she asked.

"I had a deal with someone, and then they changed their minds," Brad said, still fuming.

Brad explained that he had loaned money to a woman he knew named Aisha, and she had given him her wedding ring as collateral. But now the woman was reneging on the deal that they'd made. Liliana never saw the ring he mentioned, and Brad never explained what happened to it.

Liliana wondered if the deal that had just gone bad had anything to do with Danny Lopez. She hadn't known Brad too long before he told her about Brian Stidham and how Brian had ruined his life.

"I want him gone," Brad said. "I want him hurt. I wish he could have his eyes poked out or his fingers broken, so he can't perform surgery anymore. I'd be happy if he was six feet under."

If Brian couldn't practice medicine anymore, Brad told her, he'd get all his patients that Brian stole back.

It was around that time that Brad first mentioned Danny Lopez. Brad told Liliana that he had hired Danny to kill Brian Stidham, but Danny had gotten killed before he could carry out the contract killing.

One night, Brad drove Liliana past the First Avenue Medical Plaza and noted that Brian had his office there. Brad noted how dark it was in the complex at night, that there were no cameras. Brian left his office late at night through the back in the alley, Brad said.

"I want it to look like a robbery," he confided.

On more than one occasion, Brad even asked her if she could find a hit man. She couldn't fathom why someone would say such outrageous things to another person whom they've only known a short time. Liliana figured it was because he trusted her. She soon found out that any trust she had in him was misplaced. Liliana suspected that, although he had already proposed to her, Brad was seeing other women. Yet Brad still gave her the impression that she was the only woman he was seeing. Liliana became jealous. Once, after they parted, she followed him to the Costco store on Grant Road because she was certain he was lying about where he was going. There, she watched as Brad lovingly greeted her own cousin, Lourdes. Another night, Liliana caught him in another lie when she burst into Firecracker, a restaurant close to Brad's apartment, where she confronted him dining with another woman. Liliana made such a scene that the restaurant staff escorted her out. Later, Brad chastised Liliana for ruining a real estate deal he was working out with the woman at dinner.

Early in their brief relationship, Brad called constantly. In August, the calls stopped. Liliana confided in the volatile relationship with her co-workers, who urged her to get as far away from him as possible.

"He's crazy," her friends said.

But Liliana assured them that his plot against Brian was just talk. It wasn't serious.

Liliana was angry that Brad was ignoring her and called him, but he wouldn't answer her calls. But she knew how to get his attention. Liliana called Brad's number and left this message: "I have somebody for you." Brad called back, right away. Liliana had her daughter tell Brad that she had just stepped out with someone else. When Liliana didn't return his call, Brad called time and time again.

When the two finally spoke, Liliana demanded money. She needed $350 to pay her rent, and then she would talk to him. Brad professed to have no money, but Liliana didn't believe him. He said he was going broke, and he needed a loan for $50,000 from the medical building he owned, so he could pay his bills. But the fact that Brad was a surgeon who was very well compensated, owned a Cadillac Escalade, owned his own building and lived in a nice apartment in a good part of town made her doubt his protestations of poverty. Brad gave her the money. Liliana figured that she'd gotten as much out of the relationship as she wanted and never spoke to Brad again.

***

One day in July 2004, Lourdes received a disturbing phone call from a woman who apparently was seeing Brad.

"Are you guys still together?" the woman asked. "You know, like a personal thing?"

"No, I'm not," Lourdes replied.

"I can't believe he told me he's gonna have Brian killed," the woman said.

Later, Lourdes called Brad.

"Are you fucking crazy?" Lourdes told Brad.

"What are you talking about?" Brad asked.

"You told this woman that you wanted to have Brian killed! Are you fucking crazy? You can't do that. Why are you telling anybody else that?"

Lourdes wondered what was happening to Brad. She hadn't been with him much over the past few months as she had in the past few years, so she wondered if something in him had changed so drastically that he would go around telling people he wanted Brian killed.

Lourdes's daughter was scheduled to play in a basketball tournament in San Diego during the middle of July. Lourdes was glad to get her children out of Tucson, and herself as well, not only because the California coast is cooler than southern Arizona in the middle of the muggy monsoon season, but because the getaway fell during the week that brought Danny Lopez's birthday, July 16. Lourdes was thankful that her children had something to occupy their minds other than their father's brutal death five months earlier.

If Lourdes was looking to completely escape her life in Tucson that July, it didn't last long. Brad still called her. It was the same old stuff, with one exception in a voice mail he left her.

"Lourdes," Brad said, "if something happens to me, my life insurance policy is on my dresser. Remember, you're my beneficiary."

Lourdes called back, worried.

"What the hell are you talking about?" she asked.

"Nothing," Brad replied. "I'm just saying if something happens to me."

Lourdes didn't know what to make of the strange conversation, whether Brad was being serious, whether he had an illness he didn't tell her about, or whether he was just being melodramatic.

***

By mid-summer, Carmen Fernandez had just about talked herself into thinking that her lover's temper and threatening statements about wanting someone killed were harmless thoughts when Brad called her and demanded that she come to his office because he was upset. He'd just gotten word that his hospital privileges were suspended at Northwest Hospital, the only hospital that had taken him back so far. Carmen had never seen someone so angry. Brad threw a phone against the wall, blaming Brian Stidham for his anguish once more.

Now Carmen was concerned. The only person she had told about Brad's rantings was Carlos, her co-worker. Now she felt compelled to confide in two of her teachers, who urged her to call police. But Carmen didn't. She was still so infatuated with Brad that she refused to think that he was really serious about wanting Brian harmed. Besides, when Brad wasn't mad at Brian, he was gentle and sweet with her.

In late August, she confronted Brad. She needed $2,000, she told him, because she had bills, and she might be pregnant.

Brad gave her the money willingly, without asking for collateral or even a written agreement. Carmen was grateful and used the money to pay some bills and get an insurance policy for her cars. In a few weeks, though, Brad asked if he could get the money back.

"I'm very close to filing for bankruptcy," he told her, "and I could really use it."

Carmen believed him, despite the fact that she had driven with him to Sahuarita, a rural community southwest of Tucson, where he hoped to build a house. On the other hand, he had spoken before about needing to make more money, and his office had been broken into sometime the previous year. But Carmen couldn't afford to give him $2,000 at that time.

"If you can't pay me back," he said, "then can you find somebody to take care of Brian Stidham and give them the $2,000?"

"No, I'll pay you back," Carmen said. "I promise."

***

Surfing the Internet in August 2004, Brad found a website community of redheads called Realm of Redheads, "a fun, clean community of redheads." Brad created an onscreen name for himself, EyeGuy, and submitted a photo of himself, smiling. He listed his occupation as a physician and that he had strawberry hair and green eyes. "I am a fun loving, free-spirited kind of guy," Brad wrote. "I work hard and I play hard. I love to travel to see new places and I love scuba diving in exotic places. I live for the weekends and vacations. I have always liked being a red-head because people always remember me for that. They will remember me years after meeting me as that 'red-headed guy.' It has always made me stand out in the crowd." He listed his interests as hiking, sports (baseball, football and hockey), going out to eat, traveling and listening to music and seeing shows. Realm of Redheads also had an online dating site, Planet Redhead, for those who sought more intimate connections. Brad created another name for himself, eyeguyfromaz, when he signed up. Responding to the questions posed by the site, Brad said "anything goes" as for the kind of relationship he sought, women wanting to know his religion would have to "find out later," he didn't smoke but didn't care if his date did, he rarely drank, had three children not living with him and was "undecided" whether he wanted more and that his sense of humor was "quick witted."

Brad joined other Internet dating sites as well. One day as he was cruising Match.com, Brad thought of Lisa Goldberg, the real estate agent from Phoenix. Brad wondered if whatever relationship she had been in the previous April was still going on. And if it was, he mused, maybe he could still start something up with her. Brad sent her a friendly email, asking if she remembered him from their brief electronic exchange.

To Brad's delight, Lisa responded, saying that she was, indeed, single again. Brad called her up, and they chatted.

"I'd love to take you out to dinner," Brad said.

Lisa agreed to drive to Tucson and meet Brad at a local chain restaurant. She immediately took to Brad, and it wasn't long before the two found the time to have dinner again. They shared life stories. Brad told Lisa about his marriage and the deterioration of his medical career, which he was trying to build up again. In turn, Lisa told him that she had gone through a divorce, too, so she knew how he felt. And, she confided, she suffered from an anxiety disorder that causes her to have panic attacks. She felt comfortable telling him about this, even though it made her feel vulnerable, because he was a physician. Besides, by then she already knew he was a great fan of the HBO mob series *The Sopranos*, whose main character suffered from panic attacks.

By the third date, Lisa agreed to stay in Tucson and go back to Brad's apartment to spend the night. Things seemed to be moving a bit fast for her taste, but Lisa was willing to go along, for the moment. On only their second meeting, Brad professed his love for her.

Lisa was stunned.

"I'm not there yet," she told him.

Brad seemed all right with her hesitation. It certainly didn't cool his ardor because then, after their third meeting, he told her he wanted to go shopping for an engagement ring. Lisa was overwhelmed. Flattered—that this good-looking, hard-working doctor seemed so taken with her that he was gushing about getting married—but overwhelmed. Lisa was reluctant to return Brad's wholehearted affection, but she certainly didn't want to end the relationship.

It certainly wasn't boring to be with Brad. He could be extremely affectionate one minute and then explosive the next. One time, they agreed to stay in for the night, watching movies at Brad's place. He wanted to see *Traffic*, a movie about drug runners in which a man's wife steps in to do whatever she can to protect her criminal husband.

"You know," Brad told her as they watched the movie, "I operated on a man once who was a drug trafficker."

"Really?" Lisa said. "How do you know he was a drug trafficker?"

"He told me. He said, 'Brad, if you ever needed anything done—anything—I can make it happen for $10,000.'"

Lisa wasn't sure if this was just something Brad was making up, but he was so animated when he talked about things like that, that she just didn't care. She thought he overexaggerated, but even that was charming because he obviously was doing that to impress her. He did have a dark side, and he wasn't afraid to show it. Almost from the first time they talked, Brad talked about a deep-seated anger toward a fellow doctor, Brian Stidham. Brad admitted he had been self-medicating himself to relieve the pain from his injuries and that caused him to get into trouble with the DEA and go into rehab. Brian, Brad told her, then took all of his patients away and screwed up his life. Brad blamed Brian for ruining his life. Brad could get angry fast when the subject of Brian Stidham came up, and Brad seemed to raise the issue often.

"I want him dead," Brad told her one night.

"That's a terrible thing to say," she told him.

"Well, it's a terrible thing, what he did to me!" Brad countered. "I'm telling you, I'm gonna have that man killed."

"That's ridiculous," she said. "You don't mean it, and you know it."

Lisa tried reminding Brad that he had three kids to think about, but no matter what tactic she tried to calm him down, Brad's temper always flared when it came to Brian Stidham.

"He ruined my life, Lisa!" Brad said. "He's gonna die."

"But Brad, even you have to realize that that is TV," she said, pointing to the screen. "That's not reality. You have so much going for you. Your career is coming back together. You've got wonderful children who love you. Please, Brad, take that thought out of your head."

CHAPTER 7

As complicated as Brad's life was, Brian's was going smoothly. He had suffered a couple of minor heart attacks, but was fit enough to rebound quickly after surgery. Thanks in part to an experienced staff he'd worked with at Brad's practice, Brian's practice became a thriving business. Not only did he retain some of his previous patients, Brian's popularity among the local medical community was such that other physicians gave him the lion's share of references. Things were going so well financially for the Stidhams that, on the advice of their financial planner, they hired an estate attorney to draw up a living trust in mid-2004. Around the same time, they took out a $1 million insurance policy on Brian's life, with Daphne as the sole beneficiary.

Still, because Brad had some special skills that Brian lacked, hospitals and physicians did refer patients to Arizona Specialty Eye Care when conditions called for it. It was inevitable that the two surgeons would cross paths from time to time. If they did, nothing more than casual acknowledgments were exchanged. Brian tried not to think about the past, just forge on with the present. Still, there were persistent rumors that got back to Brian hinting that Brad was still upset about the falling out. Dr. Kevin Concannon ran into Brian one day at Tucson Medical Center in the spring of 2004 and noticed that his friend was on edge.

"It's Brad Schwartz," Brian confided. "I don't know. I keep hearing these things that ... that he's out to get me."

"Out to get you?" Kevin asked. "How?"

"He might even want to kill me," Brian said.

"Brian!" Kevin said. "That's ridiculous! I mean, I've known Brad for a few years and, as I always say, he's a bit of an odd fish. There was that deal with the drugs and all. But wanting to kill you? I just can't believe it. Are you sure he's saying that?"

"Well, no, I'm not sure," Brian said. "But it's what people are saying that he's saying. I'm wondering if I should be concerned about it. Take it seriously, I mean."

"I just don't think it would ever come to that, really," Kevin said.

"Well, he thinks that I stole all his patients," Brian said. "Which is really ridiculous because he brought me here to take all the pedes. But they're saying that he's really angry with me about that. Angry enough that he might want to kill me."

"Oh, Brian, I just don't think that's realistic," Kevin said. "I know there are murderers out there, but cold-blooded killers—it's just not what I'd expect from him. He's an educated man. He's got children. People like that just don't go around killing people. I know that in my past, I've certainly gotten very angry with my partners. And I've probably got to the point that I've thought I was so mad I could shoot them. But I never would have taken action. And I don't think Brad would, either."

"So, you don't think I should call the police or something?" Brian asked.

"And tell them what? That you've heard these rumors?" Kevin asked. "I doubt they could do anything."

"I suppose you're right," Brian said. "What could they do? They might talk to him, and it might make him even more angry, if he is that angry with me."

"Right," Kevin said. "Don't worry, kid. He'll get over it, if he hasn't already."

***

By fall, Brad's operating privileges at Northwest Hospital were reinstated, though he would have to wait for other hospitals to follow suit. Kraig Marton, Brad's attorney in his dealings with the state medical board, told Brad that once the DEA cleared Brad for full prescription-writing abilities, the other hospitals would welcome him back. Brad never failed to keep up with his obligations set by the federal court and medical board. He never missed a drug test and never once came up positive for drugs or alcohol. He continued to go to counseling and missed only a few meetings for family obligations or illness. A few of the health insurance companies also had agreed to cover Brad's patients. Each month, more and more patients were coming in to Brad's office, and he set his sights on expanding his business and building a new life for himself with a new home in Sahuarita, a bedroom community southwest of Tucson.

On Sept. 4, 2004, Tucson Medical Center sent a patient to see Brad over an injury to his right eye. Brad, though he wore an arm harness due to a shoulder surgery, performed eye surgery on Bruce Bigger on Sept. 15, 2004.

Ronald Bruce Bigger, who goes by his middle name, first came to Arizona in the late 1990s to visit a childhood friend in Scottsdale. Arizona was a big change from northern Indiana, where Bruce had grown up. Arizona was a place where only one person, his best friend, knew what Bruce had gone through. Arizona was a great place to escape the problems that plagued him in Indiana.

David and Mary Sue Bigger had only one child, Bruce. When Bruce was about 4 years old, David Bigger was critically injured after a train collided with his car. David clung to life for months, witnessed by his young son, who often visited the hospital with David's parents. Sue saw what a devastating effect David's hospitalization caused on Bruce and begged her in-laws to stop taking him there. They agreed. Eventually, David Bigger succumbed to his injuries. David

Bigger had been a manager at a local credit union, which was conducting an audit around the time of his accident. It was discovered that David, who had been an alcoholic, had been embezzling money from the bank. Though the official determination of death was by accident, many—including Bruce Bigger—suspected David Bigger committed suicide by driving his car up on the railroad tracks. Sometimes, Bruce told friends that he suspected his father was being chased by someone, who caused him to drive in front of the train.

Sue raised Bruce alone for two years on her salary as a patrol officer from the LaPorte Police Department until she married a man who had no children of his own and became physically and emotionally abusive toward Bruce. That marriage lasted five years until Sue filed for divorce. Meantime, Bruce began attending Catholic schools, where he got average grades. He had many friends and developed a reputation as a chatterbox. From the time he learned to dress himself, Bruce also enjoyed looking his best. He was athletic, playing on the high school football and wrestling teams, and liked to read, especially about his favorite subject: sports. He did get into one fight in high school, which earned Bruce a suspension. It all worked out though; eventually Bruce and the other boy became good friends. When Bruce was 15, Sue married Chris Yadavia, who had two sons of his own. The boys all got along well. Bruce had always considered Chris his father, though the marriage to his mom only lasted three years. Sue blamed Chris's lack of anger management during their divorce.

At age 18, Bruce enrolled at Franklin College, where he obtained a partial football scholarship and dreamed of becoming a short story writer, though he chose poly sci as his major. The lure of living away from home proved to be too great for Bruce, however, who leaped into the party life. At age 20 (year was 1997), he transferred to Ball State University, where his football career ended when he was injured in a car accident. By that time, Bruce knew he had a problem with alcohol and drugs. Two years previously, at LaPorte's hospital, he'd been diagnosed with addictions to cocaine, alcohol and marijuana. His doctor recommended attending Alcoholic Anonymous, get psychotherapy and perhaps a court order for Antabuse, but Bruce failed to follow up. While hospitalized for his car accident, Bruce asked whether someone could force him into drug treatment. Also that year, Bruce was devastated when his grandfather and a good friend, Susan, died. Bruce dropped out of Ball State, and though he took some classes through Purdue University's extension service, he failed to earn a degree, though he often lied and told people—including law enforcement officials—that he had obtained a bachelor's degree in finance or his master's degree.

That didn't seem to matter to Bruce, who seemed to be able to talk his way into (and often, out of) any situation. He moved to Chicago where he found employment in packaging sales. Whenever he lost a job—through closings, downsizing, etc.—Bruce always managed to land on his feet. Being in sales suited his personality, and he flourished. The problem was, though he was earning a good living, Bruce seemed to have no common sense when it came to handling money. He spent money as soon as he earned it, or he gave it away. He considered anyone who was nice to him to be his friend and would go out of his way to do favors for his friends. Bruce also frittered away an inheritance of money and property his paternal grandfather had left him. Sue fretted that she might have been too lenient on him as a child and felt sorry for him growing up as a cop's kid, but she always helped Bruce out whenever he needed a boost.

During those years, the years Bruce considers himself most successful, he was dealt another emotional blow. His father's grandmother and great aunt became ill in 1998. Bruce did whatever he could to help them, but they both died around the same time, which sent Bruce's life into a downward spiral. He sought psychological counseling for the first time, battling the depression that his mother had seen since his childhood. Bruce also began collecting DUI citations.

In 2004, Bruce was arrested for forgery after writing a check on his grandmother's account. He passed it off as a misunderstanding, but the court was less forgiving and sentenced him to three years probation after spending about two months in jail. The judge, however, granted Bruce's request to travel to Arizona to visit his best friend, but only if Arizona officials approved it and would monitor him. Regardless, Bruce took off for Arizona. Though this time, he would not go to Scottsdale. Instead, Bruce decided to check out Tucson, about two hours south of Scottsdale. Bruce had about $2,000 on him and figured that he could land a job easily when the money ran out. Bruce drove to Tucson in his mother's car and, as he had done previously, had no problem finding new friends and a place to stay. Months passed, and whatever job prospects he considered he had disappeared as Bruce wallowed in street life and drug abuse. And, much like the rest of his life, if Bruce didn't find trouble, trouble came looking for him.

Tucson police officers were dispatched around 4:30 p.m. on Sept. 4, 2004, regarding a report of an assault at a Circle K convenience store, 4702 E. Speedway Blvd. A 19-year-old man, David, reported that he and his girlfriend, Una, were walking into the store when another man confronted him and punched him in the head several times with closed fists. David fell to the ground and was kicked in the ribs. Una ran into the store to ask the clerk to call 911. Una watched as the stranger yelled at David, who was trying to get to his feet. The clerk got between the two men and ordered the stranger to leave. A surveillance tape of the incident showed David pushing the stranger back, and the stranger was lunging for David when the clerk came between them. David was taken to a hospital for treatment. The suspect left in a white SUV, the clerk reported.

Minutes later, the officer who responded to the store was told by the command center that a man named Bruce Wright called in and was "mumbling incoherently" about the incident at the Circle K. However, the officer was unable to find Bruce White or locate the SUV the assault suspect left in.

Luckily, the clerk was alert enough to write the license plate number of the white SUV down. An officer was sent to the address where the vehicle was registered. A woman said the car was her estranged husband's and told him where he was now living. The husband told the officer that a friend of his had borrowed the SUV around 2 p.m. and left a note saying he was going to Walmart. However, when the friend came back, he was upset and said he'd gotten into a fight at Circle K. The two men left the house, but began arguing. The man said he'd dropped off his friend at the intersection of Irvington and Valencia roads, on Tucson's far South Side near the airport, with all his belongings and a warning that he'd better not come back to the house.

Police records traced the suspect's identity to Bruce. The police then issued a "stop and arrest" order for Bruce on two counts of assault. He was arrested two days later. Bruce claimed that David began the fight and was mad because he had gotten beaten up.

On Sept. 9, police were called to an apartment in midtown Tucson reporting that a man and a woman were yelling and things were being banged around.

When officers arrived, they found a man described as Hispanic, though it was Bruce Bigger, sitting on a couch, bleeding from his face and head. Bruce told them that he'd been sleeping on the sofa when two black men came inside, woke him up and said, "You hit my sister!"

"I've never hurt a woman in my life," Bruce said he told the men.

The larger of the two men began hitting him, Bruce said, and they fought into the hallway when the other intruder grabbed Bruce from behind. The men fell to the floor and

Bruce hit his head. The men left in a blue Ford Escort, Bruce said. Paramedics were called and treated Bruce for cuts over his right eyelid, back of his head, left forehead and on the brim of his nose as well as scratches on his right shoulder. Bruce told officers as he was being treated that he was visiting Tucson because a friend had recently died and was bunking with a woman pal at that apartment. He had trouble remembering the woman's last name and the name of a man staying there also.

He was arrested at 4:37, but released because he had head injuries and was taken to Tucson Medical Center. He was referred to Dr. Brad Schwartz for an eye examination. Claudia Huerta and her daughter, Sharon Payne, both saw Bruce come into Brad's office, with a swollen, black-and-blue face.

Twelve days later, Bruce was in trouble again with the law. He was riding with three friends in the area of Grant Road and Alvernon Way when an undercover officer noticed the car running without a light over the license plate. Uniformed officers were called in and pulled the car over at Flower and Haskell. The driver, Dereck, said he was borrowing the car and didn't have insurance papers or registration. A records check showed that Dereck was driving on a suspended license. Bruce told an officer that they had been at a friend's house and the only thing of his in the car was an Altoid's tin. Other officers searched the car and found a crack pipe in front of the front passenger's seat, where Bruce had been sitting. Bruce was charged with possessing drug paraphernalia. Officers also found more pipes and syringes with residue, a scale and cigarette box with marijuana wrapped in tissue inside. Bruce had come a long way from his days wearing a business suit in the financial world. And his perilous journey had not yet come to an end.

CHAPTER 8

On Oct. 5, 2004, Brian awoke at 5 a.m., his usual time, after only a few hours of sleep, which was also normal for him. This day, for the first time in several months, Brian decided that he was going to lift weights. It had been a month since he'd had heart surgery, and Brian felt strong enough to do some light weightlifting before getting ready for work.

At 7:20 a.m., Brian left his home to go to the office. He had set up his self-named practice in a medical complex on busy North First Avenue just south of the even busier crosstown route of River Road. The complex had been built 30 years ago by Dr. Gerald Altschuler and his wife, Phyllis. Dr. Altschuler had his own office in the north end of the western building that formed an L with another row of offices. Brian's practice was just a few doors down from Dr. Altschuler's. The complex also had two shorter rows of offices tucked in the southeastern end of the lot.

Brian's morning was packed with patient visits. He managed to slip away shortly before 1 p.m. to call Daphne at home. Daphne wanted to bring the children in for a while, which pleased Brian, so they made arrangements. Brian usually left the office before 5 p.m., if not much sooner, but Daphne knew that he was staying late to lecture to a group of med students that evening. Brian promised to call later that day, if he had the time.

***

Across town at Brad's office, tucked away in a gathering of medical offices near Tucson Medical Center, Katherine McKenzie showed up for her appointment. Katherine was surprised when Brad interrupted the exam to make a long-distance call to the Pennsylvania medical board.

"This is Brian Stidham," Brad said. "I just want to find out if you guys have my phone number."

Evidently, Katherine surmised, the person on the other end of the phone said they did have Brian's number.

Brad slammed the phone down, cursing.

"Damn it!" he said. "I knew it! I knew Brian had ratted on me to the board."

Katherine wasn't sure what Brad was talking about, but before she had the chance to ask, Brad said he'd suspected that Brian had called the Pennsylvania medical board and told them about Brad's federal drug case. That put his Pennsylvania medical license, which is granted for a lifetime, in jeopardy, Brad explained.

"You know," Brad said, "I once did reconstructive surgery on this Mexican drug lord. He told me, 'If you're ever having problems with somebody, let me know. I can take care of them for you.' "

"What did you say?" Katherine asked.

"I told him it was tempting, but I couldn't do that to anyone," Brad said, his sweet temperament returning.

While Brad was seeing patients, his Phoenix girlfriend, Lisa Goldberg, was preparing to head down to Tucson. At mid-day, Lisa put her overnight bag, her dog and study materials for a real estate exam in her car. Lisa was scheduled to take the exam the following day in Tucson and planned to have dinner with Brad that night. Lisa arrived in Tucson sometime after 4 p.m. and drove straight to Brad's office, parking around the back, so she could leave her dog in the fenced-off yard. Brad greeted her and introduced her to Julie Herrington, an aesthetician who was opening a space in his office. Brad explained that he was still seeing patients, but

Lisa could hang out with Julie. Julie offered to give Lisa a tour of the office, which Lisa accepted. Lisa knew that Brad had a lot of ambitious plans for his office, ways of expanding his practice that would earn him more money and prestige. At that point, though, many of the plans were in boxes and blueprints strewn around the unfinished space. Julie excused herself to talk to a man who was waiting in the office. Lisa didn't know the man or had ever seen him before. She assumed he was a patient. After Julie was finished showing Lisa around, Brad was still tied up with patients.

"I tell you what," Lisa said. "It's such a long drive down here, and I'm really hungry. Is there a Starbucks around here? I'd love to go grab a muffin and coffee, something to tide me over until dinner."

Julie said yes, there was a Starbucks nearby and offered to go with Lisa. Once they were alone, Julie started asking Lisa a lot of questions about Brad.

"Look," Julie said, "I know it's really none of my business, but there are some things I think you should know about this man you're seeing."

"Like what?" Lisa asked.

"Are you dating other men?" Julie asked.

"No, of course not," Lisa replied.

"Do you think he's seeing other women?"

"No!"

"Well," Julie said. "You're wrong. I've known the man for a couple of years now, and Brad Schwartz has *never* been faithful to anyone. Not to his wife, not to anyone."

"You know this for a fact?" Lisa said. "Because we've talked about this, and Brad said he wasn't interested in seeing other women."

"He's lying to you, honey, believe me," Julie said. "Brad Schwartz doesn't have a faithful bone in his body."

The conversation left Lisa on edge.

***

Dellene Moyer, who was working in a laboratory in the First Avenue medical complex, decided to take a cigarette break around 5:15 p.m. She headed out the back of the building, which opened into an alleyway, grabbing her cell phone along the way, so she could call her fiancé. Dellene saw a Mitsubishi pickup truck to her left, which had been parked in the same spot for a couple of days. Turning to her right, she was startled to see a man wearing a light-colored T-shirt and jeans with sandy blond, shoulder-length hair that moved in the late afternoon breeze. The thought occurred to her that he might be wearing a wig, but she shrugged off the notion. She noticed that as he walked by a pillar to the breezeway leading to the front of the complex, the setting sun caught the gold rims of his sunglasses. Dellene caught a glance from the man, a glare that made her feel like he didn't think that she belonged there. He so unnerved her that she snubbed out her half-smoked cigarette and went back inside the lab, being careful to lock the door behind her. About half an hour later, when it was time for her to leave work, Dellene checked outside to make sure the man wasn't lurking there anymore. He wasn't, so she walked quickly to her car and left.

Becky Carr, who was working in an allergy clinic for Dr. Leonard Schultz at the First Avenue medical complex, was closing the office around 5:25 p.m. when a man in dark-colored scrubs entered.

"*Hola!*" the man said, using the familiar Spanish greeting.

Becky and a nurse exchanged glances, neither of them showing signs that they knew who the man was. Perhaps he was a late patient, which happened sometimes. The complex also tended to attract a wide variety of people throughout the day, some of whom ask to use the bathroom.

This man headed to the back of the office waiting room, where there was a water cooler, so obviously he knew the place, Becky figured. After taking a drink, the man left the office, and Becky continued shutting things down for the day.

Minutes later, as she and her co-workers were leaving, she glanced over toward Dr. Altschuler's office, where she saw the man sitting on a curb.

***

Lisa and Julie returned to Brad's office around 5:30, just as Brad was finishing up. Lisa followed Brad's Escalade back to his apartment, where she could let her dog stay, and she could hang out while he was at a counseling session. She decided not to say anything to Brad about her conversation with Julie until later.

***

At 5:45 p.m., Brian called Daphne on her cell phone to discuss plans for an upcoming gala. He sounded rushed, and they talked about the dress that Daphne wanted to wear. After a few minutes, they said their goodbyes and hung up. Daphne went to prepare dinner for the children and herself while Brian waited for the pizzas he ordered for his evening lecture with the med students.

***

Brad and Lisa drove over to his apartment, where Lisa would stay while Brad was attending his weekly 6 p.m. group counseling. Lisa took advantage of his absence to do a little snooping. She saw that his computer was on sleep, and, figuring she needed to get directions from MapQuest on where the real estate test was being held the next day, Lisa tapped on the space bar to bring the computer screen to life. Apparently, the last thing Brad was looking at was an Internet dating site for Hispanics. She felt like she had no option but to bring up the subject of his unfaithfulness to her after he returned.

**

Across town at the North First Avenue Medical Complex, Christine Rotelle was walking to her car when she noticed how dark it seemed to be for 6 o'clock. The sun was just setting and darkness would overtake Tucson within half an hour. Well, she thought, it is getting to be fall, so the daylight hours are going to be shorter. A strange feeling came over her, and she looked around the complex in case there was something suspicious occurring that she was sensing. Nothing but the usual comings and goings at that time of day in the complex. On First Avenue, traffic was busy as usual with thousands headed north to their Foothills homes. She climbed into her car, shrugged off the strange feeling and headed for home.

Jason Lee, a medical student at the University of Arizona, arrived at the medical complex shortly before 6 for a scheduled lecture at Brian's office. Jason parked his car next to the northern row of offices, not being sure where Brian's office was.

"Need some help?" a man in aqua scrubs asked.

Jason told the man he was looking for Dr. Stidham's office.

"It's over there," the man in scrubs said, pointing toward Brian's office. "I saw some pizza being delivered there for the meeting."

Just up the road from the medical complex, Jennifer Dainty was working the night shift, 3 to 11 p.m., at Quicksmart on the southeast corner of River Road and First Avenue. Around 6 o'clock, a man who says he locked his keys in his car asks to use the store phone. He uses the phone about five times. Jennifer later described the man as being Italian or Mexican wearing light blue, short-sleeve shirt and matching pants. He was dark-skinned and spoke with a New York or East Coast-type accent. He was in his late 30s, around 5-foot-8 medium build with short dark and curly hair and brown eyes.

"He was very excited," she said. "He'd been up for 72 hours and was using a real strong New York accent. He asked another customer for a cigarette before he left."

Minutes after the man left, around 7 p.m., a call came in to the convenience store. A man asked whether someone there was trying to reach him. Jennifer told the caller that a man had been making phone calls from there, but he'd just left.

***

When Brad got back to his apartment around 7:30, he and Lisa changed clothes and headed out to a place that Brad said had the best Thai food anywhere in Tucson.

"Brad," Lisa said. "Are you seeing other women?"

"What are you talking about?" he said testily.

"Julie told me this afternoon that you're seeing other women," she said.

"Julie doesn't know what she's talking about, and she has no business telling you stuff like that," he snapped.

They were supposed to meet up with Julie for dinner, but Brad called Julie to cancel.

Lisa felt redeemed by having Brad all to herself for dinner. Of course, his phone kept on ringing, as it always did. Julie told Lisa that she sometimes turned Brad's ringer off when they had meetings, so that she had his undivided attention. Lisa wished that she might have done that, too, when Brad told someone to meet them at the restaurant.

"It's a friend from rehab," Brad said. "I'm kind of helping him out. He's having car problems. He asked if he could come meet us for dinner. Is that OK?"

Lisa reluctantly agreed.

Tom Boager had just begun his night shift as a cab driver when he decided to cruise down Speedway Boulevard to an all-nude strip club, Bunny Ranch, where it was relatively easy to pick up a fare. Sure enough, as soon as he pulled his van into the parking lot, a man who appeared to have just crossed the street and was out of breath, flagged him down. Bruce climbed into the back seat of the van and said he needed to go to a Thai restaurant near the corner of Campbell Avenue and Grant Road. Boager pulled out onto Speedway and headed west.

"What's the name of the restaurant?" Tom asked, trying to picture the businesses in that area and coming up empty for a Thai restaurant.

"Do you have a phone?" Bruce asked. "Can I borrow it? I'll ask."

Tom passed his cell phone back to Bruce without a second thought. He barely paid attention to the conversation, but Bruce appeared to be making arrangements to meet up with someone at the restaurant. After the phone conversation ended, Bruce told Tom that the restaurant was just east of the intersection.

"I can't picture a Thai restaurant there," Tom said. "Do you mean where Yankee Doodle Pizza is?"

"I don't know," Bruce said. "I'm not from around here. But he says it's right there."

Tom turned north on Campbell, then right on Grant. He looked on the north side of the street and was surprised to see that Yankee Doodle Pizza wasn't there anymore. In its place was a restaurant called Karuna's.

"That's it!" Bruce said as they passed the restaurant.

Tom made a U-turn and drove up to the restaurant, pulling into a short driveway leading to a small parking lot. Brad saw the cab approaching and stood up.

"I'll be right back," Brad said. "Um, do you have 20 bucks for the cab fare? I promised to pay for the guy, but I've only got cards, no cash."

Lisa gritted her teeth and handed Brad a $20 bill.

Bruce scooted out of the van and met Brad on the sidewalk. They spoke for a few moments before Brad approached the cab with the money for the fare.

"No tip," Tom said to himself. "Thanks a lot."

Brad led Bruce to the back of the small restaurant, where Lisa was seated.

"Lisa," Brad said, "this is Bruce. Bruce, Lisa Goldberg."

Bruce smiled at Lisa. She recognized him now as the man who was waiting in Brad's lobby when she arrived at the office earlier that day. She didn't remember anything about Bruce's behavior earlier, but thought he was acting agitated now. The pupils of his eyes were dilated, and Lisa thought he could have been on drugs, never considering that he'd been to see an eye doctor that day. Bruce was fidgety, too, squirming around in his seat. She glanced down at his hands and noticed that his fingernails were very dirty. Bruce saw her staring at his hands and nervously apologized for their appearance. He hadn't been sitting with them long when he got up and asked the waitress for a beer.

"That's a strange thing to ask for when you've been in rehab," Lisa thought to herself.

The restaurant didn't serve alcohol, Bruce was told, so he settled for a soda.

Brad and Lisa had been finishing their dinners when Bruce arrived. Brad allowed Bruce to pick through the leftovers. Brad summoned the waitress over and asked for the check, which he paid for with his credit card. The trio then piled into Brad's Escalade and headed back to Brad's office, where Bruce had left his bike.

"Hey, how'd those scrubs work out for you?" Brad asked Bruce.

"Just great!" Bruce said.

"I wanted to go horseback riding," Bruce said to Lisa. "And I didn't have anything to wear, so Brad gave me some scrubs."

"To go horseback riding?" she asked.

Another strange thing about this man Bruce, she noted.

Lisa stayed in the Escalade after they arrived at the office. Brad and Bruce went to the back of the office, where Bruce's bike was and brought it up to the Escalade. The plan was for them to put Bruce's bike in the Escalade, and then Brad was going to take Bruce to a hotel. But, as much as they tried and as big as Cadillac Escalades are, the bike just wouldn't fit. So the men took the bike to the back yard and got back in the car. Lisa, who was pretty exhausted after a long day, would recall that Brad said something strange, but at the time, she was just too tired to care.

Instead of going to a hotel, Brad instead drove to an ATM. Once again, Lisa stayed in the SUV while the men got out. After a few minutes, the men returned. Brad seemed perturbed.

"There's only $20 in my account," he said. "I just sold a car, and I was hoping that the funds had cleared, but I guess they haven't."

Brad drove to a hotel, in hopes of getting a room for Bruce. Lisa once again chose to stay in the SUV and assumed there weren't any vacancies at the first hotel they found when the two men came back minutes later. Brad drove on and found another hotel, but again, no vacancies. However, the clerk gave them the number for the Residence Inn, which did have vacancies in the penthouse. Lisa was relieved when Brad returned to the SUV alone at the Residence Inn. Lisa breathed a sigh of relief as Brad began driving toward his apartment.

CHAPTER 9

Christine checked her watch. Almost 6:45 p.m. The young massage therapist was eager to get home. On Tuesdays such as this, she saw clients in an office tucked away in a medical complex off a busy Tucson street. She usually tried not to schedule any clients after the other employees left the office, but her client had been running late, so Christine didn't mind accommodating her. The bright red sunset that filled the western sky was soon giving to dusk, and Christine felt nervous in the medical complex after all the other employees left and night fell. Even though the traffic on North First Avenue next to the complex kept steady throughout the night, the complex's parking lot was poorly lighted, and the shadows could hide any creepy horror you could imagine.

On top of that, the complex was built near a large mall and next to a natural culvert, or wash, that carried off rainwater in southern Arizona's summer monsoon season. Vagrants often found shelter in the wash and sometimes wandered into the offices, looking for water or to use the restroom. Christine had overheard some of the women in the office talking about a man that very night who walked in as if he owned the place as he helped himself to some water from the cooler.

Christine gathered up her belongings, opened the front door and paused at the threshold, making sure there was no one outside near her. The early October evening was typical for a Tucson fall. The skies were clear and calm; it wasn't so chilly yet that you needed a jacket for the evening chill. There were just a few cars remaining in the lot, and Christine kept her eye on them as she headed toward her car. After Christine loaded her belongings into her car, she sat in the driver's seat and breathed a sigh of relief. In addition to her anxiety about the dim parking lot, she was also eager to get home and continue making plans for her upcoming wedding. But first, she reminded herself, she had to make a run to the grocery store, which was on her way home.

After shopping, Christine headed home, which was just a few miles from work. It wasn't until she was almost home that she realized that she had left her most precious belonging at the office: her engagement ring. Christine didn't want her ring to get gunked up during massages, and she didn't think clients would like the bauble on their skin, so she always removed it before client sessions. The thought crossed her mind that she should immediately turn back and pick up the ring, but Christine dismissed the notion almost as quickly as it occurred to her. One glance out the window convinced her to wait until her fiancé, Anthony, came home. When she left the office, the sky was still dusky blue, but by 7:30, it was dark and moonless.

Christine reconciled herself to settling in at home, making dinner for herself and Anthony and then enlisting him to escort her to the complex. By the time he did arrive, Christine had nearly forgotten about the ring as they dined and discussed their upcoming wedding. Eventually, though, she conceded to him that she had left the ring behind at work and wanted to get it that night instead of leaving it until the next day.

"You never know who might come through at night," she told him. "I wouldn't want someone to swipe it."

Anthony agreed to take her, and the young couple set out in his pickup truck just after 10.

As Anthony pulled the truck into the parking lot of the complex, his headlights caught an image that, at first, neither he nor Christine could comprehend. It seemed to be a man in scrubs—prone on the pavement. Anthony braked and brought the truck within a few feet of the object and verified that it was a man, lying face up, his arms and legs outstretched.

Anthony rolled down his window.

"Hello?" he called out. "Excuse me, sir, but are you all right?

Anthony motioned for Christine to stay in the car while he got out. He saw papers strewn around the motionless man.

"Hello?" he repeated. "Sir, are you OK?"

Anthony cautiously approached the man, speaking loudly, hoping to get a response. There was none. Anthony gingerly nudged the man's right shoulder with his foot. There was no reaction. Something in Anthony wanted to believe that this was not a dead man in front of him. Yet he knew that it was. Maybe it was a prank, although Halloween was three weeks away. Realizing that something was terribly wrong and not sure how he should proceed, Anthony got back in the truck and moved it away.

"Christie, he's not moving," he said.

"Is he drunk or something?" she asked.

"I don't know."

"Should we call 911?" Christine suggested. "Should we check for a pulse?"

"Yeah," Anthony said. "Check for a pulse. I'll call 911."

Christine, who had once trained to be a lifeguard and knew CPR, slowly got out of the truck and approached the man, checking for a pulse on his right wrist. His skin was not warm as she would expect it to be, but it was not clammy, either. Anthony called 911 on his cell phone and described the situation. He looked at Christine, standing by the man.

"Is he OK?" Anthony called out.

Christine shook her head.

"This person is gone," Anthony told the 911 dispatcher.

Within minutes, around 10:30 p.m., a Tucson police officer arrived at the scene. The medical complex happened to be located in a tiny peninsula of unincorporated Pima County, with Tucson's city limits abutting it. Soon, deputies from the Pima County Sheriff's Department arrived at the complex to take over. Within the hour, the darkened lot was illuminated by bright lights, a large section was taped off and the surrounding area teeming with deputies and detectives. Not surprisingly, some TV station newsrooms had heard about the suspected homicide as they were finishing up their telecasts for the night and sent crews over to document the investigation and get what few details would be released in the early hours of a murder case.

Near the body, deputies saw a motor vehicle registration renewal form, torn and bloodied, to a white Lexus—but no matching car nearby. The name on the form read "David Brian Stidham" and gave an address in a tony neighborhood in the foothills of the Santa Catalina Mountains just north of the city. The name "Dr. D. Brian Stidham" was marked above an office door about 40 feet from the body. Of the dozens of murders in Pima County each year, few of them involve someone of such standing in the community. It was obvious to the deputies and detectives that this young doctor was the unfortunate victim of a carjacking. Word was sent out immediately for law enforcement officers across town to watch for Dr. Stidham's white Lexus.

Shortly after 10:30 p.m., Deputy Jeffrey Craven arrived at the First Avenue medical complex in response to a "man down" call. As he steered the patrol car into the lot, a man and woman began waving him over and pointing toward the place where they had found Brian's body. Brian was lying face-up, his head in a southwestern direction, his arms and legs spread out on the pavement. Bloodied and torn paperwork was strewn around him. His glasses, speckled with blood, lay on the asphalt beside him.

Craven surmised that the victim worked in the medical field by the scrubs that he wore. The body appeared pale and still. Craven put on some latex gloves and checked for a pulse, finding no sign of life. As he stood up, paramedics David Latour and Cynthia Gibson drove up. The paramedics confirmed that the victim was dead, about 10 minutes after Craven arrived on the scene.

Other deputy units began arriving, so Craven directed them to secure the crime scene. Two deputies checked all the doors in the complex, looking for unlocked doors or occupants. Deputy S.G. Shafer noticed that there was one door to an office that earlier was darkened, but now appeared to have a light on within. He knocked on the door and was greeted by a tiny woman who identified herself as Dr. Thili Kulatilake. The doctor explained that she had been in her office for most of the day, but that she'd left around 3:30 p.m. to make a trip to Walmart to get cleaning supplies for the office aquarium. She brought the cleaning supplies back for the staff, then left for a medical appointment and a trip to Costco. It was 6 p.m. when she got back to the office.

"Did you see any other people or vehicles in the lot when you got back?" Shafer asked.

Dr. K wasn't sure she saw any people, but she didn't make a note of which cars were there, since there usually were a few there at that time of day.

"Did you hear any noises or commotions tonight?" he asked.

"Not until just now," she said. "That's why I opened the back door and stepped out to look."

***

Deputy S.J. Marsh arrived on the scene and was instructed to conduct an exterior sweep of the complex. Other than finding a gold 1989 Mitsubishi half-ton pickup parked in an alley to the west of the complex, Marsh found nothing remarkable. The pickup, he learned later, had been reported stolen the day before.

Marsh conducted an interview with Anthony and Christine about how they found the body and what brought them there.

"Did you see any suspicious vehicles leaving the area when you arrived?" Marsh asked.

They had not. They also didn't recognize the victim.

Christine told Marsh that she didn't want to leave her engagement ring at the office overnight because various cleaning crews come through the office, and it might get stolen. She waited for Anthony to come home because the complex was dark at night and she felt unsafe going there alone.

Sgt. P.D. McGhee arrived at the scene just as the paramedics were removing EKG wires from the victim. McGhee could tell that the victim was dead.

"Are you done?" he asked.

Yes, they said.

"Then I need you to clear out because we've got a crime scene here."

Marsh briefed McGhee and put in a call around 10:50 p.m. to the home of Sgt. Brad Foust, head of the Pima County Sheriff's Department's homicide unit.

"Deceased white male subject," McGhee said. "Looks to be in his mid-30s, lying in the middle of a medical plaza parking lot. It's possible that he's a nurse or doctor, because he's wearing scrubs and there's a hat, like the kind that doctors wear in surgery, laying near the victim's head."

Lt. Robert Kimmins, a force commander, arrived around 11 p.m. and walked cautiously over to where the body was lying, careful as to not step on anything he thought could be evidence. He noticed there were several pieces of paper from the Motor Vehicle Division near the body. They could be clues to the victim's identity, but they were face-down, so he couldn't see any names. Kimmins gently turned the registration paper over and saw the name David Brian Stidham. Kimmins jotted down the name, address and information about the car, a 1992 Lexus coupe with the license plate number 806 GPP, which he gave to another officer. The information was then relayed throughout the state in case any other officer saw the car.

After hanging up with McGhee, Foust called his five detectives—Jill Murphy, Paul Montano, William Knuth, Jesus Lopez and Chris Hogan—and told them to get out to the murder scene. The detectives take lead roles in a rotation, and it was Murphy's turn to head up the murder case. Foust left his house around 11:36 and was on the scene in 20 minutes himself. Along the way, he listened to the radio traffic to update himself on what was taking place.

Once the unit was assembled at the murder scene, Foust told Murphy, Knuth and Hogan to process the crime scene. Montano was sent to inspect the stolen Mitsubishi. Lopez, who had arrived first, already was interviewing the couple who found the body. Foust told Det. Matthew Othic, one of the members of the night detective squad who also came to the scene, to go to the convenience store at River and First to see if they had a surveillance video that might have caught something worthwhile. Othic later reported that the store's surveillance video camera wasn't working.

Just before midnight, Foust dispatched Othic and several deputies to go to the victim's home to check on the family or if the car that was supposed to be at the scene was actually at the home. From what the detectives could surmise, it appeared that there was a fatal carjacking. Shortly before midnight, Foust sent several deputies to the home address listed on the motor vehicle papers either to contact survivors or determine whether there were more victims.

CHAPTER 10

Shortly after midnight, four deputies arrived at Brian and Daphne Stidham's house. Deputy A.E. Stevens noticed that there were no cars parked on the street. The deputies knew that Brian drove a Lexus. Stevens and two other deputies, J.R. Hamilton and J.G. Ledesma, walked up to the house while Deputy Moreno went around the back to cover them. Stevens peered into the windows but couldn't see anything or hear any stirrings within the darkened house. Stevens rang the doorbell, which they could hear echoing within the house. No response. One of the deputies tried calling a phone number given to them, but got a busy signal. Orders were sent to call Qwest to interrupt the call, but Qwest said its equipment that could cut in was broken.

Stevens rang the doorbell again.

Still, nothing.

Stevens turned the doorknob. Surprisingly, it was unlocked. Stevens slowly opened the door but could only get it open about an inch and a half before a security chain stopped it.

"Hello?" Stevens yelled into the crack. "I'm a deputy with the Pima County Sheriff's Department! Is anyone inside?"

Stevens heard nothing, even after repeating himself several times.

Checking around the house, Hamilton was able to push open a door to the three-car garage, which contained a Lexus SUV. The deputies called in the license plate number, which turned out to be registered to Brian and Daphne, but it was not the Lexus they were looking for. Det. Othic arrived and told the deputies that his supervisors gave permission for them to enter the home. The deputies entered the house through the unlocked door from the garage. Othic stood guard outside the front door for security as the four other deputies entered the house through the laundry room. To the right, there was a double-door entrance to what they assumed was the master bedroom. Hamilton told Stevens to watch the bedroom door while he surveyed the open dining and living room areas. Once that area was cleared, Hamilton searched the kitchen and family room.

Stevens and Ledesma cautiously opened the door to the bedroom. Peering inside, they saw a woman sleeping on her back on the right side of the bed. Stevens shined his flashlight on the woman and shouted, "Pima County Sheriff's Department, ma'am!"

The woman slowly opened her eyes, sat up and blurted, "Is my husband OK? Was he shot?"

"Why did you ask me that?" Ledesma said, according to his report of the night.

"Because he's missing. He didn't come home."

With permission from deputies, Daphne put on some pants. Stevens noted in his report that Daphne didn't look to her left, which would be where her husband should have been sleeping. She just hopped out of bed and walked to her dresser, Stevens observed, where she got a pair of pajama pants.

"Was he shot?" she asked again.

Stevens and Ledesma, to that point, had said nothing about her husband, his whereabouts or his well-being, according to their reports. The deputies asked Daphne for some ID and escorted her to the kitchen where Daphne retrieved her purse and sat down on the floor, combing through it for her driver's license. They were joined by Moreno, who had come in from the back of the house, and Othic, from the front.

Hamilton continued his way through the house. Just off the kitchen, he came across a room with a double set of doors that was locked. He tried the next room and saw a crib with a sleeping baby inside. He continued down the hall and reached another bedroom, where a young boy was sleeping on the bed. Hamilton was coming around again to the dining room area, where he heard sounds of a woman speaking in what he would describe as a saddened type of voice. He saw Daphne seated with the other deputies.

Othic gestured for Daphne to take a seat at the dining room table, which she did.

"What's your husband's name?" he asked.

"Brian," she said. "Well, it's David Brian, but he goes by Brian."

"What does he do?"

"He's a doctor, a medical doctor."

"Where does he work?"

"He's got an office on First Avenue."

"What kind of car does he drive?"

"A Lexus sports car, white," she said. "Has my husband been shot?"

"I'm not sure," Othic said, according to his report of the events, surprised at her question since he was just about to tell her why they were at her house. "I'm afraid, though, that I do have some bad news. Your husband has been found deceased."

Daphne broke down, sobbing. She caught her breath and asked if she could make some phone calls.

"Can I use the phone in the bedroom?" Daphne asked, explaining that the house lines weren't working, so she needed to use her cell phone.

After the deputies gave her permission, Daphne raced to her bedroom, followed by Moreno. Hamilton stayed behind in the dining room, with an eye on the boy's door in case he was awakened by their voices and needed consoling.

Daphne plopped down on the floor of her bedroom and began dialing on her cell phone as Moreno stood nearby. The deputies noticed in their reports that Daphne was visibly upset, crying and shaking as she began notifying her and Brian's family about his death.

"He was probably just tired," Daphne said to a deputy in between calls.

"Why do the most horrible things happen to the nicest people?" she asked, looking up at the two deputies and smiling sadly. Daphne continued trying to reach her family without success.

"Why do the most horrible things happen to the nicest people?" she repeated.

Moreno looked around the bedroom and noticed there were some legal papers that appeared to be a will, placed on a couch next to the bed, according to his report. He called the papers to Othic's attention. Stevens and Ledesma also noted the paperwork, which was in plain view on top of a couple of magazines, in their reports.

"I don't know why the cruelest things happen to the nicest people," Daphne muttered.

Othic also noticed that there was an unplugged house phone on the bedroom floor.

Daphne said she knew a couple of people who were against her husband. Brad Schwartz, for one, she said. He'd gotten into drugs and had trouble with the DEA.

"Was it a murder?" she asked. "Are there any detectives with Brian? Was he shot or was it a heart attack?"

Speaking to a friend on the phone, Daphne said, "I was asking the police if he was just shot or something, but they don't know. I feel so guilty. I just wanted to tell him that I loved him, but I didn't want to bother him at the time, earlier today."

Moreno asked the sheriff's communications to get an emergency message through to Daphne's mother, Junja Herding, in Texas, since Daphne was having trouble getting through to her parents' house.

Moreno noted in his report that Daphne didn't seem as upset as she did earlier when they arrived.

"Do you want anything to drink?" she asked politely. "Would you rather sit down in the living room?"

Daphne also repeatedly asked how her husband was killed, according to the deputies' reports.

"Could he have had a heart attack?" Daphne asked. "He's been so overworked and busy with the kids all the time. I think he might have had a heart attack."

Stevens explained that he had no information about Brian's death.

"Can I talk to someone with my husband to see if he was shot?" Daphne asked Stevens, who wondered why she kept referring to Brian being shot as no deputy had told her he was.

"I'm sorry," Stevens said, according to his report. "I wasn't on the scene when he was found, and I don't know what caused his death."

"If he was murdered," Daphne said, according to the deputies' reports, "I know of a couple of people. I need to know if he was shot or if he just died."

"I'm sorry, I don't have that information," Stevens said.

The deputies' concerns were relayed back to Sgt. Leonetti, who in turn kept Sgt. Foust informed. Based on what they were hearing, Foust decided to send Detectives Montano and Lopez to interview Daphne Stidham.

Othic walked in while Daphne was contacting Joyce Stidham, Brian's mother.

"I know that this is hard for you," Daphne said to Joyce. "I'm sorry."

After Daphne hung up the phone, she turned to the deputies.

"I wish I could pay you for being here with me now," Daphne said.

"Do you want anything to drink?" she asked politely. "Would you rather sit down in the living room?"

Daphne sat down with the deputies in the living room as they waited for the detectives to arrive.

"Did my husband die of a heart attack?" Daphne asked. "Was he shot? Did someone hear a shot or something?"

The deputies maintained that they didn't have any information about how Brian died.

"I wonder, is it harder to lose a child or a spouse?" she asked.

Deputy Hamilton didn't know how to respond to that, he said in his report, so he just looked back at her.

"Are you married?" she asked.

Hamilton said he was.

"Do you think it's worse to lose a child or a spouse?" she asked.

Hamilton just shook his head, still unsure how to respond.

"I've never been in that situation," Moreno said.

Moreno excused himself to check around the house as the detectives arrived and began questioning Daphne. It was now around 1:20 a.m.

"Can you tell me what happened tonight?" Det. Paul Montano began. "And how did you– who woke you up, and what do you know so far?" he asked.

"Uh … I … um … think I remember hearing, um, a man talkin' by my bedroom door. I thought it could have been a dream. I don't know how long the person was there," she said,

"OK. Did they scare you?" Montano asked.

"I don't know," she said. "Brian, my husband, hasn't been home yet."

"What time should he have been home?"

"Well, I don't know," Daphne said. "Today he was, today's Tuesday, he was giving a clinic at the office, patients, and then after that, then residents were gonna come to Brian's office and … and … give 'em a lecture, so he should've been home … I didn't know …"

"It's a pretty busy profession," Montano said. "I understand it. Can you just tell me about this morning? Does he live here with you? OK. So, um, are you guys still married and livin' together?"

Daphne nodded.

"So, this morning can you tell me what time he left and what was goin' on, anything unusual, just kinda walk me through the day from the time that, you know, you last saw him this morning and what his schedule should've been. Did you talk to him during the day? Stuff like that."

Daphne began to answer his questions when the phone rang. Montano motioned that it was OK to answer.

"Hello?" Daphne said into the phone. "Yeah, hi, Daddy. I don't know how to … they showed up at my door and said they found Brian deceased, at his office. … I don't know, Dad, they came and … Yeah, I … I don't know, he was supposed to have clinic today, and then he was supposed to give a lecture after, to, um, a couple of residents and then I remember it was, like, 10 o'clock, or 15 before 10, he wasn't home, I said, 'Well, maybe he got caught up'… didn't call today … I don't know, Dad, they won't tell me, uh, actually we're talking to the detectives now, can I call you back? OK. I love you, Dad."

After Daphne ended the call, Montano picked up on the questioning.

"Did Brian receive any phone calls or anything out of the ordinary from anybody, before he left the house?" Montano asked.

"No," Daphne said.

Then Daphne blurted out Bradley Schwartz's name, the detectives noted in their report of the night.

"Did they, did they communicate today, that you know of?" Montano asked. "Bradley and your husband?"

"I don't know," Daphne said.

"But this morning you don't know if they … well, in your presence here in the house, he … he didn't receive a call from him?"

"But I know he's done that before," Daphne said. "He's called our home. It's kinda weird. He would call my husband, his office. Did you ever find out what's goin' on?"

Daphne told how she had gone to Brian's office during the day because their home computer had crashed. She took the children with her, and then took them to the park. Brian, she said, left her a voice mail message somewhere around 5:30 or 6 p.m. on her cell phone.

"So, when you left his office, was anything suspicious or weird goin' on?" Montano asked.

Daphne didn't see anything irregular, she told him.

Montano asked about which car Brian had taken to work, and Daphne told him that he took his white 1992 Lexus.

"Do you know the license plate number, by any chance?" Montano asked.

"Can you tell me if he was shot and killed?" Daphne said.

"Well," Montano said, "we don't know, because, like I said, the team is over there workin' it right now, but while they're doin' that it kinda helps to see what's goin' on, by talking about his day and, you know, people we should go, other people we should go talk to, nobody knows better than his wife, so, um … What time was he supposed to be home?"

"I don't know," Daphne said. "I was assuming, um, I know he had to give the lecture at 6, and I don't know if he ran late. That's why he called me so rushed at a quarter of 6."

"Should his car be there at the office, then, somewhere?" Montano asked. "It's a big parking lot. We haven't been all the way around the parking lot yet."

"There's only parking in the front," Daphne said.

"Where does he park?"

"Um, he usually parks catty-corner from the front door of his office."

"Could Brian have … does he have any medical history where he maybe suffered something natural?" Montano asked.

"He has ... the police officer, he said it's, ya know ... he's only nine months away ... he has had two heart attacks, smoking," Daphne said in short bursts.

She pressed Montano to tell her how they think Brian died.

"It takes a while to work the way up to actually examine fully any person found," he said, "They're still lookin' at that, so I truly don't know what to tell you about how he died. I mean, that's why I'm makin' sure I rule out anything natural, bad heart, had ... ever having seizures, um, I mean is anything wrong with him that could maybe have contributed to him passing away?"

"No," Daphne said. "He ... I know the heart attack, maybe. But he exercises religiously."

"Have you found any medication?"

"He takes something for his hair," she said. "I forgot what it is."

Daphne was asked if Brian took any other pills.

"No," she said. "He just got done with his surgery, uh, maybe a month ago. He took a lot of Valium the doctors gave him."

The detectives asked about Brian's practice. Daphne told him that in December, it would have been Brian's two-year anniversary at that office.

"Has he ever had any problems, uh, with anybody at that office?" a detective asked her. "Like an employee, customer?"

"Or past patients that weren't happy with any, you know, treatment received, anything like that," Montano added.

"Yeah, one guy," Daphne said.

"Has anybody made any threats towards him?" a detective asked.

"Brad has," Daphne stated. "Brad has said, like, 'I'm gonna kill you.'"

Montano asked if Daphne had any contact numbers for Brad. She mentioned that she knew he had hospital privileges at Northwest but couldn't get them at Tucson Medical Center or St. Joseph's because of a "drug thing."

Montano asked if Brian had sounded angry or upset, or if there was anything unusual in his voice other than being rushed when he called at 5:45.

"Nothing unusual," Daphne said.

"When he gives lectures, does he wear a suit, does he just wear ..."

Daphne said Brian was self-conscious about his "hair shine" so he often wore a hat with his scrubs.

"Does he usually carry his wallet with him?" Montano asked.

"No, he usually leaves it in the car," she said.

Brian usually didn't carry a lot of cash, she said. They had identical credit cards. Daphne showed her cards to the detective, so he could copy the numbers down.

"Just to make sure," Montano said, "Brian doesn't use illegal drugs? Or have any bad habits from his partner or anything?"

"Once in a while," she said, Brian would take pills because "he can't sleep."

After the detectives went over any body scarring Brian had—except for the scalp surgery where his hair was shaved, stretch marks on his back and appendix scar, there were none, she said—the detectives asked why the home phones weren't working.

"I don't know why the phone doesn't work," Daphne said. "You just pick it up and there's no dial tone. That one never worked because I don't ever talk on the phone very much with the kids. But the other one—I don't know why it doesn't work.

"Did you say it was a struggle?" Daphne said, pressing again for a cause of Brian's death. "Usually with a heart attack people are choking, they're not getting any air."

"We're gonna check all that," Montano assured her. "Plus, we're gonna have an autopsy. The unit is responding to the crime scene. Uh, they'll have … you know, an autopsy to … to further check anything that's visible externally."

The detectives asked Daphne about who stays at Brian's office and what time all the employees leave.

"Were you with your kids all day?" Montano asked. "Did they go to a sitter for any reason? Like, at any period, any time?"

"Yeah, I have a lady that helps me with, uh, she comes Tuesdays, Fridays, 8:30 to about 2. Sometimes she leaves at 3, and she works at cleaning, she cleans from 8:30 to about 2 o'clock, and then watches the kids for about an hour and a half."

"Does anybody else watch your kids or did anybody else watch your kids yesterday?" Montano asked.

"She was alone with him," Daphne said, explaining that she had to leave the house to shop at the grocery store around 2:30 p.m.

"What time did you come home Tuesday and stay home, Daphne?" Montano asked.

"Tuesday was yesterday," she replied.

"Mm hm," he said.

"We went to the park and to the Baby Aldrich to get some toys at the store and then got gas—"

"Did you ever go anywhere else after about that time?"

"The grocery store."

"And what time would you have gotten home from the grocery store, do ya think?" Montano asked.

"Well, the nanny left at 2:30, right around 3," Daphne replied.

"Any weapons in the house? Even collector items that won't get used, anything at all? I mean, weapons, sometimes people say they don't have guns, but they don't really fire 'em but they're collectors, collector items or somethin' like that."

Daphne said there were no weapons around.

"Is it OK with you if I walk through the house, just to—"

"I should've picked up a little bit first," Daphne apologized.

"It's alright," Montano assured her.

While Montano began his inspection of the house, another detective asked how the Stidhams were doing financially.

"Very well," Daphne said. "He just bought me a car, um, we're looking to build a house. He just put a buncha money into a surgery center. Um, yeah, we go on very nice trips."

How about any insurance policies?

"It's a coincidence, he just set that up," Daphne said, according to the detectives' report. "A couple or several months ago, but, ya know, we just finished our trust, which replaces a will. Um, and we're just now in the process of turning everything over to the trust."

Daphne was asked how much Brian's life insurance was worth.

"I don't know, actually," she replied.

"It was actually his idea first," she said. "And then, um, we were talkin' about, ya know, should a spouse get it, too? And I said, 'Well, I just stay home.'"

So Daphne didn't get a policy for herself, she said. She estimated that his policy was worth $500,000 or $1 million, the detectives reported.

The detectives wanted to know more about Brian's will. Daphne began to explain that the papers the deputies saw by her bedside wasn't his will, but their shared estate papers, according to the detectives' reports.

"We're just in the process of ... we just finished doing the paperwork for the trust," Daphne said. "And then, um, transfer stuff from the trust ... I forgot ... just reading it, actually, before bed tonight. Transferring, um, something to the trust, I think all of our paperwork, stuff like that."

"But what were you reading before you went to bed?" she was asked.

"Directions on what I'm supposed to do, I think, and I was supposed to, I have the sheet, actually ... I'll get it, but I think I'm supposed to call the homeowner's policy and have 'em transfer the stuff to the trust."

Daphne explained that she had gotten the instructions from the couple's attorney.

"Our financial planner told us to get this," she said. "It's a good idea to have. Are you sure you can't call the detective and ask how he was killed or if he– ask them if he was strangled, was he shot, was he choked?"

The detectives said they couldn't tell her.

"You need to know?" they asked.

"Yeah," she said.

"How come?"

"I just wanna know. I don't know … at Dr. Schwartz, or …"

"What do you think happened to your husband?"

"I find it really hard to believe that he's only one month older than I am, I just turned 36 October 1, that someone like that just dies. I don't think that happened," she said. "He doesn't smoke. He had a very good home life, real happy home life. I think somebody killed him."

"What makes you believe that? Do you have a gut feeling, or …"

"Because it was such a bitter breakup, and Brad was indicted and, um, he was indicted, and he would just call here and just hang up."

The detectives asked why Daphne thought Brad Schwartz had something to do with her husband's death, according to their reports.

"Maybe," she said. "I don't know if it was— you just don't die, someone like my husband, 'cause he's so healthy. I know he's healthy 'cause he made a point of telling me the life insurance was good because he had to get a blood test or something, and said it was pretty good for someone who's had a heart attack. So, I'm just thinkin' … had it been like that, the man would still be alive."

"What time did you go to bed tonight?"

"Before 10."

"It was before 10?"

"Yeah, and I thought about calling him, asking him, 'When are you coming home?' 'Cause usually he calls me, 'I'm on my way home.'"

"Is 10 o'clock, uh, normal for him not to be home or does he usually, is ... is he usually home before 10?"

"Yes," Daphne said. "He usually comes home before 6, 6:30, but he had to do that lecture around 6, and I feel so bad now ..."

"When he does give a lecture, how, how long does he usually take? Normally."

"One, two hours," she said.

"And when that happens, what time does he usually get home?"

"Between 7 and 10," she said. "I didn't call him before I went to sleep."

"What time did you put, uh, your kids—"

"I put the baby down, somewhere between 9 and 9:30, and the boy, a little after 7."

"What did you do during that time period?"

"Played with the baby."

"Just played with the baby."

"Yeah," she said. "Played with the baby, um, gave her some more bottle, cleaned the kitchen, washed the dishes, get ready for bed. ... I ... I shoulda called him."

"Do you find it odd that he wasn't home by 10 o'clock when you went to bed?"

"Yeah," she said.

"How come you didn't call?"

"'Cause ... I don't know," she said.

"Would you normally call?"

"Or he calls me, sometimes I call ... and I think I'm bothering him, 'cause I asked him ... I shoulda called him ..."

"OK, um, so you went to bed about 10 o'clock, you said. Did you look at the clock to know what time you went to bed?"

"Well," she said, "I stopped reading ... before 10. No later than 15 before 10."

"And what were you reading?"

"A parenting book," she said. "And then that stuff on the trust, what I have to do."

"OK. And, um, obviously, you ... did you fall ... fall asleep?"

"Yeah."

"OK, and then what time, uh, were you woken up?"

"This clock said 12:26, so prob'ly around then."

"OK. And can you explain to me what happened when you, you were awoken?"

"No, I ... I ... I don't know actually how long I ... I laid there," she said. "I don't know how long they were standin' there. Then I got up."

"Were you worried?"

"When I ... I ... yeah, I knew right away something was wrong, because, um ..."

"Did they knock on the door? Did they come inside?"

"I didn't hear them knock," Daphne said. "They were just standing outside my bedroom door, the door was open, and the light was on."

"What did you think when you saw them?"

"I saw the badge, under the light, and I knew something was wrong. My husband's gone, so I knew something was wrong."

"Did you say anything to the deputies?"

"Yeah, I said, I said, 'What's wrong? Has something happened, or ... or ... my husband OK?' And then they didn't answer me, I knew that was because, I just had my sister pass away about several years ago, so I know what it looks like to see a police officer's face."

"OK, so, so the first thing you ask is, 'Is Brian OK?' "

"I think so, 'Is my husband—' "

"What else did you ask the deputies?"

"'What happened?' and I remember they didn't wanna tell me," Daphne said.

"Did you say anything?"

"I shoulda called him," Daphne whispered to herself.

"Anything else that you recall tellin' the deputies?"

"I told them about the doctor."

Daphne remembered saying something to the deputies about how she's endured so many deaths in the last few years—her sister, who suffered from anxiety; Brian's father, Mac, died a year previously and then Brian's uncle a week ago.

"I don't know if you got into that yet," Montano said, returning to the room, "but did you guys ... have you had any marital problems in the last few months?"

"Mm mm," Daphne said, shaking her head no.

"Was there ever a separation?" Montano asked.

"No."

"You've always lived together?" Montano asked.

"Mm hm," Daphne said, indicating yes.

Daphne told Montano that she and Brian had been married since 1997 and in that time, neither had filed for divorce or separation.

"Did you ever file a complaint against Brian for abusing the children?" Montano asked.

"No!" Daphne said. "He would never do anything like that! He's the most mild-mannered man. He has a real introverted side. And everyone loves him in the community."

"I apologize that we're the bearers of bad news," Montano told Daphne, according to his report. "And I apologize that we're, ya know, here, you know? And we have so many questions. But I appreciate the fact that you're willing to ... to speak ... to speak to us. And that's you know ... we appreciate your cooperation, and ... and it really helps us with the investigation. Is there any reason that you would not want to talk to us at this point?"

"Uh, no," Daphne said. "I wish I could talk with the people at the office, to find out what happened."

"Uh, is there anything that—is our presence making you speak to us at this time?"

"No, she said. "I'm glad you're here. I don't wanna be here alone."

"OK," Montano said. "Because we're in your home only because you ... you allowed us in here, OK? We don't, you know, the only right we have to be here is 'cause you let us in here. For any reason you didn't want us in here, you have to tell us to leave."

"OK."

"And any reason you don't wanna talk, you have the right to tell us you don't wanna talk, OK?" Montano said.

"No," Daphne said. "Please don't go."

"OK, so I just wanna make sure that we're not here pressuring you. I mean, uh, you're kinda outnumbered. But you're not under arrest," Montano said, according to his report. "And you're free to leave any time, and you're free to make us leave your home at any time, do you understand all that?"

"Mm hm," she said.

"OK," Montano said. "For any reason you feel compelled ... for any reason you feel like we're making you do anything, we're not, OK? And it's— anything you tell us, my understanding is—and I hope you understand the same thing—is that it's because you wanna talk to us. Is that, I mean, is that clear to you?"

"Uh huh."

"Alright," Montano said, according to his report. "I don't wanna make you feel worse than you already do, you know? You're suffering a loss, and you're not under arrest, and we're not forcing you. So, OK. I'd have to say that I'm sorta confused why you said some of the things that you did say."

"OK," Daphne said.

"Um, I kinda wonder why your first impression would be, you know, 'Was my husband shot?' Can you answer that for me?" Montano asked, according to his report.

"Because I know someone who really despised him, against him, who ruined his life."

"And who's that?"

"Brad Schwartz. Because since we came here, he lost his entire practice, divorce, lost his house, and his wife left him, it was really bad," Daphne said.

Montano noted in his report that he wondered why Daphne would automatically assume that the deputies were there for her, why she didn't think that they might have been in the wrong house or why she just assumed it was something bad about her husband. Why didn't she think Brian had been in a car accident or something?

"Yeah, I thought it was a car accident," Daphne said. "Before, sometimes as a resident he used to fall asleep at the steering wheel."

"And the detectives that came before we got here, they tell me that they did not indicate where your husband was found, that they said you knew where he was found. How did you know where he was?"

"Uh, I think I asked them that," she replied. "I ... I ... I said, um, 'Is my husband OK?' And I think they said ... they were at his office, and they found him."

"Is there any way that we don't even have Brian," Montano said. "I mean, that it's not Brian. It's somebody else that's over there. I mean, it's a big complex, right? There were people there possibly for a lecture, you know, there's employees coming and going, there's other doctors that could possibly come by and talk to him, or be around, you know, for any reason."

"That was ... you mean they killed him? Or—"

"No, that's been killed," Montano said.

"Oh, that has been killed," she echoed.

"See what I'm saying? It just seems pretty positive in your mind that, it seems to me that you're aware or you're expressing awareness that Brian was found at his office, at his complex, and that he was killed, and that he was shot. Exactly what made you come to all that information?" Montano said, according to his report.

"Well," Daphne said, "just now 'cause when they, police were here, he was gone, and I know the last place he was at was at his office. Um, the reason I say shot or killed is 'cause he's really healthy, and he exercises all ... all the time ... and has a healthy lifestyle. And a man just doesn't die like that."

"You know, so again, you know, you talkin' to me, you also have the right to have counsel or an attorney if you wanted it– if you felt the need or anything like that. Because, you know, people say things and then police can use those things again– you know, what you say can be used against you and could be used against you in a court of law. I'm just, you know, people need to be advised of ... of the way it works or the system works, you know?" Montano said, according to his report.

"And if this person was killed," he continued, "then we're investigating a homicide. If we're investigating a homicide, then, everybody we talk to needs to be aware that you have the right to counsel– counsel can be appointed to 'em. You have the right not to talk, to remain silent. And, you know, that what the Miranda rights are, so, I just wanna clarify that with you. Um, do you think you need an attorney or anything at this point?"

Daphne's response was unclear to Montano.

"I'm sorry, yes or no?" he asked.

"Oh, no," Daphne said.

"OK, I just wanna make sure that you didn't mean yes, OK? OK. But, like I said, you know, it just seems to me that ... that you were aware of certain things that I don't even know yet. And I'm working the case. And it seems to me like you know something."

"I ... I know ... I know his schedule," Daphne said. "I know what he does."

"It would just sort of shock me if I went back and they told me it is him and, uh, he's been shot and, well, she just seemed to know that, you know? That Daphne seemed to know that. Even before we knew that, you know?"

"Well, 'cause ... I don't know who else coulda done it," Daphne said. Like I told him, I'm just tryin' to eliminate ... does ... does a man, 36-year-old, die like that? Someone who works in his office just dies? No. It doesn't happen. Um, I know somebody that has a strong dislike towards him."

"You're talkin' about Bradley Schwartz," Montano said.

Another detective asked whether Brian caused all of Brad's problems.

"Well, no," Daphne said. "He brought us out here, this guy."

"So why does Bradley have somethin' against your husband" the detective asked, "if your husband had nothing to do with what happened to him?"

"Well, he blames him for leavin'," Daphne said. "He thinks we should've stayed or something. Uh, he never told me directly, but I'm just assuming, because he was so busy before we got here, and he sees kids, he sees adults, does more than one specialty. And the community was just loyal to him, and they adored him, and then as soon as we got here, the drug bust came, and then all the business just left. There's pediatricians that my husband works a lot with, um, told my husband that ... that he's hurting for patients, and he's called, and he's sent people over, and you know, um ..."

"But did your husband cause his drug problem?" the detective asked.

"No," Daphne said. "But I'm assuming this went on a long time. My dad's a neurologist, and he does a lot with drugs, and Brad probably had a long-lasting problem that started before we got here. Um, I don't ... I don't know if it's over yet, um, but it was there long before we got here."

"Daphne," Montano said, "where's the clothes you were wearing before you went to bed?"

"Uh, prob'ly in my room," she said.

"Would they just be on the bed or on carpet somewhere or … or is there a hamper in there or where would they be?" he asked. "Well, let's just start with this, what clothes were you wearing today, you took off to go to bed?"

"I think I was wearing this, but, uh, actually, I was wearing this. I just put these on."

"These are what, just sweat pants or night …"

"Uh, just ling— lingerie," she said.

"Not, OK, but what clothes were you wearing today when you were out and about?" Montano said. "What clothes were you wearing before the pajamas?"

"Oh, my, um, water top and pants."

"And where are those now?" Montano asked.

"Either, uh, either in the laundry room or in my bedroom, the closet. I can show you."

"What color are they?"

"Blue, turquoise and white flowers."

"Are they … are they full length? Are they shorts? What are they, the water pants?"

"The pants go to here, and they can get wet, and then the top is like a white top, short sleeve, with some kind of print that matches the pants. And I also, I … I always carry, uh, to the park and I wear a green … it's my husband's shirt … it's a green … like a, um … and I wore this shirt to my husband's office today. Then when I went to the park, I wear the green shirt to keep the sun off, and then, when I got back home, uh, after the park, I changed again."

"May I have those?" Montano asked.

"They're kinda dirty," Daphne said.

"We can take 'em when we're done with this."

"OK."

"What kinda shoes were you wearing?"

"Uh, tennis shoes and, um, like ... black, um sandals ... and then in the house I always wear my slippers."

"When you went to bed, did you shower before bed?"

"Um, not immediately before bed, but at ... at nighttime."

"Um, let me just be real blunt," Montano said. "Any reason that you would wanna hurt your husband?"

"Oh, no!" Daphne said. "He was so good to me. He just bought me a car. I mean, he's ... so gentle and ... he has the best manners, and he's just such a good man ..."

The detectives asked if there were any legal problems between Brian and Daphne, if either had filed for divorce or accused the other of abusing the children. Daphne insisted they hadn't had any problems like that.

"And there's no reason for us to look into jealous boyfriends, jealous girlfriends?" Montoya asked. "Of either you or, um, Brian?"

"All his girlfriends would be in Texas," Daphne said.

"Any girlfriends during your marriage ... that he had?"

"No."

"Are you sure, or ...?

"I'm positive," Daphne said.

"You're positive," another detective said.

"Once we talk to the employees," the other detective said, "are they gonna tell us anything about you guys' relationship that we should know about now?"

"Any arguments today?" Montoya asked. "Any arguments in the last few days?"

"They ... they're very close to him," Daphne said.

"So," the other detective said of Brian's staff, "they wouldn't know if you guys had problems?"

"Maybe they could sense, like, I don't think my ... my husband's not the type to just ... go up to anybody and tell 'em things," Daphne allowed. "If ... there was something wrong with him, he wouldn't go up to employees and tell 'em, he'd tell me first, um, but maybe they could sense if something was wrong. Because they often buy him lunch."

"Would, uh, Brian be having any kind of a fling or an affair with any of the employees?" the other detective asked.

"No," Daphne said. "'Cause they all worked for Brad, they don't like me."

"What do you mean, they don't like you?" the detective asked.

"Well, um, I know Brad has tried to, um, get back some of the money for their vacation time, and, um, one of the employees, I think had to have an attorney. My husband wrote off the debt for that employee."

"Does your husband ever travel by himself out of town?" the detective asked.

"Yeah," she said, mentioning a trip Brian made a month ago.

"By himself?" the detective asked.

"Yeah," Daphne said, but she added that his mother was with him when Brian went to have his surgery.

The detectives were eager to find out the intimate details of Brian's life, asking Daphne who Brian was closest to, other than herself.

"Maybe Steve Cohen," she said. "Another ophthalmologist. He's not the type to— I don't think he would do that— he wouldn't go to a friend and talk about things … things like that. I mean things that would really be—"

"If he did," the detective asked, "who would he talk to?"

"Me first," Daphne said. "And then his mother, family, sister, um, and maybe Steve Cohen. Our kids play together."

"Who can verify that you were home today from 3:30 till time the police came to your house?" Montoya asked. "As in Tuesday afternoon all the time."

"Who can verify?" she asked.

"Yeah."

"I mean, I don't have anybody else here," Daphne said.

"And if we look up your phone history," Montoya said. "Who would you've talked on the phone with Tuesday afternoon, uh, up until your last phone call?"

"My husband," she said. "My family."

Daphne insisted that the only local call that could be traced to her was back and forth between Brian and herself, with the exception of a wrong number from a woman. Daphne got her cell phone and showed the detectives the most recent calls she got, from her mother, sister and one from her mother-in-law that came in while Daphne was breaking the news about Brian's death to her own parents.

"Did you tell your mother-in-law what happened?" a detective asked.

"Yeah. Oh, yeah," Daphne said.

"And how did she take it?"

Daphne said Joyce Stidham was in denial.

"What'd you tell your mother-in-law?" the detective asked.

"Just, um, they found Brian at his office," Daphne said.

"So, what did you tell your mother-in-law, exactly?" the detective asked.

"I don't remember exactly," she said, "but I ... I told her that, that Brian was dead."

"Did you say how he died?

"No," Daphne said. "I said they don't know."

Daphne's phone showed that the call from Brian came in to her at 5:36 p.m. There was another call that came in at 1:12 p.m. that Daphne didn't know who the caller was, another call from Brian's office at 12:48 p.m. and a call at 8:11 from a local business.

The detectives also looked at the calls Daphne made that day. Just before talking to the detectives, she called a local friend but didn't get hold of her. The most recent calls came, of course, to her family and Brian's after she was awoken.

"OK," the detective said after examining her phone. "What's your gut feelin'? What do you think happened?"

"I think Brad Schwartz killed him," Daphne said, according to detectives' reports. "Because he was a little psycho. He had a bad problem with drugs, um, my dad said that you can treat patients with seizures, but, uh, people like that, their brain doesn't work right. I know he didn't just pass away because of his lifestyle habits. You know, a healthy home life, um, you know, I cook so I know what he eats. I buy all the groceries. He doesn't have time for fast food or eat out, really. Like, once in a while, something, out to eat, um, he exercises ... the only thing I know, he's chronically tired."

"Eh, are you taking this ... is it hitting you pretty hard yet, or you still haven't, uh, I guess grasped that, uh, your husband may be, uh, dead right now?"

"I'm hoping ... I don't know ... I'm not really sure it's him," she said, "because someone said they don't know if his car was out there."

"Who said that?" Montano asked.

"I think you did."

"I asked you if he had a car where it would be," Montano said.

"How long has the phone been out of service?" another detective asked.

"It's not out of service," Daphne said. "It's just, you know, our house phone just doesn't work."

Daphne said the phone hadn't worked since Monday.

"Well," the detective said, "the bedroom phone was not hung up, so could it have been because it wasn't hung up?"

"No," Daphne said. "'Cause they often say to do that, uh, you know, when the cordless phones don't work, disconnect all the cordless phones in the house and reconnect them, and if they don't work, try again later. They've been unplugged for a long time."

"Have you reported to the phone company you're havin' phone problems?" the detective asked.

"No," Daphne said. "Our phones never work in our house. We've always had that problem."

"I just have some concerns about stuff," the detective said. "There's a few things out of line, you know. I mean, your husband's dead and if he was murdered, you know."

"Well, he doesn't know it," Daphne said. "He's not ... he ... he didn't just die."

"Your phone," the detective said, according to his report. "Your phone just seems to be like it's intentionally disconnected. I'm just wonderin' why it would be intentionally just pulled out?"

"Because it ... well ... we're messing with it all the time," Daphne said. "And, plus, Alexandre, the kids always push the buttons on it."

"And the officers were banging the front and back door when they were tryin' to get in," the detective said. "How come you didn't hear anybody?"

"I don't know," Daphne said. "I ... I ... I take something to sleep."

Daphne told the detectives that her prescribed medicine makes her drowsy, according to their reports.

"But once you wake up, it doesn't keep you sleepy or anything?" he asked.

"No, it ... it takes me out," she said. "I ... I found that out, it takes about 14 hours to wear off. So, I take it about between 5 and 6 and then I'm alert enough for my kids. 'Cause he has to be at school at 9."

"Well, you're pretty alert right now, for takin' it," the detective observed. "You took it Tuesday night, today being Wednesday morning, did you take it last night? Not making you pass out right now."

"No," Daphne said. "I'm ... I'm sitting down, but I was lightheaded when I was standing up in the bedroom."

"Our concerns were," Montano continued, according to his report, "that you didn't hear anybody banging on your door, that you got the wills out— that's kind of a big deal. Shut the phones off, and you seem to know things that I don't know yet. I'm just bein' honest, that I have what I would call some concern. And it makes me feel suspicious. Makes me wanna know why? If you had anything to do with your husband's death?"

"No," Daphne said, according to the reports. "I didn't kill my husband! Is that what you're imply— I did not."

"I'm implying," the detective said, according to his report, "that I'm ... I'm suspicious. I'm suspicious as to why all these things are present and if you had anything to do with it at all, or ... or ... or ha— did you hire anybody to hurt him?"

"Uh, no," Daphne said. "I mean, I would never do that. I ... we had a perfect life."

"Well, no life is perfect," the detective said. "I mean, everybody has marital, you know, tiffs and, you know—"

"I ... I ..."

"— good days and bad days," the detective finished.

"Our life is just about made," Daphne said. "He makes an extraordinary income, amount of money. He just bought me a car. We're building a house. My mother-in-law is supposed to come and ... come over in November to watch the kids, so we can go talk to architects about building a house. We don't ... he's just been really ... he's always been really good to me. We have no reason to ... there's no problems ... he's very well respected."

Daphne's phone began to ring.

"Who's that?" one of the detectives asked.

"Can I get this?" Daphne asked.

"Sure," Montano said.

"Hello?" Daphne said into the phone. "Hello? ... Uh, oh, hi, Mommy. ... Uh, I don't know ... they ... they don't know yet ... but, no, I think he was shot, Mommy, because, like, he exercises every day and it's ... gets up at 5 and he eats so healthy. ... Well, Mommy, people don't die at 37 years old. They just don't die. ... Well, they're asking me questions. ... I think it was Brad Schwartz. ... Yeah, I think so. ... Well, thank you so much, Mommy. ... Uh, I don't know ... I don't ... They're sleeping. ... I don't know what I'm ... I don't know what I'm going to tell Alexandre when he wakes up.

… Well, they don't know anything, and I wanted to go down and look."

Daphne also spoke to her father, repeating that she was confused about how Brian could have died. The fact that her life had just irreparably changed began to dawn on her. "I don't know what the heck I'm gonna do. Where am I gonna go, Daddy?

"These people think I killed him," Daphne continued, with the detectives listening in, as they noted in their reports. "Well, they're asking me all these questions: 'Daphne, I'm a little bit suspicious.' Well, they're asking me about my clothes and everything. And they said, uh, this guy's, well, basically telling me I'm, 'You're lying,' 'cause he said, 'No marriage is perfect.' We had a perfect marriage."

Daphne then told her father that she had taken a prescription medicine earlier that night, which prevented her from waking up when deputies entered the house, according to the detectives' reports. (Prosecutors would later characterize the medicine as "sleeping pills.")

"They're saying how come you didn't get up. They were knocking at the door. I didn't hear it. Well, did they do that to you about Yvette? Did they?" Daphne asked, about the time her parents were notified about her sister's death. "Well, they asked me about the life insurance. And about our wills and everything. Well, Daddy, I'm really just shaking, you know? Is it worse to lose your spouse or your kid?"

Daphne worried about how she would tell the children their father was dead and repeated her suspicion that Brad Schwartz had killed Brian.

"I know this guy, Brad, I know he hated us, Daddy," she said. "Well, he's unstable."

Daphne told her father that someone that night brought up a complaint she'd filed against Brian, though there is no mention in any public record about that. Daphne denied she'd filed a complaint or that Brian did anything to cause her to file a complaint, but quickly moved on to thinking about Brian's health and how he could have died.

Her father apparently expressed concern about how she was doing. She mentioned that she had pills for insomnia, as well as another prescription drug.

"I don't know what the heck I'm gonna do. I'm ready to fall apart," she told her father.

"Daphne," one of the detectives said, "we're almost done here ..."

Daphne ended the call and faced the detectives again.

"I understand you need to talk to your parents," the detective said. "We just have a couple of more questions and then we, you know, we will be done here."

"Um, I swear I did not kill my husband, if that's what you think," Daphne blurted, according to the detectives' reports. "And, money-wise, um, I don't need any money, 'cause my parents have a lot of money. My sister has a lot of money. We don't, I don't need that."

"Did you hire anybody to hurt your husband?" the detective asked, according to reports.

"No."

"OK," he said. "The reason we have to ask these questions, you know, somethin' happened to your husband. It's our job to initially invest— you know, we're investigating the death of your husband. So right off the bat, we always talk to the family and ascertain what they know. And you gotta see our point of view of some of the things that have come up, you know, thus far. So that's why we're asking these questions. And we just need to cover all this right now.

"Um, the one question I do have for you," he continued, "you told your father that your ... that your husband was shot. Why do you keep saying that?"

"Well, I, uh, I guess I was wrong because he just said, 'No, Daphne, that does happen. Some, some men just have a cardiac arrest or an irregular heartbeat and just die.' And I used to ask him that, you know ... 'Daphne, that, that's a possibility.' I said, 'Well, how come you never told me that before?' 'Cause he knew my husband was always overtired. And I think in general when you're overtired, your body breaks down, easy. It just doesn't hold up very well. And he goes, 'Daphne, he only said I feel fine.'"

"Who, again, um, why would you say that he was shot?" the detective persisted, according to his report. "I'm just curious."

"I guess ... I don't know," she replied. "'Cause it's nothing ... I, I, I didn't think that someone like my husband, uh, a man with those kinds of habits, healthy habits, can just die. My dad just corrected me. 'Daphne, I've seen him at the office,' and he just talked to my mother-in-law ... it, it is a possibility. But I didn't know that before. So I said, 'Well, it's not true.' And before I went to bed, I had a, a feeling that maybe something was just not quite right."

"OK," the detective said. "Can you—"

"I guess he, 'cause he wasn't home," Daphne continued. "And, you know, the lecture starts at 6, and it's almost 10 o'clock, and he's still not home and ...".

"So," the detective said. "So, you had a feeling something may not, was wrong or somethin' like that?"

"Well, yeah," she said. "'Cause he usually calls me, and I said, 'Well, you know,' and I didn't ... I was so tired, overtired, and, and I, it takes a lotta energy to keep up with two kids. They're active. I get so tired and my hus— my son gets up sometimes at 6 o'clock, sometimes 4 a.m. ..."

"'K," the detective interjected. "Uh, how's your relationship with your in-laws? 'Cause I noticed that they haven't called at all."

"Oh, yeah, they've ... my mother-in-law's called. She just, just, 'Daphne, just do what you have to do and call me when things settle down, and I'll get a first flight out.'"

"OK," the detective said.

"I can tell you we do have a perfect marriage," Daphne said. "'Cause my husband and I read a lot of self-help books—

don't sweat, don't sweat the small stuff at work, don't sweat the small stuff about money, don't sweat the small stuff. And I read a lot about parent effectiveness, training, about those things ..."

"You gotta understand, we hate to ask these questions," the other detective said.

"No, but I'm correcting that we had a ... mm ... almost a perfect marriage," Daphne said.

The phone rang again. Daphne answered it, telling her friend that she'd call back soon.

Montano asked if detectives could see the prescription drug that Daphne said she took earlier in the evening, according to their reports. Daphne agreed to show them the bottle. There is no public record that deputies looked at her pill bottles or the clothes that she wore that day.

"OK," Montano said. "Reference reading the will last night. Who had you doing research on that? What're you tryin' to do with that?"

"My husband," Daphne replied. "He told me to do it. He, he has a ... there's some stuff that we need to transfer from the ... some accounts to the trust, has to be under the trust, I think. And my husband did, like, four or five, and I was supposed to do my ... he asked me to do that last week, and I didn't do it ... was gonna do it."

Daphne told him that Brian had told her to complete a list of about 10 items that the trust company had asked them to do to wrap up the trust. Daphne said they used the same lawyer who had drafted Brian's contract with Brad Schwartz, who also forced Brad to take down the sign on his office that said Brian still worked there after the two split.

After Montano and the others got the names of the people who helped Brian and Daphne with the trust, they wrapped up the interview. It was two hours since they had begun, and the phone began ringing again.

Deputy Stevens was the only one remaining of the original four who had first arrived at the house. After

Montano's interview was finished, Stevens went outside the house to speak to a representative from the Victim Witness program, who had been called to the house to help Daphne with anything she needed. Stevens escorted the volunteer inside and introduced her to Daphne.

A couple of hours later, Stevens would write down his observations and impressions of the night.

"During the majority of my interaction with Daphne Stidham," he wrote in conclusion, "she appeared to be rather calm and did not cry from what I saw. The only time she appeared upset was upon the initial notification that her husband was deceased. The remainder of the time, she appeared to be calm and very lucid."

Every deputy who stepped into the Stidhams' home that night believed Daphne either killed her husband or had something to do with his murder, according to their official reports. But from that night on, the focus of the investigation would be Brad Schwartz.

CHAPTER 11

Some six hours after Dr. Stidham's body was found, a team from the Pima County Medical Examiner's Office arrived to examine and transport him for an autopsy.

By dawn, the deputies and detectives were finished documenting what evidence they could locate in the parking lot. The fire department was called to wash away the blood that had pooled beneath Dr. Stidham's body, just as office workers began arriving. While many of them didn't arrive in time to see deputies in their parking lot, they knew something was wrong because police tape was still strapped around a trash bin and trees near where Dr. Stidham had been found.

By morning, Dr. Stidham's staff already was aware of his death. His office manager had been called by deputies around 2 a.m. to punch in the alarm code to the office, so detectives could determine whether anything leading up to his death had started in the office. She sent word to the others and they, in turn, called others in the medical community, so by midday on Oct. 6, 2004, almost everyone in Tucson who knew Brian well learned that he had been murdered. Brad was in surgery on Wednesday mornings, including the morning after Brian was killed, but he talked to two staff members separately, both of whom told him about Brian's untimely death. Brad expressed shock to his employees upon hearing of his colleague's demise.

The Tucson media latched onto this homicide with gusto. Editors who were numbed by a constant barrage of gang fight murders and drive-by shootings saw the uniqueness of this stabbing death and sent reporters out to fetch anyone who knew Brian. As more and more people found out about the murder, the pressure on the Pima County Sheriff's Department to name and find a suspect grew. Who would want to murder Brian Stidham, a man who seemed to be universally loved and respected? And where was his car? His wife and children were found that night, sleeping safely in their beds, fortunately. Brian's young family captured the heart of Tucsonans, most of whom had never heard of the surgeon before his death. Three bank accounts were set up to receive money from anyone who wanted to cushion the blow of the children's despair by making their financial future a bit easier.

Brian's funeral was held in Tucson. His family and friends from Texas were pleasantly surprised to see how many of his patients and their parents took the time to come to pay their respects. Many of them took the hand of Brian's mother, Joyce, and tearfully related how Brian had saved their child's eyesight. Often, they added gratefully, he did it for free because they couldn't have afforded a surgical procedure that expensive.

"I didn't have insurance," one mother said. "And he said, 'That's cool. Someday, if you can give me something, that's fine. But your little girl needs to see.'"

In the days following the brutal murder of Dr. Brian Stidham, the residents of Tucson looked among themselves for the killer walking freely. Some in the community thought they knew who had slain the popular children's eye surgeon. Most did not. The shock felt by Tucsonans when they first heard that someone had stabbed Brian to death just to steal an old Lexus that was not even top-of-the-line was small, though, compared to the shock that came with the accused killer's identity and the reason some said Brian Stidham was killed.

***

While the autopsy on Brian's body was being conducted, across town, Rachel Atkinson was fretting about the appointment she had made for her son to see him. Rachel called the office around 9 a.m. to cancel the appointment but couldn't get through. Before she could call the office again, Brad called, knowing that she had made the appointment.

"I'm sorry. I can't do it," Rachel told him. "I just can't go through with it. I'm going to cancel."

"That's OK, Rachel," he told her. "If you're that uncomfortable with it, then go ahead, cancel or reschedule the appointment. Call me back when you're finished and tell me what they said, OK?"

Brad seemed rushed, but it was Wednesday, and he was expected at surgery.

The next time Rachel called, she got the answering service, which surprised her. She would have thought that the office opened at 8 a.m. or 9 so she could speak to one of Brian's staff. The answering service told her that all the appointments for that day were cancelled and had to be rescheduled. The office was not open that day because Brian passed away the night before.

In shock, Rachel called Brad right away. He was floored.

"Something must be wrong," Brad told her. "That can't be right. Call again. Look, I don't want to talk about this on the phone."

"But what abou—"

"You don't have to do anything you don't want to do, OK?" Brad interrupted. "I can't talk about this now. We'll talk about it later. I've gotta go. Bye."

Rachel didn't call Brian Stidham's office again. She knew that there was no reason to.

***

Julie Herrington was getting her 10-year-old daughter ready for school when she heard the news around 10 a.m.

that a man was found slain the previous night at a medical complex on North First Avenue. Julie had come to know Brad fairly well while she was preparing to open shop in his office. Brad liked to talk, and Julie had heard about the fallout Brad had experienced with Brian Stidham a couple of years ago. She also knew that Brian had an office on First Avenue. The news that a man was slain in that area concerned her. As far as Julie knew, Brad had confided everything about his life to her. He had told her about problems with the girlfriends he was seeing, problems with Lourdes, problems with his former mother-in-law who had recently wrecked his Camry. Yet, Julie reflected, Brad had spoken very little about Brian Stidham. Julie couldn't even be sure of what kind of relationship the two man had, other than employer-employee.

Her curiosity aroused, Julie called the one man she thought could fill in the pieces of the puzzle: Wendell Hunt. Julie and Wendell, a lieutenant with the Tucson Police Department, had met a decade ago at Tucson's popular country bar, The Maverick, when he was sent there on a call. They had stayed in touch over the years as friends, but the previous December began dating and having a sexual relationship. Wendell searched through TPD's computer system and found nothing. Wendell then called the Pima County Sheriff's Department's communication center, which verified that the victim was, indeed, a David Brian Stidham who had an office in the complex where he was murdered. Without knowing what the autopsy said, police believed that Brian had been shot to death because knife wounds are often mistaken for gunshot wounds without close inspection, Wendell told Julie.

"What about the car?" Julie asked.

"What car?" Wendell asked.

"The doctor's car," she said. "Do you know what happened to it?"

"I don't know anything about a car," he said. "They didn't say anything about it. Julie, why all the questions?"

"I'm curious," she said.

"Well, I'll see what I can find out and meet up with you later," he said.

When Julie arrived at the office around noon, Brad was already there. He broke the news to her that Brian Stidham had been killed. Julie told Brad about what Wendell had learned, including that Brian was shot.

No, Brad told her. Brian was stabbed to death, not shot. Before long, Brad excused himself. He had some errands to run, including going to the bank, where he withdrew $10,000. Minutes later, he called Bruce on his cell phone.

***

In addition to calming Julie's fears, Brad also dealt with Lourdes, who was getting increasingly suspicious of him. Over the next two days, Brad called Lourdes frequently, and the conversation was always the same.

"Lourdes, I had nothing to do with it, please believe me," he would say.

Lourdes refused to side with Brad, and she knew that upset him.

"Brad," Lourdes said. "First of all, you've lied to me all the years that we've been together. You were unfaithful, and you know you said this repeatedly."

"Don't say that," Brad said. "Lourdes, don't say that over the phone. Let me see you. Stop saying that over the phone. I didn't do it. Lourdes, I didn't do it."

"Just leave me alone," Lourdes told him.

She was afraid to tell Brad that she was thinking of calling the police, for fear that
he might harm her or the kids.

***

As news spread of the murder and the ensuing investigation, calls began coming in to TPD and the sheriff's department. Most of the tips led nowhere.

Sgt. Foust got a message to call Liliana Bibb, who wanted reassurances that her identity wouldn't be spread around.

"I need protection before I say anything else," Liliana said.

"I can't make you any promises," Foust told her. "But I'd like to talk to you, if you're willing. Even if you have information that's pertinent to our case, I might not be able to arrange any protection."

"Why not?"

"Well, a variety of reasons," he said. "It might not be warranted, or we just might not be able to handle it."

Liliana was still cautious, but she agreed to speak to him. Foust thought her information sounded remarkably similar to tips received earlier in the day on an anonymous line.

"Did you call 88-CRIME earlier today?" he asked.

"Yes," she admitted. Actually, Liliana had her sister call 88-CRIME, but she was listening in. "I was scared, at first, to call. But the more I thought about it, the more I knew that I needed to call in myself."

Foust made plans to interview Liliana in person the next day.

***

After Lisa Goldberg's real estate exam, she met Brad for dinner at a restaurant near his apartment called Noodles.

"How'd it go?" he asked her.

"OK, I think," she said.

The pair chitchatted and had a nice dinner before Lisa headed off for home. Brian Stidham's name never came up.

***

Even though Carmen Fernandez had stopped dating Brad Schwartz in August and had not spoken to him since September, she remembered how often he'd spoke of wanting revenge against Brian Stidham. The day after Brian's murder, Carmen called Brad.

"Tell me you didn't have anything to do with it," she asked him.

"I didn't, Carmen," Brad said. "I had nothing to do with Brian's death."

"What if the police come to me?" she said. "What should I do? What should I say?"

"Just stay away from them," he said. "Don't talk to them.

"Remember," Brad said, "I know about your family. Don't go to the police."

***

At a quarter to 10 Wednesday night, Tucson police Officer D.E. Martines was cruising through the midtown area as part of Operation Safe Streets and helping to search for Brian's missing car. Martines was assigned an area between Fort Lowell Road on the north, Pima Road to the south, Campbell Avenue to the west and Swan Road to the East. He was passing through the southern parking lot of the Bellevue Tower Apartments on Dodge Road and Bellevue when he spotted a 1992 white Lexus SE400 with the license plate matching the one sought in the murder. Martines, who was driving a marked patrol car, parked nearby and called in the sighting. Unmarked units from the Pima County Sheriff's Department were dispatched to the scene immediately to begin surveillance that lasted throughout the night.

***

Julie and Wendell were finishing their dinner when he got a phone call that Brian's Lexus had been located at an apartment complex in his district.

Once again, Julie peppered Wendell with questions about the murder, something she'd never done in the past on other cases.

"When are the police going over there, to get the car?" she asked.

"The SO's just going to watch it for awhile," Wendell said. "They want to see if the killer comes back to it."

"Where is it?" she asked.

"At an apartment complex on Dodge and Speedway," he replied.

"That's odd," she said. "Who lives there?"

"Honey, I don't know," he said. "It's not my investigation. They were just giving me a courtesy call about it. I really don't know more than you do. Although you seem to know things about this *before* I do."

Julie shrugged it off as hunches.

"What's really bothering you?" he asked.

"I think," she said, now voicing her greatest concern, "that Brad had something to do with this. And if he did, I don't want to have anything to do with him."

"I think you're overreacting," Wendell told her.

***

Undercover deputies had kept an eye on the Bellevue Tower Apartments throughout the night, just in case the killer decided to return. No one ever did approach the vehicle, so the surveillance was called off around 9 Thursday morning. A deputy approached the car and noticed that not only were the keys in the ignition, but there appeared to be blood on the driver's side of the car and inside the Lexus as well. The deputy also spotted a cell phone in plain view.

Det. William H. Knuth Jr. spoke to a woman who said she lives adjacent to the complex and keeps her motorcycle parked underneath the awning at the Bellevue Towers. She walks over to the apartments frequently to check on her bike.

"I've seen that Lexus here before," the woman told Knuth.

The woman said the driver was an older man, probably in his 50s, with gray hair, mustache and glasses.

***

As tips kept coming in to 88-CRIME and the sheriff's department, Sgt. Foust got some interesting news: someone who works for Brad Schwartz, the rival doctor Daphne Stidham spoke of on the night of the murder, is dating a police captain. Foust jotted the information down as another angle to explore.

***

"Lisa," Brad said, "Brian's been murdered."

Lisa Goldberg was stunned. She wasn't sure if it was the news itself or the matter-of-fact tone in Brad's voice as he called that evening.

"Oh my God! What happened?" she asked.

"He was killed," Brad said. "On Tuesday night. Remember Tuesday? That was the night we went out to dinner at Karuna's."

"No, no, it can't be!" she exclaimed, bursting into tears. "Brad, everything that you've said about Brian … Brad … Brad … did you have anything to do with Brian's death?"

"Lisa," Brad said calmly, "I have nothing to gain from Brian's death. And remember, you're my alibi."

Brad told Lisa that he feared a woman he knew, Kim, was talking to police about him.

"God help me if she does," Brad said. "She's psycho."

Trembling, Lisa hung up the phone, not wanting to hear any more details.

Brad tried calling her back, but Lisa refused to pick up the phone. He called her cell phone. He called her house line. She curled up with a pillow, sobbing, as he left message after message for her to call him back. Lisa was terrified. She kept replaying Brad's conversation in her mind and going back over their steps that night. Did Brad kill Brian? She wondered. No, he couldn't have, she was with him that afternoon, all evening and spent the night in his apartment. But that Bruce guy they met up with, he did creep her out. And Brad had spoken of having Brian killed.

At 11:30 p.m., Lisa summoned up her courage to make a phone call, only it wasn't to Brad, it was to the Pima County Sheriff's Department. Lisa was put in touch with Sgt. Foust, whom she told about her fears that Brad Schwartz might have had Brian killed. Lisa told Foust about having dinner that night with Brad's friend, Bruce, and how they had held conversations out of her earshot that evening. Foust asked her to describe this Bruce fellow.

"Italian," Lisa said. "In his 40s. He had what I can only describe as a fake New York accent."

Lisa said he was about 5-foot-10 to 6-feet-tall and weighed about 180 pounds. He had dark hair and an olive complexion. He wore a button-down blue shirt and jeans. Brad told her that he'd met Bruce in Nar Anon classes. That explained, Lisa thought, how someone like Brad, a surgeon, would meet someone like Bruce. But it didn't explain, she said, why Brad would want to hang out with him.

"He told me that he was from the Midwest," Lisa said. "I didn't trust him, and I don't think he was using his real name."

Lisa told Foust how they went to Brad's office to fetch Bruce's bike, then to an ATM machine and several hotels. After dropping Bruce off at the Residence Inn, she said, she and Brad went back to his apartment.

***

On Friday morning, Det. Knuth began following up on the claims that Brad Schwartz and Bruce Bigger went to area hotels on the night of the murder. He drove to the Residence Inn and made contact with the operations manager, who provided him with a list of people who had checked in that night. There, at 10:52 p.m. on Oct. 5, was the name "Bruce Bigger." The manager also gave Knuth a list of phone calls made from the room, a copy of the receipt paid through American Express and other expenses charged to the room. Knuth took down the name of the woman who worked the registration desk that night and left to go to the Sheraton, where he obtained a surveillance video showing two men entering the hotel. One of the men he recognized as Brad Schwartz.

Later, Knuth contacted the woman who had worked the desk at the Residence Inn that night. She said she had gotten a phone call from a man asking if there were any rooms vacant. When she said there was, the man asked for a hold on a room. About 10 minutes later, two men arrived. While the man who paid for the room was quiet, she said the other man seemed frustrated and agitated. He told her that he hated Tucson. The clerk described the other man as being 5-feet-10 inches tall, in his early to mid-40s, with brown hair and a medium to heavy build.

"He had a dark complexion," she said. "He might have been Italian. And he spoke with an accent, maybe a Boston or New York accent."

The clerk saw the dark-haired man wave to the man who paid for the room as he left in a large white SUV. The dark-haired man went to his room, but returned about 10 minutes later. He asked where he could get food, and she pointed to a small market in the lobby.

"Do you want anything?" he asked her. "Because I can pay for it."

The dark-haired man bought an armload of food from the store and chatted along the way.

"I'm having a bad day," he said to her and other hotel staff. "My rental car caught on fire."

While the man was shopping, a call came in for his room from a woman. The dark-haired man took the call, then retreated to his room, she said. A little while later, the dark-haired man returned to the lobby and asked where he could get a soda. He was with a woman the clerk described as white, around 5-foot-8 with dirty blonde hair.

"He made me very uncomfortable," the clerk told Knuth. "I asked the security guard to come over when he was there."

After interviewing the clerk, Knuth proceeded to another hotel, where he obtained another surveillance video from the night of the murder in which a man matching Brad Schwartz's description is seen at the hotel lobby desk with a man matching the description of the dark-haired man seen at the Residence Inn. The man who was working the desk that night remembered that the dark-haired man was in his middle to late 30s, wore a gold chain and had a New York or New Jersey accent. There weren't any rooms at the hotel, but the men were able to find a vacancy after calling another hotel and left, the clerk said.

Around 11:30 a.m., Detectives Kelly Anderson and Chris Hogan went to speak to the man who owned the stolen Mitsubishi found behind the medical complex. The man said his truck was stolen sometime between Sunday night and Monday morning. He had last seen it where it was parked on the street in from of his house.

The detectives then went to Karuna's restaurant, where Brad Schwartz was supposed to have been dining the night of the murder. According to the waitress who served him, Brad and a lady who wore a princess-cut diamond ring arrived together and were joined by a man who arrived in a taxi. The waitress recognized Brad from a photo. Brad wore slacks and a dress shirt, but removed his tie during dinner. After a while, she said, Brad went outside to make some calls. The other man arrived about half an hour after Brad and the woman did. The other man wore khaki-type shorts and was about 35 years old. When the man first arrived, she said, he spoke with Brad outside for a while before coming in and sitting down.

***

Lisa Goldberg was settling down to take a nap at her Phoenix home. The emotional pressure from the last few days had been almost too much to bear. Plus, Brad was constantly calling her. She kept replaying the events of the night of Oct. 5, hoping she would remember some detail that would erase her suspicions about Brad. Then she remembered something that she had meant to tell Sgt. Foust, so she called him.

"It was shortly after we got into the Escalade after dinner," Lisa said. "Brad said to Bruce, 'How did those scrubs work out?'"

***

That night, Bruce arrived at the apartment belonging to two gay friends of his, Chris Corley and Chris Carney. Bruce flashed a large roll of cash and said he wanted a rental car to go to Las Vegas and party.

"Where'd you get so much money?" Chris asked.

"Ah, you know, I got connections to the Mafia," Bruce boasted. "My uncle, he owns this high-class restaurant here."

***

Julie Herrington arrived at Lisa Oien's home to pick up her daughter, Aurora, who had been playing with Oien's daughter, a classmate. Other than the fact their daughters were friends, Julie and Lisa had something else in common:

men in their lives who worked in law enforcement. Lisa is married to Jim Oien, an officer with the Arizona Department of Public Safety. Julie was dating Wendell Hunt. Lisa and Jim were at their daughter's orchestral recital earlier in May 2003 when Julie showed up with Wendell. The Oiens were shocked because they knew that Wendell was caught having sex with a woman on duty and videotaping the act as well. Wendell wasn't on duty the first time the Oiens saw him with Julie, but he came to another recital with her in his uniform.

On this October evening, Julie arrived as the girls were finishing their ice cream sundaes. Julie waited for Aurora and struck up a conversation with the Oiens about the murder that was dominating the headlines.

"I've got inside information," Julie confided, telling them that Brian was stabbed in the back of the neck, execution-style while kneeling down either when he was killed or when he was found.

Brian didn't put up a fight, Julie said, and there were no bushes where he could hide from his attacker. In addition, Julie related, Brian left work every day at 4 p.m., yet he was killed at his office at night. The Pima County Sheriff's Department, Julie said, spent only an hour or so at the scene investigating. On top of that, Julie said Brad Schwartz was a suspect.

"I'm Brad Schwartz's prime alibi," Julie told the Oiens for some reason. "I was having dinner with him that night."

The Oiens were shocked, to say the least. They both had been reading stories and watching TV reports about the case and were aware that what Julie knew had not yet been reported. Knowing that Julie was dating Wendell Hunt, Jim Oien contacted the sheriff's department, fearing that Hunt was leaking information to Julie. Some details of the story Julie told were clearly not true, but enough of it hit close enough to home that the sheriff's department launched an investigation into any involvement Wendell Hunt had with the murder case.

Shortly after the murder, Kim Collins, who was Brad Schwartz's medical transcriptionist, contacted a friend with the Tucson Police Department, Sgt. Ed Shaffer. Schwartz's pattern of dictation on the day Brian died was odd, Collins said. She got suspicious when she learned that Brian had been killed that day. She and her husband knew that Brad hated Brian because they both worked in the office before, during and after the practice broke up in 2002. Shaffer had to get permission from Sgt. Brad Foust of the sheriff's department as well as his supervisor, Lt. Hunt, to talk to the Collinses. Shaffer told Hunt that he'd have to get overtime to talk to the couple. Hunt admitted knowing the Collinses, which raised a red flag with Shaffer.

"Be careful what you say about the case to Hunt," Shaffer was warned by another supervisor.

***

Lisa Goldberg, the events of the week still wracking her brain, called Sgt. Foust around 9:15 Saturday night.

"He's still calling me," she told him anxiously. "He knows what's going on. He knows that you've been talking to someone named Julie and how she thinks that he's involved with all of this."

Foust had already become aware that Brad Schwartz might have inside information about the investigation, but he didn't want to tell Lisa about his concerns.

"I'm worried," she continued. "Brad told me he was coming up here to Phoenix tomorrow. What should I do? I'm afraid he might hurt me. What if he thinks I've been talking to you?"

"Don't meet him if you're worried about that," Foust said.

"Have you guys been following me?" she asked.

"No," Foust said. "Why do you ask?"

"It just seems like, over the last several days, that a black SUV has been following me around," Lisa said. "I have the license plate number, if you want. There's a Mexican man driving it, with a red baseball cap."

Foust took down the information.

"If you're worried about your safety," Foust said, "I'd suggest spending the night at a friend's house tonight."

Lisa took his advice and arranged to visit a friend that night. Foust asked if she would call him later and let him know that she had left her house safely, which she did.

***

In Tucson, Rachel Atkinson had some suspicions of her own, but she didn't voice them to Brad. Their conversations in the days following Brian's murder didn't quell her fears, either.

"Hey, would you do me a favor?" Brad asked her one day.

He sounds nervous, she thought.

"If anybody asks you, could you tell them that I gave you $2,500?"

"Why?"

"Just do it for me, as a favor," he pleaded.

"What if they ask why you gave that to me?" she asked.

"Just say that you needed it to pay some bills or whatever," Brad said.

"Why would someone ask me that?"

"It's just some accounting error or something," Brad said. "There's some money that I can't account for. I told you that I sold the Camry, right?"

"Right."

Brad explained that because Joan's mother had wrecked the car, there were some problems in trying to sell it. He threw around some numbers, which didn't seem to add up for Rachel, but she acted as if he were making sense and agreed to say that he loaned her $2,500.

***

Sunday morning, despite the misgivings Lisa had relayed to Sgt. Foust, she met Brad at a Phoenix department store, so he could shop for some office items. Though she had told Foust that she was willing to wear a wire to capture their conversation, Lisa wasn't wired up. She had mixed emotions when Brad walked up to her, smiling. Lisa realized that she still cared for this man, who had confided in her the deepest of the darkest of secrets that any human being could have. Lisa feared that he could detect that she had already spoken to the police. If he did, he certainly didn't show it. Lisa kept up the pretense as long as she could before she reached out for his hand and tucked a note she'd written earlier in his palm. Brad opened the note and read it:

Brad, the police have contacted me and have questioned me. The police are looking for you. You need to leave me alone. I've already gone and talked to them and I told them the truth.

Brad folded the note back up and handed it back to her.

"OK," he said. "I understand. But I want you to know, Lisa. I had nothing to do with this, OK? I had nothing to do with Brian's death."

Lisa never spoke to Brad again. He never called her again.

Later, Lisa called Sgt. Foust and told him what happened. She also told him that the police officer Brad knew was named Wendell. Lisa's call cemented Foust's fears that information was getting leaked to a murder suspect.

***

Rosalia Humo, like almost everyone in Tucson, had heard about Brian Stidham's death. She also feared that Brad had something to do with it. On one hand, she wanted to stay as far away from him as possible. Maybe she used to run with gangs, but it looked more and more to her like he was capable of carrying out a hit, and if he could, then it'd be nothing for him to come after her. But her curiosity got the better of her, and she dialed the number that he'd left so often at her grandmother's house. He sounded surprised to hear from her and asked how she was doing.

"Any trouble with your eyes?" he asked.

"No, they're fine," she said.

"That's good."

"I was just calling because, well ... I was just reading about Dr. Stidham and what happened to him," Rosalia said.

"Yeah," Brad said. "He sure got what was coming to him, didn't he?"

"Well, I was thinking about what you said before, about asking me for help," she said. "So I was wondering if maybe you—"

"No," he said calmly. "No, I didn't have anything to do with it."

Unconvinced, Rosalia called 88-CRIME after they hung up.

***

Around 11:30 Sunday night, Sgt. Foust got a call at home regarding a woman who wanted to pass on information about the case through a sergeant at TPD. Foust, who had worked with this particular sergeant before, called him and learned that a woman named Rachel had contacted them about the murder. Foust thanked the sergeant and called Det. Murphy, the lead investigator, to give her a heads-up that he was going to call this woman to find out whether she had good information to give them.

Foust was greeted on the phone by a woman who sounded extremely nervous. As they spoke, he could hear a small child whimpering and crying in the background.

"I'm dating this man, Dr. Brad Schwartz," Rachel said. "And he's said things to me in the past that make me worried, especially since I heard about this other doctor who died."

"Would you be OK with some detectives coming to your house to speak to you?" Foust asked. "Based on what you're telling me, we really would like to come talk to you in detail about this."

Rachel agreed and gave her address.

"They should be there soon," Foust promised.

"It doesn't have to be tonight," she said. "I could meet them in the morning."

"No," Foust said. "We'd really like to get this done this evening."

Later, Detectives Murphy and Montano arrived. Rachel told them her concerns and that Brad had recently asked her to lie about getting a loan from him for $2,500. He sounded nervous and paranoid, Rachel said, and on the verge of tears. Rachel told them how Brad sometimes got emotional, including once when he was breaking up with her.

"He would get upset, and he'd cry a little bit," she told them. "He would get overwhelmed with different stuff."

Rachel told them how Brad would talk about wanting Brian harmed. She felt guilty, she told the detectives, because he had confided that in her—and no one else, to her knowledge—and she had done nothing.

The next day, Murphy told Foust that Rachel would be willing to talk to Brad Schwartz and try to get more information out of him, with police officers monitoring the conversation.

Rachel did as she promised and continued to talk to Brad, trying to get him to reveal any involvement in Brian's death.

"Have you ever thought of just giving up?" she asked him. "Just leave and find someplace new."

"No, never," he told her. "I'm going to stay in town and fight back. I don't have anything to hide. I didn't have anything to do with this."

***

On Monday evening around 9, Det. Murphy set off for the Tucson Police Department's Midtown Substation at 22nd Street and Alvernon Way accompanied with Detectives Montano and Lopez and Sgt. Foust. The team had gotten word that a police lieutenant might be having an affair with a woman named Julie who works with Brad Schwartz. Foust wanted very much to talk to this Julie, but he didn't want to call her at work, which could spoil the investigation. He was also concerned that Lt. Hunt might be passing along information about the investigation to Julie, who could easily relay that to Brad Schwartz. At the station, Murphy and Montano sat down with Hunt after a brief explanation of why they were there.

Hunt confirmed that he was dating Julie Herrington, told her where she lived and gave them her phone numbers.

"Do you think she'll talk to us?" Murphy asked.

"I doubt it," he said. "Julie's smart. She plays things close to the vest, you know? And she doesn't much like people like us."

"Has she spoken to you about the murder?" Murphy asked.

"She hardly has spoken about anything else," Wendell said, adding that it was unusual for Julie to ask so many questions about a case.

Wendell expressed his concerns that Julie seemed to have information about the murder that he didn't have. At first, he told them, Julie suspected that Brad had something to do with the murder. But over the last few days, he said, she was just as sure that he had nothing to do with it.

Nevertheless, Murphy and Montano set out for Julie's house to question her, with Lopez and Foust remaining to interview Hunt.

Wendell said he knew that Julie performed some type of facial treatments, but he wasn't sure what it was called, that she'd known Brad Schwartz for a couple of years and he often called her throughout the day and well into the night.

"There were times that I thought there might be something going on between them," Hunt said. "But she says they're just friends."

About an hour later, Hunt's cell phone rang. Wendell ignored the call, silencing the phone. A few minute later, Lopez noticed the phone was vibrating.

"It's probably Julie," Wendell told them, "because your detectives should be at her house by now."

Wendell glanced down at his phone to check the number that was calling him.

"No," he said. "It's not Julie. It's him. Brad."

Wendell reached over to a landline and dialed his voice mail, putting the call on speaker phone so the detectives could listen in.

"Wendell," the voice said. "This is Julie's friend, Brad. I don't know if you know this or not, but detectives from the sheriff's department are at her front door now at fucking 10 o'clock at night. Julie called me and wants you to call her or me."

Wendell frowned.

"That's very weird that he called me," he said. "I've never spoken to the guy or even met him before."

Foust asked Wendell if he would call Brad back.

"Sure," Wendell said, dialing the number using the landline with the speaker phone.

"Hey, Brad," Wendell said when he picked up. "This is Wendell."

"Hey, Wendell," Brad said. "Thanks for calling me back. Why the fuck would detectives be at Julie's house this fucking late at night?"

"When we get information on a case, we follow up," Wendell said calmly. "That's what we do. They're just interviewing people."

"Do you know about me and Brian?" Brad asked.

"No," Wendell said.

Brad explained that the DEA began investigating him just when Brian came to work for him.

"I couldn't practice for 10 months and it cost me $2.5 million dollars," Brad said.

But Brad hadn't spoken to Brian in two years, he insisted.

"The last thing in this world that I wanted was for Brian to die," Brad said.

"Who would want him dead?" Wendell asked.

"I have no fucking idea," Brad said.

Brad acknowledged that he had a bad reputation in the medical community.

"I'm just tryin' to make a living," he said. "Why the fuck would I want to do pediatric ophthalmology? You know, what I'm really interested in is plastic surgery. There's a lot of money in that. You know what I'm talking about. Like getting Julie to come in and work her magic. That's what people pay for.

"I swear, I have not spoken to Brian in two years," Brad continued. "Look at his wife. Two months ago, she came to me and asked me about life insurance. She's fucking weird, you know.

"Was it a carjacking?" Brad said. "Fuck if I know. Who's going to say anything bad about a dead guy who takes care of kids? Someone killed him."

"Well," Wendell said, "they must have something if they're talking to Julie."

"I was with Julie and another girl the night of the murder," Brad said. "I was with Lisa Goldberg, from Phoenix."

"Now, I'm talking to you as a police officer," Wendell said, a statement that concerned Foust, who took it as a warning signal Hunt was hinting to Schwarz that he had better watch his words. "What did you do the night of the murder?"

"I was with Julie all day," Brad said. "I went to dinner with Lisa at Karuna's near Grant and Campbell."

"The police can verify this information," Wendell said. "Would anyone recognize you at the restaurant?"

"The waitress would remember me," Brad said. "I eat there a lot. I paid for the dinner with my American Express card."

"Save the receipt, OK?" Wendell asked.

"Lisa's flaky," Brad offered. "She's got a few screws missing."

Brad told Wendell how he'd gone to his group counseling meeting before dinner and spoke to Julie on the phone before going to dinner. Afterward, he and Lisa went back to his apartment.

Foust passed Wendell a note asking him to find out whether there was anyone else with them at dinner.

"Yeah," Brad said. "A friend, this guy Bruce, came by."

Brad explained that he had met Bruce in NarcAnon.

"What's Bruce's last name?" Wendell asked.

"Lickavoyer," Brad said, lying. "Something like that. I can't pronounce it."

Brad said that he and Lisa were at Karuna's until about 10 p.m., when they went to a hotel, and he paid for a room for Bruce with his credit card at the Residence Inn at Speedway and Wilmot.

"You're going to need to account for your time on the night of the murder," Wendell said.

"I didn't do anything," Brad insisted. "Why are you guys looking at me? Dude, I do not have money to pay someone, and I wouldn't do anything to jeopardize things because I've got little kids. No one deserves that. It doesn't matter if someone shook his dick at a group of little kids, no one deserves to die like Brian did. I know I've got a history, but I've told everyone on my staff to tell the truth if the police come asking about Brian."

***

Though Liliana Bibb had already spoken to the sheriff's department, the question of whether Brad had anything to do with Brian's death intrigued her. She boldly called Brad on the evening of Oct. 12, to see if he would tell her anything. The subject of Brian's brutal murder wasn't far from Brad's mind, either. Somehow, the conversation got around to DNA evidence. Liliana had been raped as a child and knew that law enforcement officials got her DNA off of the rapist, so she wondered aloud to Brad about whether DNA could catch Brian's killer.

"But," Brad said, "what if the murderer wore something that covered him all up? If he wore a suit that covered his whole body? Then they wouldn't be able to find any DNA on him."

Any hopes that Liliana had of Brad confessing to the murder were dashed. He insisted he had nothing to do with it.

***

Around 10:15 a.m. on Oct. 13, detectives Montano and Gary Burns visited Brad's office, where they talked to four employees. They learned that Brad had a patient named Ronald Bruce Bigger who was injured in an assault at the Circle K at Speedway and Swan. Burns verified the information about the assault in the police database.

Around 3:30 p.m., Kathleen Bright-Birnbaum, a criminalist with the sheriff's department, took latent fingerprint impressions taken from the murder scene and compared them to a set of finger and palm prints belonging to Bigger.

None of the fingerprints matched his.

Around 4:35, detectives Anderson and Burns took a photo lineup with Bruce's picture included to Jennifer Dainty at the convenience store. Dainty picked out Bruce's photo, circled it, and signed and dated the form as they asked her.

***

Robert Wetzel met Bruce Bigger through a friend, Theresa Morales. Robert knew that Bruce had recently arrived in Tucson, and while he didn't seem to have a job, usually had enough money to spend on partying, which always included the new friends he made. Sometimes, Robert knew, Bruce's mom would wire him money. Theresa needed a car, so Robert let her drive his white Volvo. One day, Bruce and Theresa told Robert that they wanted to take the Volvo to Las Vegas. Bruce had recently come into a large amount of money, and he wanted to treat his two friends to an all-expenses-paid trip to Vegas. That sounded good to Robert, especially when Bruce assured him he had enough dope to last the trip. Bruce was even kind enough to give Robert a grand to spend as he wished in Vegas. When the money ran out, the threesome had to return to Tucson.

**

Brad drove to Joan's house on Oct. 14 to hand over her alimony check, which he knew she wasn't going to like very much that month. Instead of the usual $6,500 he normally gave her for alimony, Brad brought her $3,300.

"I don't have enough money to pay you this month," Brad said.

Of course, Joan was upset. But given that this was the first time he'd ever come up short on the alimony, she didn't figure she had that much to complain about.

"It's your mother's fault," he said.

"What? How can this be my mother's fault?" Joan asked.

Brad had recently loaned his 2003 Toyota Camry to Joan's mother, who got into a fender bender. Joan's mother paid him for the damage, but when Brad tried to sell the Camry that month, he got $3,000 less than his $19,000 asking price.

"Your mother devalued the car by wrecking it," he said. "That's the difference in your check this month."

CHAPTER 12

While media reports about Brian's death questioned why anyone would want to kill such a nice, popular children's eye doctor, behind the scenes suspicion was building quickly around Brad Schwartz and his resentment following Brian's departure from the practice in 2002. Joanna Brenning, who was engaged to Dr. Mark Austein, Brad's friend, called 88-CRIME with her suspicions. Another woman who was seeing Brad around that time, Kim Seedor, also called the anonymous tip line. Perhaps the person who felt this tension building up around Brad more acutely than anyone else was Lourdes Lopez. In the days following Brian's murder, Lourdes struggled with the notion that someone she had loved dearly could be a cold-hearted killer. When the burden became almost too much to bear, she called her good friend, Paul Skitzki, a former colleague from the Pima County Attorney's Office. Paul was living with Nicki DiCampli, also a prosecutor. Lourdes and Nicki were the best of friends, but in her emotional state, Lourdes now wanted Paul's quiet reasoning over Nicki's compassionate friendship. Lourdes often turned to Paul when she needed someone to calm her down.

Lourdes was right to call Paul. She knew what his reaction would be before she even called him, however. She knew that he would urge her to call law enforcement with her suspicions. She knew that she should. But she needed a gentle nudge in that direction. Perhaps she was hoping that Paul wouldn't think she needed to tell the world about her terrible secret, about the times that she heard Brad say that he hated Brian, that he wouldn't kill Brian himself, but that he would hire someone to kill Brian and make it look like a carjacking to throw off suspicion. Perhaps if Paul just consoled her, and told Lourdes that the idea that Brad would actually follow through with such statements was ludicrous, then Lourdes could lay her suspicions to rest.

"Lourdes, you've got to tell them about this," Paul said, with urgency in his voice. "You know what you have to do. You used to be a prosecutor. You know how this works."

"I know, I know," Lourdes said, crying. "But, um, what if they already know? What if they already suspect him, I mean, what if he told someone else, too, about these things, and they've already gone to the police?"

"I wouldn't be surprised," Paul said. "But it still doesn't matter. Lourdes, you know him better than any of us. I'd like nothing more than to turn him in myself, you know how Nicki and I feel about him. But it's not our call. It's yours. You've got to call them, Lourdes."

"I know, I know," she whispered.

"If you're uneasy calling them directly, then you can call 88-CRIME or 911, you know," Paul suggested.

88-CRIME was the Pima County Attorney's Office's anonymous tip line. Callers are given numbers and if the information that they turn in eventually leads to a conviction, a reward could be given to the caller.

"Yeah," Lourdes said, sniffling. "I could do that."

"Do something," Paul urged her. "Lourdes, if anything, do it for yourself. Get it off your chest. But do something, OK?"

"OK, Paul. Thanks," Lourdes said.

That night, two nights after Brian Stidham lost his life, Lourdes thought about what Paul had said, but yet she took no action. To make matters worse, Brad kept calling. Lourdes couldn't help but let him know that she suspected him of having something to do with Brian's murder because of all the threats that he had made, which started a big argument between them.

"I can't believe you don't trust me!" Brad said. "You give all your clients the benefit of the doubt. You believe in the system, innocent until proven guilty. Yet you automatically think that I had something to do with this!"

"Brad, you said you were gonna kill the man!" Lourdes countered.

"Don't say that on the phone, Lourdes," Brad begged. "What the fuck is wrong with you?"

"Why?" Lourdes said. "Because it's not true or because you know it's true?"

"Don't fuckin' say that, Lou!" Brad said.

Brad knew just which buttons to push to make Lourdes feel bad, and he was using them on her now.

"You're the only one that I trust," he said. "You're the only one that cares about me. You're the only one that has ever loved me."

His words made her sob.

"I can't trust anybody," Brad continued. "I can't trust anyone."

The next day, Paul's urgings weighed on Lourdes' mind. She called him on Friday, and Paul again stressed the importance of calling the police even if they already suspected Brad.

Lourdes tried her best to work through her morning calendar and push the horrible events of the week out of her mind but wasn't very successful.

Adding to her stress was the fact that Brad did not let up on the phone calls. She avoided answering them, but she knew that she could not put him off forever.

"I'm ready if the police come and talk to me," Brad told her.

He said the threats about having someone kill Brian weren't serious.

"I was mouthing out," he said. "I was just mouthing out with this. I didn't mean any of that stuff. I didn't mean it. I just felt like I didn't have any control in my life. This is the one thing I could control. I didn't mean any of it, Lourdes. That situation with Danny was nothing. It wasn't anything."

"How could you have given him money?" Lourdes asked. "You're not a generous guy."

"Well," Brad said, "I figured if I gave him money, then maybe w— you and I could be closer. I felt guilty."

"What do you feel guilty with Danny about?" she demanded.

"I don't know," he said. "I just did."

***

Around 11:30 a.m., Lourdes picked up the phone and called someone else she trusted, Dawn Barkman, the public information officer for the Pima County Sheriff's Department. Two hours later, Dawn returned the call. The two women had worked together often when Lourdes was a prosecutor and had a friendly relationship, though they hadn't spoken in a couple of years due to their busy schedules.

"I really need to talk to you," Lourdes said, holding back tears.

"OK, shoot," Dawn said.

"No, in person. I don't want to do this over the phone," Lourdes said, sobbing. "I don't want to get involved in all of this, I really don't."

"All of what?" Dawn asked.

"An innocent man's life has been taken, and I can't live with this anymore," Lourdes said. "It's about Brian. Brian Stidham. And he's got two small children and a wife, and it's just horrible! But I want to talk to you, Dawn. I need to talk to you. I trust you. We always worked well together."

"Sure, Lourdes, sure," Dawn said. "Right away. I can see you right away"

The two women arranged to meet at Lourdes' downtown office at a quarter to three. Dawn made arrangements to bring Det. Jill Murphy with her, telling Lourdes that it was important to have someone from the homicide unit there as well. Lourdes agreed.

When Dawn and Jill arrived, Lourdes had calmed down somewhat and apologized for the office's air-conditioning unit, which was efficient but loud. Lourdes told the women that she would try to speak loudly, so the tape recorder Jill brought with her could pick up her statement clearly.

"I did call Dawn Barkman," Lourdes began, "because I've known Dawn for a few years, and I really trust her judgment, and I trust, she's a very good officer. And, um, I, I really needed to explain to her the information that I have about this case. I'm very reluctant to come forward, um, one, because I still have, as I indicated to you earlier, a pending case of my own, which complicates things only in that I have to involve pretrial services, and I don't like having to do that.

"And number two," Lourdes said, "it's really difficult because I know that the information I have is gonna affect this person that I care a lot about. Um, so I'll just let you know that I know Dr. Schwartz. Um, I know that he had hired Dr. Stidham to work for him, and Dr. Stidham stopped working for him probably two years ago. I've had an ongoing relationship with Dr. Schwartz for several years now. It's been on and off, but it's been personal and romantic."

Lourdes took a deep breath as the two other women watched her carefully.

"When I heard the news on Wednesday that a person had been killed at First and River," Lourdes continued, "identified as a man in a medical plaza, and that his Lexus was missing, I suspected it was Dr. Stidham. And the reason that I did that was because I know that Dr. Stidham's office is there, and I know that he drives a Lexus and, unfortunately, I had my suspicions that Dr. Schwartz wanted to have him killed."

Jill glanced at Dawn, hearing the words from the mouth of woman who had been intimate with Brad Schwartz, confirming what Jill had been hearing for days from the lips of others who had known Brad from a farther distance.

Lourdes told the women how, after the day of Brian's murder, she tried to go about her normal business. She had depositions to conduct from 9:30 a.m. to 4 p.m., but as she was heading back to her office that afternoon, she couldn't help but call Brian's office.

"I called his office pretending to be a parent that needed to see the doctor just to see if it was him," Lourdes said. "And I was hopin' to God it wasn't gonna be him. And sure enough, they said there was a tragedy, and that Dr. Stidham had been killed.

"So I immediately knew that it was, it was probably Brad. And, I don't believe that Brad Schwartz actually killed Dr. Stidham. I believe that Dr. Schwartz had somebody or a couple of people kill him. And that's because he had said to me over the last several months that he was gonna kill him. He was very upset about the fact that Dr. Stidham had left the practice and took his entire pediatric ophthalmology practice. The doctors in town felt very comfortable sending their patients to see Dr. Stidham because Dr. Schwartz obviously had a pending federal case. He had an addiction. He admitted to it."

Jill let Lourdes continue, without interruption. Lourdes said that Brad was forced to have regular drug testing and that his solo practice was suffering because the pediatric patients were being sent to Brian, not him.

"His practice basically went to nothing," Lourdes said. "And he was losing money. And he was ashamed. And he was upset. And he was angry. And he was, and he ret—, re—, repeatedly ... and I have to be really careful about my words. I don't wanna mislead you. ... Repeatedly told me that he was going to kill Dr. Stidham.

"And I never thought he would actually do that," Lourdes said, leaning toward her attentive audience. "Over the last several weeks, I'm gonna say, because I don't know exactly when I confided in other people about my concerns."

Lourdes told them how she called a friend before Brian's murder to beg a favor, to call Brian's office and warn him about Brad's threats.

"And then one thing led to another, and ... and ... you know ... you get busy, and I figured, maybe I'm overreacting, so I'm not gonna scare him. The worst that could happen, he'd call the police. The police would say, 'Who do you think it is?' They'd probably, he probably would say Schwartz or somebody. The police would go talk to Brad and then that would be it. Right? That would be the worst that would happen. But I, we didn't follow through with it. And I confided in another friend and said, 'I'm really worried that he's gonna kill somebody,' and that friend told me, 'Lourdes, he's just talking. That's not, that's not gonna happen.' and I heard the news, and I said, 'I hope to God,' I was telling Dawn that I hope I am wrong. I hope that I'm overreacting, that I am absolutely dead wrong because number one, this is a person's reputation, their livelihood, their, their life. I don't want to have anything happen to Dr. Schwartz that shouldn't happen to him, but at the same time, there's a person that's dead who didn't deserve to die. And Brad had told me that he was gonna kill him in his office. It was gonna be like a robbery or a carjacking, that there would be more than one person, and that he would be dead. That's what he said."

"Did he say, you know, how he was gonna have it done?" Jill asked.

"No, never said a gun. I have never seen Brad with a gun. I know he has a bat. I know that he has, 'cause I think in T–, in Taiwan visiting his son a long time ago, like those stars, those ... throwing stars. I've never seen him with like, um, switchblades, or, or, or g-, or knives other than kitchen knives. I've never seen him with any weapons of any kind, ever. Again, just a bat that you, that you can use as a weapon, if you'd like. And I never overheard conversations with him, you know, with people suggesting these things, never, never, I mean, I never saw anything other, I never knew anything other than his desire to have this happen. And that's where I'm at. And, again, that's why I'm so hesitant to, was so hesitant to call you because it's not like I have a picture or a phone number or a name of somebody that I could tell you, 'Go call 'em up.' And I … I just … I just know that, uh, he … he had somebody do this to him."

"Have you talked to him since?" Jill said.

"Yeah," Lourdes mumbled, "Yeah …"

"What's he saying?"

"After this happened, after I found out, I think it was Wednesday, right? I'm like, I can't even remember that, Wednesday is the day it was told on the p—, on the rep—, on the television, and I was still in my deposition. That night he called me and said, 'I need to come over to your house to show you something.' By this time, I was pretty hysterical inside, and I was really worried that he was gonna come to my house and sorta look at me to see how I was doin'.

"See, Brad trusts me," Lourdes said. "He doesn't trust anybody. He trusts me partially because of what's happened between the both of us. And I never took a plea to testify against him. So he's always trusted me with everything, with his children, with his family."

Lourdes told how Brad came over to her house the day after the murder and had been constantly calling her, professing that he had nothing to do with Brian's murder.

"I didn't tell him, 'I'm gonna call the police,' because I'm afraid of him. I am," Lourdes said, adding that she feared he might hurt her children.

"And I don't think you should tell him anything right now," Jill said.

"And I wasn't gonna!" Lourdes said. "I didn't wanna antagonize him, you know? I wanted him to think that all I'm doing is just, I feel really horrible, and I'm not gonna say anything. That's … that's what I wanted him to know. And it's been really hard because he called me this morning and said, 'Please help me do my QuickBooks, 'cause I do that for him.'"

Lourdes explained that she often helped Brad with his accounting. She also felt it was important to say that when she and Brad broke up in May, it wasn't an amicable split.

"It was very ugly," Lourdes said, telling Jill about how Brad had staked out her office to take back the car he had given her.

"About when did you guys break up?" Jill asked.

"We broke up in May," Lourdes replied.

"And have you spoken to him on any sort of a regular basis since then?" Jill asked.

"Yeah," Lourdes said. "I mean, not really regular. Um, he was tryin' to get back with me. I was tellin' him to fuck off, that kinda thing. But in the last month and a half, he's been really tryin' to make amends. And I said ... I just don't believe you. I don't trust you. I mean ... and ... and that's a whole other situation. You know, I just don't believe him. And these conversations that I'm talking about, about him saying he's gonna kill him, were constant. They were."

"About when did they start?" Jill asked.

"They pretty much started just in passing and saying right after he got indicted, and ... and ... and Brian went and did his own practice. You see, Brad went to a rehab for four months, I think."

Lourdes explained how Brad went to Rush after leaving Cottonwood in 2002, and she would occasionally visit him in Illinois. Their off-and-on relationship continued through May and, Lourdes confided, she knew that Brad had told someone else that he would like to see Brian dead.

"It was a woman he was seeing," Lourdes said. "He just blames Brian for taking his practice, for taking his role here, for kinda coming in and being like the new guy, who everybody loves and trusts, and ... and he just ... he's angry. He's just ... he's as angry as can be. He's just angry."

"So," Jill said, "you know Brad Schwartz pretty much better than anybody I've talked to."

"I know him better than anyone in this whole world," Lourdes stated.

"Is it your opinion," Jill asked, "that this anger has turned into somewhat of an obsession?"

"Yes," Lourdes said emphatically.

"And this is because he started talking about it quite often?"

"Yeah," Lourdes agreed.

"Alright," Jill said, "would he talk about wanting, um, Dr. Stidham dead, you know, every week, every day or what was the frequency?"

"I … I would imagine that when we were together, and remember, we broke up in May, it was, there was a period of time where it was pretty much every night when we would get ready to go to bed … and … I just … it was constant."

Brad would say, "I'm gonna fucking get him. That fucking guy's gonna die. He's gonna fucking die," Lourdes said.

"And," Lourdes said, "he always asked me about evidence. I used to be a prosecutor. I'm a defense lawyer now. I'd share cases with him, never people's names, but … you know … your file is open. You can see pictures and … how do the police do this, and how do the police do that? And that's also because he's curious about that stuff, you know. So he would ask me questions about, um, 'What would happen if they found child pornography in his office?' You know, just to get him framed is what he wanted. He wanted him to be humiliated. And the … the … the conversations also said, you know, he's gonna get his."

"And you said that he had mentioned in specifics that he wanted it done in the parking lot?" Jill asked.

"No, not the parking lot," Lourdes said. "In the office."

"In the office?" Jill asked. "And at night, or …?"

"Not, well, he never said at night," Lourdes said. "But it would make sense that it wouldn't be during the day when people could see it. But it was specifically at his office. And it was gonna be a robbery or a carjacking, so where … uh … I would … again, I'm assuming … not that he said it, that he would take the money from him or, um, his car, you know, something of his personal property. I even suspected it would be a break-in at his office. It was definitely gonna be robbery or a carjacking, so that it would appear as though it was random, and it was just … you know, a victim, and it wasn't anything else. You know, I just … I just suspected there were some people that were helping him, you know, people that I didn't know very well, that were … but they weren't shady characters. I mean, Brad doesn't associate with shady people like drug addicts. He doesn't do any drugs. He doesn't drink. He's not that kind of person. Um, he's got money, he's got power in that he's a doctor, I mean."

"How is he financially now?" Jill asked.

"Now?" Lourdes said. "I mean, the last time I did his books, he was doin' really well. His practice was really getting better. It was, which again, is my hope that, oh, well, that whole anger thing? It's over. I would tell him repeatedly, you know, 'You need to let your anger go. You need to just let it go.

"I was actually gonna marry him," Lourdes admitted. "I was doing classes to convert to Judaism and part of the reason that I did it was so that he would sit with me."

Despite the lessons that Lourdes was learning at the JCC about forgiveness and peace, Brad was anything but.

"Who was it easier to blame?" Lourdes told Jill. "Other people. You know, he hates other people around here, you know, other doctors."

Lourdes told Jill about a local plastic surgeon and ophthalmologist that Brad expressed anger toward because he competes with them.

"I remember him say, you know, fucking people, not that he ever said those people are gonna die. But, I mean, he was angry with 'em. And with Brian, it was like …"

"Was it different with Brian?" Jill asked.

"It was different with Brian," Lourdes said. "Because he felt like Brian was completely disloyal to him. He was really offended and pissed off that Brian would come to this town, and Brad did give him the entire pediatric practice. Brian walked into an established practice, and he did a good job, and when Brad first left for rehab, whatever, however long he was gone, Brian kept things going for his patients, and then I'm sure Brian thought, 'I can do this on my own. This guy got, you know, charged in a federal, you know, drug thing. I think I'm gonna leave.' And I think that's what he did. He left. He had to ... he had to worry about his own family."

Lourdes said she would try and console Brad by telling him that he could show Brian and everyone in Tucson that he could survive without him, even thrive.

"I don't know if you even know him," Lourdes said.

Jill shook her head.

"But Brad is an extraordinarily gifted doctor. I mean, he is really gifted. He's extremely well trained. He's one of only 20 in the country that can do what he does because of his neurology training, his plastics training, his pediatric ophthalmology and all the training that he's done. He's extremely bright. He was the valedictorian of his class. He's bipolar. He gets two hours of sleep a night."

"Does he take his medication regularly?" Jill asked.

"I don't know," Lourdes replied.

"Has he ever been known for, to perhaps get off of it?" Jill asked.

"After awhile, after you start noticing people's behavior, when I would note that he was actually easy to deal with, not antagonistic, he would follow through, not lose patience with the children, I figured he was on his meds, but then he wasn't as productive as he was. You know what I mean?"

"Right."

"He needed to sleep. He needed to eat. He couldn't see 80 patients and still have time to do this and the other. You know what I mean?" Lourdes said.

"Right."

"So the trade-off, I believe, was he would rather have the craziness in his head, but, my God! He got to do everything. He would do surgery. He would see the patients. People would call. You don't understand. Patients love him. He is a … a phenomenal doctor."

"Oh, I know that," Jill said.

"You know, he's just as angry as can be. I have never met anybody that has been so consumed with anger and hasn't been able to try to be productive about it, 'cause I get angry. I mean, I was … I wasn't happy about what happened to me. I could've easily turned it around and said, 'I'm gonna blame other people.' But you know, you realize you've made a mistake. You take your lumps, and you move forward. That's what I did. You know, I'm not … I'm not proud of what happened. I'm not proud. I was ashamed that I was in the paper. I was ashamed I was arrested. I was ashamed that my children, you know, had to know. But you have to move on. And you can't blame other people. And that's what I told him, that he had to do. And I was very close to his kids."

Lourdes admitted that she took Brad's oldest son, Ari, with her and her son to the Greek festival that fall. Ari spent the night at Lourdes's house.

"I really care about his kids," Lourdes explained. "And I absolutely care about him. But Dr. Stidham is dead. And I can't imagine what he went through. And … and this is real personal, too, because my ex-husband was murdered in March, and he was murdered in Nebraska, and he was shot and killed, and I had to tell my children about that. And I had to make the arrangements for the burial and the body, and … and it's real personal, you know what I mean?"

"Yeah," Jill said.

"Like the … what the kids are going through," Lourdes continued. "The fact that they don't have their father anymore and … and I just feel like, you know … Daphne … the children … they don't deserve to have that kind of trauma and, you know, in their lives."

"Yeah, she's pretty much still in shock," Jill said about Daphne. "And I think it's sinking in."

"I think we met once, one time, and I talked to Brian when he used to work with Brad, and he was really a nice guy, very soft-spoken, a very quiet individual. When you would see him and Brad together, it was like … I … I don't know what … uh … maybe like, um, the odd couple because Brad was so quick and reactive, and when there was a diagnosis that was real tricky, Dr. Stidham was really cautious. He wouldn't … he would be almost afraid to say, 'This is what your child has, a tumor,' and Brad, on the other hand, was like, 'Look, I've been trained. You have a tumor. You need to have surgery.' And he was always right. I mean, he saved people's lives."

"Does he have any, do you know of any pending lawsuits that Brad has?" Jill asked.

"Oh, yeah," Lourdes said. "That's a matter of public record. I mean, he's got malpractice insurance lawsuits from, stemming from the fact that he admitted to the medical board that he had been using Vicodin, and I believe the people that are suing him believe that he did surgery on them during those times. So he's got, I think, two pending suits right now. And then he was going through a divorce, too, with Joan, and it was really ugly. You know, I pretty much helped him at the end with … he didn't have an attorney. I didn't represent him formally, but I, obviously, I read all the pleadings, and I told him what he needed to do, and Joan and I have grown to have a lotta respect for each other. I mean, 'cause she knows how much I love her children. And she said, 'I may not like you, Lourdes, but I know that you love, that you love,' and they're so wonderful. They're so wonderful."

"Does he have joint custody of the children?"

"Yeah, yeah, and he's really good with them," Lourdes said, smiling. "It's like the Dr. Jekyll and Mr. Hyde. If he was a bad dad, if he hurt them or was completely impatient with them or short with them or not kind, this would be so much easier to accept, but it's like there's a part of him that when he is challenged, when he is, and he feels like his livelihood is challenged, he'll do anything, you know?"

"Yeah," Jill said. "So did he ever consider pickin' up and going somewhere else and startin' a practice?"

"Yeah, yes he did," Lourdes said. "I think he just ... I think he thought about doing that very recently, going to Las Vegas. That's why he kept going up there because he was, there aren't many doctors trained like him in, in Vegas, I think, and he would actually do very well. But his business is here. He owns the building. His children are here. I mean, it would ... it was gonna be too much trouble. And then, plus, when we broke up, he wanted me to go up there with him, and when we broke up, I mean, he wasn't gonna be able to do it by himself. I mean, he still asked me to marry him. I mean, he still loves me. In his mind, he believes that. You know, and I just ... after what happened in the federal case between us, no, I realized I can't cover things up for him. I ... I can't ... and this is ... um, I hope that you guys lead ... you do your investigation and you realize, 'Wow! That's a lot of stuff, but he's innocent.' That's what I hope happens. He'll hate me for it, but oh, well ..."

"Well, you have to do what you have to do," Jill said. "Just, I mean, the fact remains that he told you these things, and, you know, he apparently told this person the same stuff. In a nutshell, that's what the murder looked like, everything that you said, that he told you."

"That's why, when I heard more about they recovered his car, and, you know, it's not really as random as people think ... and I was ... I knew the minute that I heard the news that morning, I knew it was him. I knew and I prayed to God. I'm a defense lawyer, you know, I've got ... I got people accused of murder that I represent, but I have been struggling with this for the past two days, and I just want you guys to know what I know, and if … I mean … he's just begging me to have dinner with him tonight, but I said I can't. I cannot look at him. I can't. I just can't, and … and I know that he's worried that I'm gonna break down and do what I'm doing right now."

"Do you think he would harm you in any way?" Jill asked.

"Yeah," Lourdes said. "Oh, yeah."

"You do?"

"Yeah."

"What do you think he would do to you?" Jill asked.

"I think he would kill me because if he thinks that I'm the only person that can put him in prison, then he'll kill me. He loves me, but he'll have to kill me. See, I don't know," Lourdes said forlornly.

"That's what he said to you, or…?"

"I've had people ask me if … if I need to move, and I haven't told the children about any of this, obviously, 'cause I don't want to scare 'em. They're already, from what happened with their father, they don't trust the world. They're very sad that their father was taken from them in such a brutal way, 'cause he was … his head— half of his head was blown off. And we did, well, the best they could at the funeral. You know, so I don't like to bother them, and then when Brad and I broke up, it was ugly. I mean, he took my car, and the next day, I mean, that day, I … I couldn't pick up my children."

"Has he ever been physically abusive with you?" Jill asked.

"Oh, yeah," Lourdes said.

"He has?"

"Oh, yeah," she said. "We got into it last July, and there was a city court case that was dismissed ultimately, after his surgery. It was always about women. That's what it was about."

"Has he had surgery recently?" Jill asked.

Lourdes confirmed that Brad recently had an operation on his left shoulder.

"I don't want you to get the wrong impression," Lourdes blurted. "I've tried to ... to stay as much away from him as possible, but we are like intertwined in some weird, I mean, the furniture that you see in here, he gave it to me, but it's ... it's his. Do you know what I mean?"

"Yeah," Jill said.

"He helped us set up our office, you know. I help him with his QuickBooks. I take care of his kids. He has Daniel, my son, come over to his house, so he can see him feed the python that he had, you know, and I ... it's like I tried to completely break it off, and I couldn't do it. Because it's ... you know ... there's just something wrong with me on that level."

Jill had to ask a burning question, and she was blunt about it.

"Do you still love him?" Jill asked.

"Of course I do," Lourdes admitted. "Of course I love him. I ... I know that I can't ever trust him, or be married to him, but I love him to death. I wouldn't do anything to hurt him, not one thing. If there was anything at all that I could do ... I would protect him, but Dr. Stidham is dead, and he didn't deserve to die. He didn't."

"No," Jill said.

"That poor man," Lourdes said.

"Now you had told me," Jill said, "that you don't think Brad did this himself."

"No, never was physically because of the surgery," Lourdes said. "There's no way he could do it."

"OK."

"I mean, he could barely, he could barely move it. It was so ... it ... he was in such pain, and I felt so bad for him. I actually just saw him on Sunday, I think, and we were talking about his arm, and, you know, this constant ... 'Come on, Lourdes, give me another chance.' 'No, leave me alone.'"

"OK," Jill said. "Has he ever talked about how he would get somebody to do this for him?"

"He would … that he would just pay them," Lourdes said.

"Has he ever mentioned to you that he, um, tried to follow through with this before and it fell through on him?" Jill asked.

"No," Lourdes said. "No."

"Has he ever said, you had mentioned that he said he'd have more than one person do this?" Jill asked.

"Yeah," Lourdes replied. "Guys. *Huachos*. People that didn't have any reason to give a shit. I mean, can you b— imagine that I had conversations like that with him? I'm … I'm sitting here, and I'm thinking, 'What the hell was that all about?' It was my way of dismissing it, like, 'Don't be stupid. You can't do it. You cannot hurt someone."

"Well," Jill said, "and we don't know that he had anything to do with it."

"And we don't know," Lourdes said. "We don't know."

"So …"

"I … again, I hope," Lourdes said.

"We just have to gather the facts," Jill said, "and, you know, obviously, we need to know everything that you know. So this is good that you're coming forward."

Lourdes also felt it was important to say that Brad had given money to her ex-husband, Danny. Brad said it was to help out with Danny's new baby. But later, Danny's girlfriend told Lourdes that she suspected that Brad had asked Danny to kill Brian, and that's why the money was exchanged.

"And I was shocked," Lourdes said, "because I had never sus—"

"Danny's girlfriend said that?" Jill asked.

"Yes," Lourdes said. "Yeah. Now, this was her suspicion. She never said for sure. And then when you start thinking about it afterwards, you start thinking about conversations that he had, Brad had said he and Danny went to Brad's office with another guy who had a degenter— degenerative eye disease of some sort. The guy had just gotten out of prison. And Brad was gonna help him by treating him. And I think that was the guy that was gonna help kill Dr. Stidham with Danny, and I'm sick to my stomach to think that I married somebody that would do that. And that guy was either gonna do it or Danny was gonna do it with him. And then I found out also that this person is actually in custody up in Nebraska because he was one of the people that was in the car when Danny was killed. So, if in fact that actually happened, that conversation, that man may know something."

After Danny died, Lourdes said, she was comforted when Brad promised to let his anger go as well as the fact that the men she suspected would kill Brian were either dead or behind bars.

Jill asked Lourdes when was the last time she looked at Brad's bookkeeping records, which was in September.

"But you … you didn't see any financial distress goin' on there or anything like that?" Jill asked.

"Well," Lourdes said, sighing, "there's always been financial distress. What I have seen is a progression of it finally kinda goin' up. You know, finally there's money in there that you can see he can earn a living. You know, 'cause he pays, I mean, $11,500 a month in alimony and child support."

"Wow!" Jill said. "That's a lot!"

"It's a huge amount of money," Lourdes said. "But he gets a disability, um, he gets a check every month from the disability company, for it's been like a year now. So that check goes right to her. So he never has to worry about that, which is good, because the children didn't have to move from their house or anything like that. And they live in the foothills. I mean, they live very nicely. It's been … how does he live? You know, he's been angry because he can't buy a house, you know?"

"He lives in an apartment?"

Lourdes said Brad's apartment was a ground-floor unit at a gated complex on Camp Lowell and Swan roads.

"So how many times have you spoken to him since, um, Dr. Stidham's death?" Jill asked.

"He came over to my house Wednesday," Lourdes said. "He called me twice that night. He called me yesterday once, twice, three, four times yesterday. And he called me today, four, five, six, seven, eight times, nine times."

"And what's the general gist of those conversations?"

"The general gist is ... is he's ... is he wants to talk to his friend. He needs his friend. Me," Lourdes said. "He needs me to help him. This has got to be a hard time for him."

"Have you ever confronted him about, you know, this whole mysterious thing about maybe Danny was gonna do this thing with Dr. Stidham?" Jill asked.

"He said that it wasn't gonna, it wasn't gonna do ... he wasn't doing anything. He just basically said nothing. You know, 'I didn't do anything. We weren't gonna do anything.' But I know for a fact that he had this guy go to his office, and he checked his eyes. Because I believed it was gonna be ... that was part of the exchange of the money, of the compensation, 'I'll always take care of your eyes.' 'Cause apparently this guy just got out of prison. He only speaks Spanish. I mean, he's a bad guy, he's a really, really bad guy."

Jill asked if Brad had any buddies.

"I know that he does have friends that he confides in that are part of his group," Lourdes said, "but I never met them. Yeah, that's again part of the reason why our relationship went to shit, was because there were people in his life that I didn't know. I didn't know what they were like. You know, people who are obviously recovering addicts, either for Vicodin or cocaine or whatever."

Lourdes told Jill that she was glad that Brad went to rehab and had to attend weekly group counseling. At least, Lourdes told Jill, on counseling days, she knew where Brad was.

"He was so, uh, unbelievably unfaithful to me," said Lourdes, unaware, perhaps, of the fact that she had started an affair with Brad while he was still married to Joan. "I mean, he had a lot … a lot … a lot of affairs. Like, a lot. Many. Many, many, many. Not just one person, it was … so there came to a point where I didn't even believe if he went to the store. And that's part of what I'm struggling with right now. I wonder to myself, am I unfairly judging him because of what's happened to us personally and the fact that I have not trusted him and I'm making more of this than what it is? And, like I said, I hope that I'm wrong, but …"

"Well, what does your gut tell you?" Jill asked.

"My gut tells me that he had this man killed," Lourdes said.

"Yeah," Jill said. "And, I mean, he would be unfaithful to you and, you know, screw around and lie and do, you know, God only knows what. So when it comes down to him telling you, 'I want Dr. Stidham dead. I'm gonna have him killed, blah, blah, blah,' at the time did you really believe that? That he would do that?"

"Not that," Lourdes said. "Not at that time."

"OK."

"I thought he was just, in a way, I was happy that he was expressing his anger to me. He wasn't keeping it bottled up. He was sharing it with me. But, of course, I am the classic co-dependent person who thinks that she can fix everybody she loves. So I thought if I help him through it, by the classes, by being with the children and being a family and, however it is that he grew up, he says there was no love there. Now, I don't believe anything, you know. I thought to myself, if I just help him through this anger with his counselor and his therapist and his psychiatrist, you know, he'll be all right. At least he's vocalizing it. At least he's not internalizing it. So I didn't think at the time at all, but then it started to get very repetitive and then the whole situation with Danny and then Danny dies. And I'm like, 'What in the hell is happening to my life? What, why am I in the middle of this? Why is this happening to people that I love and care for?' And it got to the point when I told my friend about it."

"Right."

"And I asked him, please call anonymously. He was gonna do it."

"Are you willing to give me the friend's name?" Jill asked.

"Yeah," Lourdes said. "If you need it. He's gonna hide his brushes with the law. You know what I mean? He's a good guy. He's worried to hell about me. You know, he thinks that I'm gonna ... something's gonna happen to me and, you know, he was somebody that I was gonna be engaged to. I mean, I was very close to him. His name is Jeff Fairbanks and actually, I think he's a fireman now at Rural Metro, part-time. And he also works construction. ... I didn't want to involve Jeff in anything because, you know, he doesn't like police officers very much. I don't think so."

"Everybody loves police officers!" Jill joked, making Lourdes laugh. "We're all wonderful, you know."

"I shouldn't say that," Lourdes said. "That's really unfair for me to say that. And only because he's had some situations. No felonies. No felonies whatsoever."

"You can't blame yourself—" Jill said.

"I'm not blaming myself for being a good person," Lourdes said. "And having a good heart. I realize that I let this person control so much of my life and that's why I got into trouble a few years ago. And I thought to myself, I can sit here, and you guys can do your investigation on your own, and I cannot tell you. And it will eat me up inside. Because I know I have to tell you. You know, and here I am. And I'm not happy about it at all."

Lourdes also admitted telling someone else about Brad's threats, though she was reluctant to name Paul Skitzki.

"Don't worry about it," Jill said.

"It makes it more trouble for him at work," Lourdes said. "You know where most my friends are at."

"I do," Jill said. "And I understand. You're not the first person who has brought up Brad's name."

"I wasn't surprised by that," Lourdes replied.

"Yeah, and, um, we are lookin' at him," Jill said.

"What should I do, Jill, when he calls me again?" Lourdes asked. "'Cause he will. He's the kinda guy that will not, I mean, I told him, you can't just come to my house that day that he showed up. Don't come to my house. He shows up."

"I wanted to talk to you about that," Jill said. "'Cause frankly, I'm … I'm worried about that, I am. Um, I think that he … my personal opinion is that if, if he had this done, he is going into a panic mode right now. Because he has told people that he was gonna do this. And now he's trying to make sure that people won't talk. And I think he's freakin' out a little bit. And so that leads me to believe that he's a bit unstable right now. So I am a little concerned. I'm worried about your children. I don't have any easy answers for you on what we can do for you in the meantime. And I don't know. This can drag out for months. You know how things go."

"Oh, I know how things go," Lourdes said.

"And, so obviously, until I get probable cause to arrest him, he's gonna be out."

"I hate to say it, Jill, but he's probably gonna be really busy with the hospitals right now because Dr. Stidham is gone, all of the pediatric calls are gonna go to him. So in many ways, that's better because he's gonna be occupied with that. That's what I was thinkin' about."

"Now, I need you to think about this," Jill said. "It's completely your option, but something that we can do is we can have you confront him on the phone."

"Yeah."

"Or in person."

"I know."

"With a wire."

"I know."

"This is something you don't have to do," Jill said. "But if he's gonna tell anybody that he did it, it's probably going to be you. Because I imagine you're pretty much the one person in his life that he deals with he can actually tell."

"Yeah," Lourdes allowed. "I know."

"So I want you to think about it, alright?" Jill said.

Lourdes couldn't fight her emotions anymore and, thinking about how Brad had tried so hard the night before to convince her that he had nothing to do with Brian's death brought Lourdes to tears. She told them how much trust he put in her.

"But, you know, my children lost a father," Lourdes said through her sobs. "And I can't imagine what Daphne is gonna do now, you know? And it's ... it's a different ... this is not Vicodin. This is not shoplifting. This is not covering somebody because, you know, he took something from the store. This is somebody's life that is gone."

"Yeah," Jill said. "Dr. Stidham was a very promising young physician."

"He was a nice man, too," Lourdes added.

"He was a nice man."

"He wasn't a bad guy, Jill," Lourdes said. "He just wasn't a bad guy. You know, he wasn't the kind of person that talked about other people, or, you know, I realize now how uncomfortable it must have been for Dr. Stidham because I was there in the beginning, and I didn't know Brad was married. And here he is, having an affair with me and this ... I mean, I can imagine that poor guy, what he felt like. But he never ... he's just a nice man. You know, he was a nice man."

"Well, and it was a very brutal murder," Jill said. "It wasn't clean at all. So I would really like to find out who did it."

"Who did it," Lourdes echoed. "I know you would."

"Very much so," Jill said. "Because I can't, you know, I'm like you, I ... I don't ... when somebody innocent gets killed, I ... I can't sleep at night. It bothers me."

"And I feel horrible about what happened to my ex-husband, but there's a part of me that realizes, you know, if you're involved in drug dealing, that's a risk that you take. And I don't sleep better knowing that, but it just, you know, I think it's a risk that he thought of. And unfortunately, the cards came up differently for him. But you know, Dr. Stidham wasn't out there tryin' to score some dope. You know, he wasn't picking up a prostitute. He was going home, you know?"

Jill once again asked Lourdes to think about confronting Brad on the phone or in person with a wire.

"But if he does call me, what should I say?" Lourdes asked.

"Have you considered getting a restraining order?" Dawn suggested. "I know it's not gonna stop him from calling you, but do you realize that if he makes contact with you after you get a restraining order, every time he has contact with you, it's an aggravated charge. So if he keeps calling you, he's gonna get contacted every time by the police and get charged. What you'd have to do is make sure it's recorded, your conversation."

"OK," Lourdes said, trying to calm herself down.

"Every little thing can help you," Dawn added. "And I would hate for something to happen to you or your children because this man is crazy."

"I'm truly sorry," Jill said to Lourdes.

"Yeah," Lourdes said. "I shoulda known better."

"Well ..."

"That's what everybody tells me," Lourdes said.

"Hindsight is always 20/20," Jill said.

Jill assured Lourdes that they wouldn't arrest Brad until they had much more information implicating him in the murder.

"If he's guilty of doing this," Jill said, "then he needs to be in jail. He doesn't need to be out. And can you imagine if he is the one who set this up, and he is the one who hired somebody to do this. And he gets away with it. Can you imagine how powerful he's gonna feel? Can you imagine?

He's gonna think like, that he's unstoppable. So think about that. And think about your own self and your own well-being."

"Had it not been outside of his office, the carjacking situation, I would never have instantly thought it was him," Lourdes said. "I would have thought, you know, 'Gosh, you know, car, a car accident or rock climbing, or, you know, or poisoning or something like, oh, my God, how horrible!' But I never would … because it happened like this and this is exactly the way, in my mind, he said it was gonna happen, I mean."

"And I also have to ask you this," Jill said.

"Uh, huh?"

"If it comes down to us arresting him, will you be willing to testify against him?"

"I'm not gonna do it with a smile on my face," Lourdes said, "but I have to do the right thing. And the right thing is following through. And if that means testifying, I have to, I will."

CHAPTER 13

On Oct. 15, Det. Anderson was assigned to talk to Chris Corley and Chris Carney to trace Bruce Bigger's steps following the murder. Anderson was told about the Friday night party, how Bigger had come to their apartment with a lot of money. Bruce wanted to party in Vegas, Anderson learned, but transportation was a problem. Nobody could rent a car, so eventually Bruce took off with a mutual friend and a woman believed to be his girlfriend, Theresa Morales. Anderson brought back a tan polo shirt Bruce had worn at the apartment.

Meanwhile, Deputy Brian Cleburn got information about Theresa Morales and the white Volvo she was believed to be driving. Cleburn was told that the Volvo belonged to a man who lived in the Picture Rocks area, an eclectic rural community west of the Tucson mountain range. Cleburn set out to find the man and his Volvo.

Around 3 p.m., Sgt. P.V. Leonardi told Deputy S.F. Almodova that detectives wanted to talk to a Theresa Morales who was known to hang out in Picture Rocks. Almodova headed out to the area along with who officers from the fugitive recovery unit and two probation officers. Almodova drove down the road where Morales was said to be living on, continuing past the paved section down the dirt road. Just past the address, he saw a woman lying down in the dirt road. She looked over, saw the patrol car approaching and got up. As Almodova passed by, he recognized Theresa. Nearby, Almodova saw the white Volvo was stuck in the road, having unsuccessfully cleared a water main.

As Almodova radioed in the information that he had found Morales, he saw a man he recognized as Bruce Bigger in the car. Almodova pulled up to the Volvo and ordered Bruce out. Both Theresa and Bruce were handcuffed and taken into custody.

Bruce had several warrants out for his arrest. Theresa had a misdemeanor warrant from TPD.

Deputy Cleburn arrived and walked over to the patrol car where Bruce was sitting and introduced himself. Cleburn had spoken to Bruce on the phone before. He noticed that Bruce had a small cut under his left eye.

"What happened?" Cleburn asked.

"Ah, Theresa was drinking last night, and she got a little crazy," Bruce said. "She's been actin' crazy since then."

Bruce said Theresa began fighting with him as they were driving to Picture Rocks and began hitting him. He defended himself as best he could, but still managed to get scraped, he said.

"Do you want to press assault charges against her?" Cleburn asked.

"Nah," Bruce said.

Cleburn walked over to the car where Theresa was being held. A welt below her right eye was beginning to swell, and she had a scrape about two or three inches across her left shoulder.

"Do you want to press assault charges against Mr. Bigger?" Cleburn asked.

"No," she said.

Both Bruce and Theresa were taken to the main sheriff's office on Benson Highway for questioning and then booked into the Pima County Jail.

***

With the suspected hit man arrested, the Pima County Sheriff's Department turned its attention on Brad Schwartz.

Around 9:45 p.m., deputies met up at the area of Fort Lowell and Swan roads to coordinate the effort to arrest him. Deputies weren't sure whether Brad was in his apartment or not. Nevertheless, the decision was made to go to there and, if Brad was home, arrest him. The team made its way to the apartment complex and found Brad's unit. Two deputies, a sergeant and fugitive squad detectives went to the front door while two other deputies secured the rear of the apartment.

Deputy J.L. Rockwell, who was one of the officers sent to the back of the apartment, looked through a sliding glass door and back window and saw a man walking back and forth.

When deputies didn't get a response at the front door, a detective called Brad's phone, only to get the answering machine. The detective didn't leave a message, but several minutes later, his own phone rang. Brad was calling the unfamiliar number back, having seen it on his Caller ID.

At first, the detective pretended that he had just called the wrong number until he was sure that Brad was calling from inside his apartment.

"Is this Bradley Schwartz?"

"This is Bradley Schwartz," Brad said.

"Dr. Schwartz, we're from the Pima County Sheriff's Department. We need you to exit your apartment through the front door."

"OK," Brad said. "I will."

As Brad opened the door, the deputies recognized him as their target. Brad, clad in blue scrubs, walked out the door with his hands up and was ordered to his knees.

"Is there anyone else inside?" Westmoreland asked.

"Yes, a woman. Her name is Lisa," Brad said.

Lisa was called outside as Deputy Cleburn handcuffed Brad.

"Um, you should know, I just had shoulder surgery," Brad said. "It's still pretty tender."

Cleburn used two handcuffs locked together to restrain Brad.

"How's that?" Cleburn asked. "Is your shoulder OK?

"Yes, thanks," Brad said.

Through the open door, a friendly yellow Lab came scampering out of the apartment, circling Brad.

"That's Scooby," Brad said.

Scooby sniffed the pants of the men and the occasional hand stretched out in greeting. After Scooby approached Cleburn, the deputy placed the hairs left on his hand into a sheet of folding paper, just in case it was needed as evidence.

"Lisa," Brad said, "could you take Scooby, please? And tell Joan to come get the snakes and turtle."

Lisa told deputies that she would tell Joan to take the dog as well.

After Brad was taken away, deputies were waiting for a search warrant to be obtained when Joan Schwartz arrived around 11 p.m., asking if she could take the turtle and snake that were in the apartment. Joan was not allowed to go inside because the apartment was being guarded, so no evidence could be tampered with.

"Have you spoken to detectives yet?" a deputy asked her.

"No," she said.

Another detective contacted detectives to find out if they wanted to speak with Joan Schwartz. Det. Kelly Anderson said he was on his way, but it would take some time.

"I can't stay," Joan said. "I've got kids at home. I can't stay that long."

Joan left the deputies with her contact information.

Before the patrol car carrying Brad to sheriff's headquarters had left the complex, Sheriff Clarence Dupnik made sure that both daily newspapers and all three TV newsrooms were notified that the man suspected of ordering Brian Stidham's death was in custody and would be escorted into headquarters, should anyone wish to photograph him. No news outlet missed the opportunity to catch Brad Schwartz in his perp walk.

The next day, detectives Gary Burns and Knuth arrived at Brad Schwartz's apartment around 8 a.m. The homicide unit had discussed getting a search warrant the previous night to look for evidence, but decided around 11 p.m. that because the unit had worked long hours that day, it would be better to get the warrant and search the apartment the next day. About a quarter after 9, Joan Schwartz stopped by, hoping to pick up the turtle and snake, which were her children's pets.

Joan told Det. Burns how she and Brad had been married for about 11 years, then separated. The divorce was final in January, she said. She said she got about $10,000 a month in alimony and child support in two checks around the 15th of each month, although the check he gave her on Oct. 14 was short because of the crash with the Camry. Joan also told him that Brad gets disability pay because of his shoulder injuries.

After Joan was allowed to leave with the turtle and snake, the detectives continued searching the apartment as well as Brad's Escalade. Burns told the ID tech to take photos inside the driver's door area, the pedals, floorboards and seats. The Escalade was loaded onto a flatbed tow truck and hauled to the sheriff's department's vehicle bay for more forensic processing.

After the detectives finished searching Brad's apartment, they drove to his office, opening it with one of the keys found on the Escalade's key ring. The detectives logged some evidence and left about two hours later.

***

Brad was led into a small room with a table at the Sheriff's Department.

"Uh, I guess you can't take my handcuffs off?" Brad asked. "My shirt's on backwards."

In his haste to answer the door, Brad had quickly pulled on some scrubs without paying attention to detail.

"We'll do that in a sec, OK?" the deputy said, then pointed to a table. "Right over there."

"OK."

"Just have a seat, and we will be right back with you," the deputy said. "And we'll try and take care of whatever you need, OK?"

"OK."

After the deputy left, Brad reached into his pants pocket for his cell phone, which the deputies had not taken. He managed, despite the handcuffs, to call Mike Piccarreta, the attorney who represented him in federal court.

"Mike," Brad said, "I'm at the sheriff's office. Please. They just arrested me. Yeah. Please come quick. Sheriff's, main sheriff's office on Benson Highway. No, um—"

"No calls right now, all right?" the deputy said, interrupting.

"OK," Brad said. "Yes. It was just kind of vibrate—"

"Oh, OK," the deputy said, then took the phone. "We're gonna just hang on to this for a minute. Put it right over here, you know where it is."

The deputy left. Within minutes, the phone began vibrating. Brad walked over to the phone and, still handcuffed, answered it.

It was Piccarreta calling back.

"Hello?" he said. "Yeah, yeah, I can't really talk on it, though. Yeah, I can't, OK? Here's the officer right here, Mike."

Det. Murphy walked to see Brad on the phone. She, of course, was familiar with Piccarreta, one of Tucson's high-profile attorneys. Murphy told him that Brad would be booked into the jail, and she would leave the room if he wanted to talk to his client. Murphy left to get keys to the handcuffs, so Brad could use the phone.

"You got a couple sets on, huh?" she said, noticing the pair.

"I just had shoulder surgery," Brad explained. "I can't get my arms close together. Do you mind if I take my shirt off and flip it? It's, it's backwards."

"No, that's fine," Murphy said.

Murphy struggled with getting the handcuffs off. Brad suggested that he could take his shirt off with just one of the cuffs on him, joking that he didn't want to violate any protocol for shirt removal. After everything was settled, Murphy left the room so Brad could presumably talk to Mike. Instead, he called Lourdes.

***

Lourdes didn't know how much of this she could stand. It had been a week since she'd spoken with Jill Murphy. Against Dawn's advice, Lourdes didn't take a restraining order out on Brad. And still, he continued to call, asking for her to believe he didn't have anything to do with Brian's death. Asking for her back in his life.

"Lourdes," he told her that day on one of his calls. "Please, Lourdes, I want you to come back. I do. And I'll do anything. I'll tell you everything. Please, Lourdes, come back. I won't hold anything back."

"No, Brad," she said. "No, just leave me alone!"

On Oct. 15, Lourdes' son didn't go to school because it was grading day. So Lourdes took him to work with her. She was planning on going to fulfill a community service duty at the Boys and Girls Club and was set to leave work about 5 p.m.

"Come on, Mom!" her son said, impatient after a day of hanging out at his mother's office. "We've gotta leave. We're gonna be late!"

Lourdes gathered up the papers she needed to review that night and loaded up the car. As they were leaving, her son pointed out the window.

"Isn't that Brad's Escalade, Mom?" he said.

Lourdes glanced at her rearview mirror and her heart stopped when she recognized Brad's large SUV. She stepped on the gas and hurried away as quickly as she could, grateful that she was just moments away from having a confrontation with him. He'd left her two voice mails and two e-mails that afternoon, begging her to call him, and she didn't want to.

Later, after Lourdes got home, fed the kids and was preparing for bed, she flipped on the news to see images of Brad, in scrubs, being led away in handcuffs. She was shocked, yet relieved. There would be no more phone calls, she thought. No more begging for her to believe him, come back to him. The jig was up.

Then the phone rang. It was Brad.

"Hi," Brad said.

"I saw on the news that you've been arrested!" Lourdes said.

"Yeah," Brad said. "Yeah. Yes, so I want you to be my attorney."

"No, Brad, I can't," she said.

"Why not?" he said, beginning to panic. "Why not? Why?"

"Brad, I just can't," she insisted.

"You're the best!" he said. "Why not?"

"Isn't Mike your attorney?" Lourdes said.

"I want you to work with him."

"No, Brad."

"Why not?" he pleaded. "Tell me why. I need you to help me defend my life here."

Lourdes still refused.

"Why not?" he asked again. "No, I need your help."

"You don't need me," she said.

"That's not true," he said. "No. I need your help. I need your help. I need your help to help me."

"Brad—"

"Yes, you can!" he said. "You're the best. You're the best, no, you're the best. I need your help. I need you to do this with Mike. Please."

"No, Brad," she insisted.

"Please," he persisted. "Do it for my children. No, do it for my children. Help defend me, Lourdes. I need your help. This is your job. This is what you do. If you were going blind, you'd come to me, and I would help you. And I'd help your family. This is my life. I need your help."

Lourdes again refused.

"Why not?" he asked. "Tell me why. I want you to help me."

"Brad, I can't," she said. "I've got to go now."

"Don't ... don't do that to me," he begged. "Don't leave me. Please, don't! Lourdes? Please work with Mike. Please! You are the ... you are the best."

"Brad, don't," Lourdes said. "You know I can't do that."

"Why not? That's your job. That's your job, Lourdes. That is your job. You know that. That's what you swore to do. You tell me every day you take people on that you don't believe and ... and you did it with this guy with the church, OK? Why did he deserve your representation and I don't? So I deserve less than that? I'm asking you to do, I'm asking you, I'm asking you to do your job, to help me. You are the best. I've seen you. I've heard you. Please work with Mike, please. I'm asking you. Please."

"Have they told you what the bond is?" she said.

"Probably a million dollars," he replied.

"So post it," Lourdes said.

"What? Are you crazy?" he exclaimed. "How am I gonna post a million dollars? My life's over. Lourdes, help. Lourdes, help me do this. I need your help. Mike is good. You're the best. You're the best. If ... Lourdes, if you were going blind or your father was going blind, or your mother was going blind, you would come to me. I'm asking you, I'm asking you to do what you're trained to do and help me. I'm asking you. I'm begging you. I'm pleading with you to help Mike. I—"

"Brad, I can't!" Lourdes said.

"No, you can!" he said. "Yes, you can. I don't believe that. You can. If you want to, you will. That's what you swore to do. You do criminal defense. Whether you believe the person is innocent or guilty or not, you do that. You've told me, that is, everyone in this country has the system that you tell me, everyone in this country deserves equal representation. You've told me everybody in this country deserves, OK? *Deserves.* I need you to do this. This is ... Lourdes, this is the rest of my life here. I need—"

"Brian's dead, Brad."

"That's not my doing!" Brad stressed. "That's not my doing! I have nothing to do with that. That is not my doing."

"Brad, I can't. I just can't represent you. I have to go now," she stammered. "I don't want to talk to you anymore. I don't want to see you. It's over."

"No!" he said. "You know and I know that is not necessary. Lourdes, please don't ... don't ... don't say goodbye to me like this. I need your help. I need your help on this, please! Please."

"Brad, it's over," she said. "We're over."

"Lourdes, I understand that," he said. "But I'm ... our relationship aside, you're—"

"No, Brad, no."

"Why? This is ... you're the best," he pleaded. "You're— then, well, let me ask you a question. In addition, in lieu of our relationship or our ... it's a long word, but the fact that we've had a relationship, don't you want to see me not go to jail?"

Just as she had felt all through their relationship, Lourdes knew that Brad could see right through her.

"Did you not call me back all day today 'cause you knew this was happening?" Brad asked. "Listen, OK? I'm not asking you to primarily be responsible for my defense, but I want you to be with Mike there—"

"Brad, no, I can't," she said. "I won't."

"Please," he said. "I'm asking you, please. I've seen you work miracles with juries, OK?"

Murphy opened the door and leaned in.

"Are you still talking to Piccarreta?" she asked.

"Yeah, well, my other attorney," Brad said.

"You have another attorney?"

"Yeah."

"OK," Murphy said. "Is Piccarreta not gonna represent you—"

"No, he's the main ... he's the main guy," Brad said. "Lourdes is my attorney in certain matters. I was asking her to work with Mike on this case, too."

"OK. What matters is she your attorney?"

"She's been my attorney on all legal matters," he said.

"OK, um, I'm Det. Murphy, by the way," she said.

"I spoke to you before."

"That's right. Um, I'm assuming that, uh, you know your rights, but I'm going to read them to you anyway, all right?" she said.

"OK."

"OK. You have the right to remain silent. Anything you say can and will be used against you in a court of law. You have the right to the presence of an attorney to assist you prior to questioning and be with you during questioning, if you desire. If you cannot afford an attorney, you have the right to have any attorney appointed for you prior to questioning. Do you understand these rights?"

"Yes," Brad said.

"Do you want to answer any of my questions?"

"Not without my attorney," he said.

"OK," she said. "What's gonna happen now is—did Mike want to come down here and talk to you before we booked you?"

"No, he's gonna come down tomorrow," Brad said.

"What's gonna happen now is we're going to, um, I'm going to do some paperwork, and then we're gonna take you to the jail and book you in. Um, this is a first-degree murder charge. I need you to understand that. All right? I'm assuming somebody told you about that ahead of time."

"No," Brad said. "They didn't."

"No one said anything to you on the way down here?"

"No."

"You're being booked in for the murder of Dr. Brian Stidham."

***

Not long after deputies were dispatched to arrest Brad and Bruce, Pima County Sheriff Clarence Dupnik sent word that the media were to be notified that the murder of Brian Stidham had been solved. Print photographers and TV camera operators rushed to the sheriff's headquarters, 1750 E. Benson Highway, to take pictures of Brad being led into the building—the infamous perp walk.

"We've had tremendous cooperation from the community, especially from the medical community," Dupnik told the *Tucson Citizen.*

"Schwartz, his character is such that the medical community suspected him from the very first," Dupnik said.

Even the sheriff's own doctor asked why Schwartz hadn't been arrested, Dupnik told the *Citizen.*

Dupnik said numerous tips were called into the 88-CRIME tip line and 25 detectives worked on the case around the clock.

Bruce Bigger was arrested for Brian's murder also, he announced.

Off the record, Dupnik also told reporters that Brad Schwartz was bipolar. He hinted that there were court documents with "interesting information" about Brad related to a federal case. The sheriff seemed to take great delight in telling the press that the murder suspect had been naked in bed with a woman when deputies came to arrest him.

"I ask people to keep an open mind on this case," Mike Piccarreta told the *Citizen*. "Everything that they've been told in the Sheriff's Department media campaign will not be proven. It seems to me the Sheriff's Department has gotten their exercise by jumping to conclusions.

"They have never heard his side of the story," Piccarreta said of Brad. "And now they won't hear his side of the story until the trial."

Piccarreta, in fact, had been trying to arrange an interview between Brad and Det. Murphy in the days preceding Brad's arrest. But Dupnik's office didn't seem interested in making the appointment.

"I trust in the system that all of the truth will come to light within time," Lourdes told the *Citizen*. "He is an exceptionally well-trained doctor, and I'm sure many of his patients will tell you that."

At the time of Lourdes's statement, the public was aware only that she was a former prosecutor-turned-defense attorney who had dated Brad. The public was also learning about malpractice suits filed against Brad in the wake of his federal case. Laurie Espinoza gave a deposition in which she said he was often tardy, drooled and fell asleep—sometimes during conversations—visited his truck several times each day to pop pills with Mountain Dew and returned from those visits "bouncing off the walls." Sometimes, she said, he had to be awakened to see patients.

More details were revealed when search warrants and other public documents were filed in court.

"What the search warrant really highlights is the lack of evidence," Piccarreta told the *Citizen*. "There's no physical evidence connecting Dr. Schwartz or apparently, the other gentleman, to this act. Two, there's no confession to indicate that they did that. Three, their motive could fall apart under the scrutiny of a grammar-school detective. And four, there was no such ongoing animosity that would lead one (doctor) to cause physical harm to another. Their relationship ended years ago without any litigation."

Piccarreta said Brad had given Brian his pediatric patients, and there was a "reasonable explanation" why a phone call from the convenience store was placed to Schwartz's cell phone.

"But I'm not going to announce it now," he said.

***

Even though Lourdes had done what she knew was right—contact the sheriff's department about her fears—the events of the week and how tangled up her own life was in it all weighed on her. The weekend after Brad was arrested, Lourdes contacted her friends for comfort. One of those was Brad Roach, the prosecutor she called for help when she and Brad Schwartz fought in his car. Brad Roach is a bear of a man with boyish, tow-headed features. Lourdes had resisted talking to Brad Roach about Brad Schwartz because she knew her friend always distrusted her former fiancé. Brad Roach thought Brad Schwartz was narcissistic and a general bad influence on Lourdes. After the incident at the convenience store, Brad Roach never spoke a kind word about Brad Schwartz.

"It's shocking the number of—when you consider how large Tucson is—it was shocking the number of people, aside from Lourdes, who, when all the federal stuff happened and it made the papers, approached me and said that they had a friend who had dated Dr. Schwartz during this time frame. Also, the number of women that he had been dating. It was just an amazing number of people that came to me and approached me about that," Brad Roach told Det. Jill Murphy. "I saw him with his children, which ... I didn't see him abuse his children, but I saw him with his kids and ... and it seems to me he ... he ... his kids were an ... an accessory for him. That was the feeling I got. They were useful in ... for him to appear like a good dad, but ... um ... he didn't show any affection or ... or kind of the contrary towards the kids, which kind of creeped me out."

But it wasn't until after Brian Stidham's death that Lourdes told Brad Roach about the threats Brad Schwartz had made previously.

"Calm down, Lourdes," Brad Roach said, hoping that her hysterics made it sound much worse than the situation was. "Take a deep breath and tell me again, what did Brad say?"

"He was going to kill Brian, Dr. Stidham," Lourdes said. "He was going to have him killed."

"Oh, my God, Lourdes!" Brad said. "When did you know this?"

"He used to say it a lot," Lourdes said. "I can't remember exactly when."

Of course, Brad Roach had known about the doctors' split. Lourdes had told him that Brad Schwartz was angry about Dr. Stidham starting up a practice. But Lourdes had never intimated anything this serious about the anger.

"I'm afraid, Brad," Lourdes told him. "I'm afraid for the life of my kids and myself."

"I can't say as I blame ya, Lou," he said. "Has he called you?"

"He hasn't stopped!" she said, sobbing. "I don't know what to do! I talked to Jill, Jill Murphy, and I told her what he said. But I don't want him to know that I went to the police! What am I gonna do if he gets through to me, how am I gonna face him knowing that I've talked to the police and because of that, he might get arrested! He's gonna know it, Brad. He's gonna see it in my eyes. He's gonna hear it in my voice."

"Lourdes," Brad Roach said, cautiously, "do you seriously think he did it?"

"I do!" Lourdes cried out. "Yes, Brad, I think he did do it! The next day, I … I talked to him and … I don't know what it was, but … I was hoping that he would show me a sign that he didn't do it, but Brad, I could tell, I know he did it! I think what he was doing is sounding me out, to see what I was thinking, to see if I would still have faith in him and not turn him into the police."

"Jesus, Lou," Brad said. "Jesus, I think maybe he did, too."

***

The call that Carmen Fernandez dreaded the most eventually did come on Oct. 26. Det. Murphy identified herself and began to ask questions about Brad Schwartz. Carmen told Murphy how she'd met Schwartz and how their relationship evolved.

"During that time," Murphy asked, "did he ever say anything about Dr. Stidham? Or did he ever say anything about having something done to Dr. Stidham?"

"I don't know anything about that," Carmen lied, fearing Brad's wrath herself.

***

Whatever concerns Aisha Henry had about the things that Brad confided in her, she kept to herself. It wasn't until Oct. 26, just after she had started a new job as a customer service representative for a phone company, that the sheriff's department contacted her. Aisha dreaded talking to them, but she supposed it was inevitable. Detectives Hogan and Lopez showed up, unannounced, at her office. Even then, Aisha wasn't ready to tell them everything. She didn't know how the detectives knew that Brad had given her money, but when they asked her about it, she lied and told them that he had loaned her the money. She fed them a story about Brad wanting her husband to come over to his apartment and do some repair work. Eventually, though, the detectives wore her down, and she admitted that she took the $1,500 after agreeing with Brad to have her husband hurt Brian. Aisha stressed to them that she had no intentions of carrying through with the plan. And, Aisha told them, Brad never talked about wanting Brian killed, only harmed in some way. He never asked her to find someone to kill Brian, she said. Yes, she had to admit to herself, she was taking advantage of Brad, but then, she reasoned, he was taking advantage of her good-hearted nature, too.

**

Not everyone who knew Brad Schwartz was happy he was arrested. Kerri Delorme, who'd helped Brad open the APES office when he first came to Tucson, followed news of the case over the Internet from her out-of-state home.

"This is a sad, sad story of losing control of your life," she wrote in an email to the *Citizen*. "Not knowing when to walk away. I remember a man that was so excited to come to Tucson, looking forward to raising a family there. Only great things lay ahead for him. He had come there with the aspiration of being one of the best and respected eye surgeons in the area. He loved the thought of going to local grade schools to do free eye exams for all the children that couldn't afford eye care. He had embraced the community. Volunteered his time as much as possible. WHAT HAPPENED? Would he have come to Tucson knowing this would happen?"

Kerri, at least, was willing to acknowledge that Brad had only been charged with a terrible crime. But even that must be ripping his family apart, she wrote.

"I met his wife and children," she added. "He had such a beautiful family. How does she tell the children that once their father was a brilliant doctor, and now he is accused of such a crime? So, so sad. He has a mother, father and brothers or sisters that now have to deal with the guilt of not seeing this coming. Could they have helped stop the spinning in his life? I doubt it. I know Dr. Schwartz, and he is very independent, very stubborn and is always right. But that doesn't give way to the responsibility that the family must feel."

***

Some who were close to Brad in Tucson also were reeling from the recent events. Not everyone pulled their support. One woman in particular, Kristen Pedersen, continued to display her affection for Brad through jailhouse visits and letters.

"Well, here I am," she wrote in an Oct. 28 letter, "another day ending and another night that I will cry myself to sleep. I would give just about anything to have you here with me. I broke down today and read both the morning and afternoon papers. Just a little article on your so-called 'hitman.' Nice little record he has. Nothing that can prove that he's a murderer though. What is your take on him? Do you think they have the wrong guy in his case, too? To be honest, I don't know too much about him. Once he's someone you met in a substance abuse program, next he's a former patient of yours, then a self-employed medical equipment salesman. Which one is it?"

Kristen even got to the point where she called a reporter from the morning paper to express her disdain for a story that was written, she told Brad.

"I think I want to talk to you now about how I feel about you," she wrote to Brad. "I love you!! You have literally had my heart from day one. There was just something about you. Even knowing that you had 10 girlfriends at once, including me. I still somehow thought that it was me that you loved the most. Am I a total retard or what? Besides being lovers we were such great friends. We had something that you didn't have with anyone else. I was, and still am, your biggest fan—even when you hated me. I really don't believe you hated me. You were putting on some sort of a 'show' for Lourdes, so she wouldn't be insecure. At least that is my interpretation of that dumb situation. Is it at all entertaining to you?"

Kristen even fretted that Brad wasn't able to keep up with the New York Yankees.

"My heart breaks when I visualize your current situation!!! Please stay strong! Know that I am thinking of you, missing you, loving you, praying for you. What would I give to watch a movie, eat some peach sorbet, pluck some fat chin hairs? You have no idea!!! I miss you Brad!"

She signed her letter with three X's and three O's.

***

"Happy Halloween!" Bruce said, calling his mother, Mary Sue Yadavia, in Indiana, collect from the Pima County Jail.

"Hello," Sue responded.

"It's a big trick," Bruce said.

"Big trick," Sue said.

"And it ain't no treat," Bruce said. "Did you have, uh, trick or treat this weekend?"

"The kids are going around now," Sue said.

"You got your headlight—your porch light on?"

"No, I forgot about it," she admitted. "I've been working. I had today off, but I'm trying to recuperate from working all weekend."

"Any good news from Indiana?" he asked.

"Not yet," she said.

"OK," he said. "Um, what I was going to—Oh, Ma, whenever, if you do have an opportunity to send anything, you have to make sure you send it in a prestamped envelope."

"A prestamped envelope?" she asked.

"Yes, it can't have a stamp on it. They send it back."

"Why?"

"I don't … I don't know," he said. "That's just what their thing is, OK?"

"Yup. OK."

"All right, somebody sent me a bad letter."

"Who did?" she asked.

"I don't know who."

"What, an anonymous letter? For goodness' sake!"

"They said they're gonna do something to me," Bruce said. "Watch my back."

"Well, how wonderful."

"That fucking doctor is really something I think," he said.

"Sounds like a real piece of work," she added.

"Whoever though, mom?" Bruce said. "He's a—you know, what, what exactly have, has the paper thing said? Do you wanna talk about this or no? If it's too much, that's fine. I didn't even know who was murdered till, I don't know, four days ago, five days ago. Right before I called you. Just because they told me not to talk to—nobody was walking to me, you know."

"And that's the best way to keep it," Sue said.

"Is it?"

"Yes."

"OK, well, when you don't know shit, it ain't hard not to say shit, you know? Although, I did wake up the other morning and just sat there and thought, if they don't have my prints and if I didn't have a weapon and this and that and everything, why am I sitting in here? I sh—"

"I guess they said that, uh, you were seen," Sue broke in.

"Yeah, my lawyer said that. Said I was at a gas station."

"Right across from that doctor's office," she said.

"Oh, and they told me it was First and River," he said. "I don't even know where that is. My attorney said it ain't—that don't mean nothing."

"He said you went there and said your car's broken down and you asked to use the phone and you called that other doctor," she said. "The one that's in jail."

"Well, I could—that's what it said?"

"Uh huh."

"I did do that one day," he admitted.

"Said you were wearing a scrub."

"What's a scrub?" Bruce asked. "Like the doctor stuff, right?"

"Yes. And that was the day the other doctor was killed."

"Oh," Bruce said. "Oh, so I see why that's relevant."

"Yeah," Sue said. "A lot of circumstantial stuff."

"But a lot of circumstantial stuff adds up to … to something," he said. "I mean, that's pretty damning."

"And it said you had dinner with Dr. Schwartz that night," Sue said.

"Yeah, I've had dinner with him five or six times though, you know what I mean? That's the same day. He told me, don't worry about the car, just come over there. Never mind, I shouldn't say that. I shouldn't say nothing over the phone. You know, it doesn't say anything about the other times that we had met at, uh, other restaurants and had dinner, right? It didn't mention that time we had double-dated. It doesn't mention anything like that."

"No," she said.

"Right," he said. "Well, 'cause I'm sure they don't know about it. Maybe they do now."

"Maybe they do, now."

"Is that bad?" he asked. "I just better shut up."

"Yeah."

"OK, but listen to this. They got a guy in here that's, uh, saying he's a preacher, right? So naturally he's my roommate, right? Well, he's from Jamaica, but he's a preacher. But he got busted with a house with all this, I don't, I don't know, a couple thousand pounds of marijuana."

"Right," Sue said. "That'd be a Rastafarian."

"No," Bruce said. "He said he's no Rastafarian. He says he's a Christian. And he's, but he's this Catholic turned Christian. And then he says all Catholics are faggots. And then he started saying all this other stuff. You know, he's talking about he wants welfare, uh, he starts talking about, uh, the United States, they, you know, he's bitching that he wasn't getting no welfare. He's not even a citizen here. You know, he's here on a visa and this and that and everything else. So and then he started it again this morning. Well, he got pissed off, because I told him that Catholics wrote the Bible. And then this morning, he started again and I told him, you got two strikes against you, pal, don't go for number three. I just gotta … I gotta shut up. I just can't believe it. So then, this is my conspiracy theory, though. He's, they started a fake church in Jamaica. It's being funded out of Brooklyn by the Taliban. OK, so donations are being sent back from the United States through this church to Jamaica that says it's a Christian church. Then those funds are going to the Taliban."

"The Taliban?" Sue said, surprised at the mention of the insurgent group.

"Yup," Bruce said. "I think he's a terrorist. Oh, he's talking the other night, in, in all seriousness about how good of a guy Saddam Hussein was. That, um, Saddam Hussein hadn't killed all those people in Iraq, that it was his sons. His sons were evil, not him, OK?"

"Oh, Christ!" Sue uttered.

"Yeah, he's Taliban," Bruce said. "I'm bunking with Taliban, Ma! I'm telling you, I'm figuring it all out right from here. I'm gonna—by the time I get out, Tom Ridge is gonna be calling me."

"Oh, you think so, huh?"

"Mom, I'm so sorry," Bruce said. "I know this has to be hard. I can't even imagine. I just can't. I wake up everyday and I, I just don't know how to think or feel, you know? I had a dream today about Gideon."

"About Gideon?" she said, smiling at the thought of the beloved family dog long since dead.

"Thinking about it makes me tear up, you know?"

Bruce told his mother that he wasn't planning to call his stepfather or stepbrothers.

"I just, I just don't see it," he said. "I'm sorry. I'm just, I'm sorry that I called you, but I needed you to know. Boy, this place reminds me, jail doesn't smell good."

"It doesn't, does it?"

"Oh, man, you know what? They don't even shower people out when they come here," said Bruce, apparently more accustomed to more hygienic jails than the one in Pima County.

"No?"

"Yeah, I don't know how they don't have things going around here," he said. "But this ain't the way I wanna spend the rest of my life."

"I hope not."

Just then, an inmate Bruce had befriended motioned that he wanted to speak to Sue.

"I just wanted to hear somebody's voice real quick," the inmate said. "'Cause I haven't talked to anybody in a while. So, God bless you."

"Thank you," Sue replied.

"I think he's a good kid," Bruce said. "He's from the Bronx."

"What's he doing out there?" Sue asked.

"He come out here, he was in the service and, uh, opened a restaurant and everything when he got done here. Oh, man, he's crying! Oh, man. And, uh, I don't know, I think he beat somebody up pretty good."

"Oh, God," Sue said, sighing.

"Yeah, but, um, anyway, I'm, I'll talk to you later," Bruce said. "Maybe not. Maybe. OK. If anything good or bad happens, I'll definitely let you know. But that's gotta be in a prestamped envelope."

"OK."

"And, uh, hopefully you can, hopefully at some point, I know I stretched you, Ma, in your funds, but hopefully at some point you'll be able to go and get those taxes and that thousand dollars will be able to help you."

"OK," Sue said, knowing he was referring to his tax refund.

"All right. God bless you and have a great weekend," Bruce said. "Happy Halloween, OK?"

"OK."

"All right, bye now."

"I love you," she said.

"Bye," he said. "I love you, Mom."

***

In the wake of the arrests of Brad Schwartz and Bruce Bigger, Daphne Stidham hired one of Tucson's leading criminal defense attorneys, Natman Schaye, to represent her in connection with the case. Schaye didn't explain why Daphne hired a criminal defense attorney, but he issued a statement on Oct. 19 to the media:

> I am writing to let you know that this office is representing Daphne Stidham and her family in connection with the murder of her husband, Dr. David Stidham. As I am sure you understand, the family is devastated by this horrible crime. Family members are grateful that those responsible have been arrested and jailed. It is the hope of the family, and particularly of Daphne Stidham, that these individuals will be convicted and imprisoned for the rest of their lives.

We have no further information to provide at this time. Should you have any questions, please contact this office. Please do not attempt to contact Mrs. Stidham or members of her immediate family directly.

Thank you for your anticipated cooperation,

Sincerely,

Natman Schaye

On Nov. 12, 2004, Daphne Stidham issued a statement through Homicide Survivors:

To citizens of Tucson,

I would like to express my heartfelt gratitude to all you individuals, patients and the medical community for your overwhelming support and generosity. Because of you, I was able to sustain myself during this trying time, after the senseless and vicious murder of Brian.

Brian and I had a brief and wonderful, loving life together.

A number of special people in the medical community have devoted their time and help. I would like to thank Drs. Steve and Rosa Cohen, our dear friends for everything.

I look forward to thanking each and every person, individually.

Dr. Sam Sato has assumed Brian's practice. He possesses the same dedication, experience and loving care that Brian provided to his patients. We appreciate the continued support from patients and the medical community.

The staff at Brian's office have stayed strong and supportive. Thank you for your help and hard work. Your choice to stay and work for Dr. Sato has helped ease the transition to the new ownership, tremendously.

Thank you all.

Bless you,

Love, Daphne, Alexandre and Catherine

Dr. Joseph Miller, another local pediatric ophthalmologist, also helped with Brian's patients following his murder. A pediatrician, Dr. Mary Cochran, organized a Dec. 4 walk at one of Brian's favorite hiking spots, Sabino Canyon, with a plaque to be placed there in his memory. Tucson Medical Center helped fund her efforts. In addition, the Pima County Pediatric Society helped provide seed money for an 88-CRIME reward. The president of the pediatric society, Dr. Mehul Dixit, a pediatric nephrologists, ordered that each October of the group's meetings would be devoted to pediatric ophthalmology, in Brian's honor.

***

In mid-November, Bruce Bigger made his first court appearance, shuffling into the Pima County Superior Courtroom in shackles and an orange jail uniform. Print photographers and TV cameras awaited him. Instead of flinching from the publicity, Bruce smiled at the cameras and joked about his widely distributed jailhouse mug shot.

"I'd do anything to erase that image," he joked.

The news of his arrest made its way 1,900 miles home to LaPorte County, whose criminal justice system was familiar with Ronald Bruce Bigger.

"He was not a skinny guy the last time we saw him," Bob Schuster, the county's chief probation officer told the *Citizen*. "He was stocky and had a round face. When we saw the Tucson photo, it was like looking at two different people."

"It did indicate drug use," LaPorte County prosecutor Kim DeWitt said.

"He was a con man," said DeWitt, who had prosecuted several cases against Bruce. "He would try to come across as a highly intelligent person. He liked himself a lot."

Bruce's legal troubles seemed to mount up after he filed for bankruptcy in South Bend, Ind., in 2002, the *Citizen* reported. That August, he was charged with forgery and check fraud at LaPorte County Circuit Court. A month later, he was arrested for theft in Michigan City, Ind., on Lake Michigan. Then in October, he was wanted for failing to show up on the forgery and check fraud charges. He was arrested late that month in Michigan City and LaPorte for check fraud and forgery.

In 2003, Bruce took a cross-country trip to visit his best friend in Scottsdale. He couldn't even keep out of trouble halfway across the country, racking up traffic charges in Apache Junction. He spent much of 2003 crisscrossing between Indiana and Arizona.

"To us, he was a thief," DeWitt told the *Citizen*. "He was an arrogant young fellow. There was a cockiness, an annoyance about him."

And, apparently, a loner as well.

"Every time he came to court," Schuster said, "he appeared by himself."

When Bruce was sentenced on a fraud charge, he thanked the judge for allowing him to travel to Arizona, where he said he was employed as a packager, the *LaPorte Herald-Argus* reported.

"This case has helped me to slow down and realize what is important in life," Bruce told the judge. "I'm ready to take care of this and be done with it."

On Dec. 5, 2003, Bruce pleaded guilty to a burglary charge in LaPorte. On Jan. 23, 2004, he was sentenced to three years probation, with the provision that he could be transferred to Arizona if he was accepted there. Bruce was ordered to spend some time in the county jail, but he was out by summertime. By July, a warrant for his arrest was issued for failing to comply with conditions of his probation.

***

In mid-December, Bruce Bigger consented to an interview with local TV station KGUN in which he denied killing Brian Stidham, breaking down into tears several times throughout the course of the interview.

"I'm not the guy they're looking for," Bruce said. "I'm tired of being lied about. It's time for me to stand up for myself."

By that time, reporters had been told that a convenience store clerk near the murder scene had identified Bruce as a man dressed in scrubs that night acting suspiciously.

"I went to a gas station?" Bruce told the TV reporter. "Gimme a break! I don't even know where First and River is!"

He also denied having driven Brian's Lexus after the murder.

"My prints aren't in that damn car," he said. "I should not be here. I did not do this. I don't believe Brad did it."

Bruce did admit dining with Brad that night and getting a hotel room.

"We went to a hotel because I had two girls," he said.

He also explained why witnesses would say that he had lots of cash in an envelope with him in the days after the murder.

"I have an inheritance," he said. "My mother wires me money from Indiana. If I had $10,000, I would have been out of here.

"I am not to bear whatever is being concocted outside these walls," Bruce said. "I know I didn't kill nobody."

***

Kristen Pedersen continued to support her troubled lover. She even teamed up with Joan Schwartz at least once on a weekend visit at the jail. And Kristen arranged to send newspapers to Brad in jail, so he could read what was being said about him and everyone else involved in the case and an upcoming hike at Sabino Canyon in Brian's memory.

"As for Lourdes," Kristen wrote on Dec. 2, "what a hooker. (She really does look like one.) She sure is drawing a lot of attention to herself. I have heard in the past that she was staying with you (after the drug charges) to get payback. (literally — $$$) She makes me ill. I am wondering when the media is going (to) start in with this Dec. 4th memorial walk? Probably tonight — it's 2 days away. I would do it, but I know too many people — and doctors … and friggin' news anchors, too. That's all I need. So instead I'll just say a silent prayer for Brian. He did not deserve to die — and the way he died — so brutally! I hope he died quickly — not slowly. I wish I could make the world understand and see things through my eyes. I know you didn't do it (or have it done)."

Within a couple months of the arrests, rumors about who would get to tell "the other side of the story" were circulating around town. Richard Parrish, a local attorney and author of a few novels, positioned himself in hopes of talking Brad (or Joan) into hiring him as Brad's attorney, so he could churn out a book by the end of the trial. It didn't work.

"I need to ask you some questions about book rights," Kristen wrote to Brad in late November. "I need to talk to a writer — someone who can write a biography (about you) and a publisher will get it locked in so no one else will. I think everyone's attitude is 'Brad's story is going to be in my book.' (including your ex-girlie Lourdes). No way! Same with the attorney R. Parrish — he wants to write about the experience of being your lawyer."

***

The arrests of Brad Schwartz and Bruce Bigger dominated the headlines and newscasts of the Tucson media. Among those who watched the reports carefully was Stephanie Nagel, the woman who had met Brad at the federal courthouse, who was then sitting in the Pima County Jail on a county charge of fraud. Stephanie had shrugged off Brad's bizarre request to hire a hit man as part of misguided fantasy, but now she could no longer ignore his statements. In late December 2004, Stephanie signed a plea deal for three to five years in prison with no probation possible. The judge, though, had the option of giving Stephanie up to 12 years in prison, which frightened her. Maybe if she had good information about a murder, she reasoned, she could get even less. She asked her attorney, Richard Parrish, to arrange a meeting with the sheriff's department.

On Feb. 24, 2005, Det. Jill Murphy arranged for a free talk with Stephanie, her attorney and Assistant Pinal County Deputy Attorney Richard Platt in which no guarantees were made about what sentence Stephanie would be given, although her assistance in the Stidham murder case would be noted.

* * *

Once it became clear that Brad would not be released from jail pending his trial, the task of closing his office and settling the financial matters had to be dealt with. Joan Schwartz took on the onerous duty, with some help from Henry and Lois Schwartz, who arrived in January 2005. As Henry walked into Brad's office, he was dismayed to see that a beautiful mural that had been painted on a wall to make pediatric patients feel more comfortable had been painted over, to de-personalize the office for its next occupants. Henry set about organizing Brad's files into boxes. He noticed one folder marked "loans" and peered inside to see if there was something that needed taking care of. Among the papers was one marked with the name Danny Lopez. Henry knew that Lourdes's son was named Danny and that Brad's son, Ariel, had befriended him.

"What was Brad doing making a loan to a kid?" Henry thought to himself. It didn't make sense to him, so Henry put the paper back and closed the folder.

***

Though investigators were unsure the night of Brian's murder how he was killed, the autopsy showed that Brian had been stabbed about 15 times. Yet no one knew where the murder weapon was. Around 9 a.m. on Oct. 18, Sgt. Foust asked Deputy R.D. Roach to meet him at the intersection of Alexanderwood and Home. The sheriff's department had received an anonymous tip that the knife used to kill Brian Stidham would be there. Foust, Roach and other homicide detectives scoured the area but found no knife that could have killed Brian. That weapon would never be found.

Meantime, technicians continued to search Bruce's belongings and Brad's Escalade.

Inside Bruce's luggage, Det. Anderson and Hogan found clothing, toiletries and souvenirs. Some items had Las Vegas logos. Most of the clothing appeared to be brand new and unworn. A cooler contained a bloody tissue, which was repackaged in a new envelope for blood testing. One bag contained women's athletic shoes with a red substance on the tips and socks, which were stuffed inside the shoes. Later, testing showed the red substance wasn't blood, and the tissue likely was used for Bruce's bloody nose.

Inside the Escalade was a Palm Pilot, which had numbers for Bruce Bigger. There was paperwork regarding Brad's bank account and Brad's wallet, which had lots of credit cards and some cash. The detectives used Luminol, a chemical that reacts with bodily fluids, to see if there was any unseen forensic evidence. Three small areas were illuminated, all close together on the middle seat on the right side. The areas were circled with a red marker, and the section of the seat cut out and placed into evidence. Tests were negative for DNA for Brian and Bruce.

The Volvo also was searched. Detectives found items that you might find after a trip to Las Vegas. Luminol was used, but it didn't react with anything.

CHAPTER 14

Outside of the Pima County Sheriff's Department, the name of a suspect—certainly one in such a high-profile crime—would be known to very few people. Undoubtedly, the Pima County Attorney's Office would have been informed almost immediately about the impending arrests of Brad Schwartz and Bruce Bigger. While no one could have known about Bigger, surely Schwartz's name rang a few bells in the office. County Attorney Barbara LaWall, after all, had lost one of her best mid-level prosecutors, Lourdes Lopez, when she became entangled with Schwartz and the federal drug indictment.

Tucson, for all its worldly, big-city crimes, remains a small-town community. That's no more apparent than in the legal community, where grandfathers, fathers, sons and daughters often share the family business; where prosecutors marry cops; married judges serve in separate courtrooms. So it should have come as no shock to anyone that when a prominent surgeon who was once engaged to a county prosecutor is arrested, the ripple effect would fan out quickly.

Yet, to the general public, it would have appeared that LaWall either was ignorant of or willing to overlook the fact that one of her former prosecutors—and in extension, at least a handful of current prosecutors—might have enough of a connection to the case as to constitute a conflict. You would expect that any first-year defense attorney would leap on the fact that there was a connection with the office and the defendant, Schwartz. So wouldn't a first-year prosecutor also question whether there was a conflict?

At any rate, once Schwartz and Bigger were booked into the Pima County Jail and details about the case began leaking out, there were two questions before the Pima County Attorney's Office: Would they seek the death penalty against Schwartz and Bigger? And can they even prosecute the men, given that Schwartz was once engaged to Lourdes Lopez, one of Schwartz's main accusers?

Word on the street was that Rick Unklesbay, who then headed LaWall's criminal division, strenuously argued to keep the case, which he believed was a perfect capital murder case.

Three days after the arrests, on Oct. 18, prosecutor Brad Roach approached David Berkman about his upcoming Halloween party that weekend. Roach was enjoying "star" status at the Pima County Attorney's Office. He was assigned to the special victims unit that prosecutes sex crimes and crimes against children. For all the seriousness of his job—and Roach was good at it—he was also a likeable fellow whose annual Halloween party not only was highly anticipated by friends and colleagues, but also was a good fund-raiser for children's charities. Those in the legal community in Tucson, whether they were prosecutors or defense attorneys, might square off against each other daily in court, but at nights and on weekends, often partied together. Even though Lourdes had suffered some disgrace in her professional life, she had not been shut out of its social scene. Lourdes was among the guests invited to Brad's party and, considering that her ex-fiancée had just been arrested in a first-degree murder case, Brad wondered about whether Lourdes should come to the party.

"You need to 'uninvite' Lourdes Lopez," Berkman told Brad.

"I don't think I can do that," Brad said.

"Tell her she's not welcome and then let me know when you've told her that," Berkman ordered.

Later, Berkman told LaWall, who was out of town that week, that Brad Roach wasn't happy to hear that he should not allow Lourdes at his party. However, Berkman did say that his directive to "uninvite" Lourdes had been passed along.

On Oct. 20, Brad Roach called the State Bar of Arizona's hotline for ethical questions. What he told the Bar's attorney, Karen Clark, would be hotly disputed later. Roach says he called because he was concerned that the Pima County Attorney's Office had an obvious conflict with handling the Schwartz case and was not "conflicting" it out to another agency. LaWall's attorney said in court documents later the Bar told her that he never brought up the Schwartz case and posed the question as if he had a conflict in a case, so the Bar's attorney directed him to the state's ethical rules. LaWall once considered Roach a rising star in the office. When the *Tucson Citizen* interviewed LaWall about a story on how her office often loses good prosecutors to other agencies that pay better, she suggested talking to Roach as an example of a young prosecutor she wanted to keep but who struggled to pay law school bills while raising a family. That fall, Roach's stature took a 180-degree turn.

Within the next few days, Berkman became aware that other prosecutors—Paul Skitzki, Nicki DiCampli and others—knew Lourdes Lopez as a friend and had met Schwartz. Berkman called all the prosecutors to a meeting on Oct. 19 ordering that anyone who had any knowledge about the Stidham murder or relationships regarding Lourdes Lopez or Brad Schwartz to come forward.

LaWall was told on Oct. 25 that Roach, Skitzki and DiCampli had information either before or after Brian's murder in connection with Schwartz. But none had gone to law enforcement authorities before Schwartz's arrest and had not notified their supervisors with her office. To LaWall, these omissions and the fact that Roach had withheld information Lourdes had told him about Schwartz, was a serious breach in ethics as prosecutors. LaWall launched her own investigation into the conduct of her prosecutors, which included notifying the sheriff's department about her suspicions. Roach,

DiCampli, Skitzki, Janet Altschuler—whose parents own the medical complex where Brian Stidham was slain—and perhaps other prosecutors were interviewed by LaWall's investigators and the transcripts forwarded to the sheriff's department, which subsequently interviewed the prosecutors.

The question of whether LaWall should recuse her office from prosecuting Schwartz and Bigger figured prominently in her investigation of the prosecutors' actions. If there were a conflict, LaWall knew, she'd have to find another agency willing to take on an "expensive, resource-depleting, complex, lengthy and protracted prosecution." And, she would have to break the news to Stidham's family. Some of LaWall's top prosecutors were against sending the case out of county and allegedly were eager to file a notice to seek the death penalty against Schwartz and Bigger if they obtained convictions.

On Nov. 9, 2004, Daniel J. Benavidez, LaWall's spokesman, issued a terse press release:

> Pima County Attorney Barbara LaWall has determined that a potential conflict of interest exists in the first degree murder case against Dr. Bradley Schwartz and Ronald Bigger because prosecutors in the Pima County Attorney's Office could potentially be called as witnesses.
>
> Therefore, the Pinal County Attorney's Office will be taking over the case.
>
> Arizona State Bar's Rules of Professional Conduct prohibit further comment on the nature of the conflict.

With the prosecution out of her hands, LaWall turned to the question of what, if anything, should be done about the prosecutors who had gotten themselves involved in the case.

On Nov. 16, LaWall informed all four prosecutors that she intended to fire them and that they were on administrative leave pending the final outcome, during which time they could plead to keep their jobs. The word of the dismissals spread quickly throughout the city to the media. Roach claimed that LaWall helped fuel the fire by calling Terry Gonzalez, a reporter with KGUN Channel 9, to announce she had sent the bunch packing. LaWall maintained that Dan Benavidez told her Gonzalez called him out of the blue and must have been told by one of the prosecutors, most likely Roach, that they were given pink slips. LaWall also thought that there could be no other reason for the media to call other than Roach telling Gonzalez. Gonzales told LaWall that Roach didn't call her. Months later, Gonzalez testified that LaWall called her.

On Nov. 23, LaWall held "pre-action" meetings with the four prosecutors to give them an opportunity to explain their actions, which is a requirement under county rules. Afterwards, she reduced the discipline for Roach, DiCampli and Altschuler to a 15-day suspension without pay, but confirmed she would fire Skitzki.

All four prosecutors appealed their discipline to the county's merit system commission. Roach, Skitzki and DiCampli agreed to a public hearing together, but Altschuler requested a private, separate hearing. She would later drop her appeal.

***

On Aug. 20, 2005, Roach filed a complaint with the State Bar of Arizona alleging Pima County Attorney Barbara LaWall violated ethics rules when she testified before the merit system commission. In response, LaWall hired attorney Mark Rubin, who said Roach's allegations were "unfounded."

"There was no lack of candor or perjury on Ms. LaWall's part," Rubin said.

LaWall, Rubin said, never spoke to Gonzalez or any other reporter on Nov. 16, the day she moved to fire the four prosecutors. In addition, Roach's claims that he was disciplined because he called the State Bar's ethics hotline on Oct. 20 was "preposterous" since LaWall first learned of his call during his Nov. 23 pre-action meeting. Rubin said LaWall only talked to Gonzalez in December, that Benavidez, her communications director, called Gonzalez on the day the attorneys were told they were being fired. During an exchange between Roach and LaWall during the merit system commission hearing, Rubin said, LaWall wanted to say something about how the media heard within 15 minutes of the dismissal notices while Roach was concerned that LaWall shared personnel information with members of her staff. "Mr. Roach took a truthful answer to an inartfully-worded question, placed it in a different context, called it a lie and claimed Ms. LaWall violated the Rule of Professional Conduct and committed perjury," Rubin wrote. "Then, when Ms. LaWall tried to clarify her answer, he was not interested in hearing from her."

Just as the merit system commission chairwoman, Georgia Brousseau, was inclined to believe that LaWall didn't initiate the media interest in the attorney dismissals, the State Bar later concluded that LaWall didn't lie and violate ethics rules. Roach, who later ran unsuccessfully against LaWall for her office, asserts to this day that LaWall was worried about the media coverage on her office and how the public perceived her as an elected official and that concern drove all of her actions and statements.

CHAPTER 15

If there were such a thing as a typical career criminal, Dennis Duane Walsh would be it. His youth was plagued with drug abuse that carried over into his adulthood. While serving time in prison, Walsh's father died of a heart attack, which tormented Dennis. He was released from prison on an aggravated assault case in May 2003 and moved in with his mother, who was living in Patagonia, a rural southern Arizona community. Later, he moved in with a girlfriend who lived in nearby Sonoita. When he wasn't using drugs, Dennis could be a sociable and friendly person. The townsfolk in Patagonia liked him during sober times, because he was always willing to lend a hand when needed. His girlfriend owned some properties and paid Dennis with cash for remodeling work. He also found side jobs, which gave him more cash that he used to buy drugs. He lived off and on with his girlfriend for several months but also stayed in motels, with friends and in his car. Once he started committing robberies, he moved frequently to avoid arrest. By the fall of 2004, Walsh was preying upon Tucson to get money to feed his drug habit.

On Oct. 3, 2004, Walsh walked into the Michael's craft store, 3161 W. Irvington Road, on Tucson's South Side, and placed a note upon the counter that read: "This is a hold up, give me all your money, don't fuck up, don't call anybody." The clerk gave Walsh money from the register, and he left. Later, he walked into the Michael's store at 1161 W. Irvington Road. He grabbed a shopping basket and went to the third register, where he handed the clerk a note that read in orange print: "Very quietly open your drawer and give me the cash. I am armed." After receiving $79, Walsh left.

Seven days later, Walsh entered a Circle K convenience store at 4160 N. First Ave., toward the North Side of Tucson, strode up to the counter and demanded all of the money in the store. The clerk thought it was a joke, but Walsh demanded that the clerk open the register drawer and give him all the money, plus a pack of Camel filter cigarettes.

About 7:25 in the evening of Oct. 12, Tucson police were called to the Quik Mart convenience store in the 1800 block of East Prince Road regarding an armed robbery. The clerk said a man approached the counter asking for a pack of cigarettes.

"Why don't you just give me all the money that's in the drawer?" Walsh asked, pulling up his shirt to expose a black handgun.

The clerk opened the cash register and gave Walsh all the money, then watched him run away.

Three days later, around 4:30 p.m., police were called to a Chevron station at 1285 W. Ajo Way, back on the South Side of town, for another armed robbery. The two gas station clerks told police the man, later identified as Walsh, pointed a blue semi-automatic 9mm gun at them and demanded money from the register. After he got the money, which amounted to $192, Walsh drove away in a truck, whose license number was taken by the clerks. The truck, it turned out, had been carjacked just minutes before the robbery.

On Oct. 17, around 10:40 a.m., police were called to another Michael's store at 4070 N. Oracle Road, again toward the North Side of Tucson, about an armed robbery. The clerk said the robber approached the counter with a basket of items.

"Is that all you need?" she asked.

"No, I'm robbing you," Walsh said, pulling up his shirt to reveal a handgun. Walsh pushed aside some items in the basket and indicated that she should put the money from the register there, which she did. He ran out of the store to a car in the parking lot with his basket of goods and nearly $194.

The next day, around 6:10 p.m., police were called to the Walgreens pharmacy at 3180 N. Campbell Ave., on the northern edge of Tucson's Midtown section, about a robbery. The clerk said a man came to the counter with four toys and asked for a carton of cigarettes.

"Put the toys in a bag and give me the money," Walsh demanded. "I'm robbing you." Walsh put his hand at the side of his waist, the clerk said, but didn't say he had a gun. "Give me all twenties," he demanded. After getting the cash, Walsh left.

On Oct. 20, around 6:05 p.m., police were called to another Walgreens, this at 3910 E. 22nd St., back on the South side. The clerk said a man—identified as Walsh—came into the store, picked up a basket and filled it with a number of items. After about 20 minutes, Walsh approached the register.

"Aw, shit, man!" Walsh said. "I'm gonna have to rob you. I'm sick, and I need cash for a fix." Walsh lifted his shirt to show a handgun tucked into the waist of his jeans. The clerk shifted to the right side of the register, where the silent alarm was.

"Aw, man!" Walsh said. "You stepped on it, didn't you?"

Walsh dropped the basket and fled, without taking any money.

About half an hour later, police were called to the Quik Mart store at 1850 E. Prince Road, the same convenience store that had been robbed on Oct. 12. The clerk, who was not the same one who was robbed before, reported that a man came up to the counter and said, "Just give it to me. Don't make me grab it," lifting up his sweatshirt to reveal the pistol grip of a gun. The clerk gave him $120, and the man left.

Three days later, around 3:11 p.m., police were called to the Quicksmart convenience store/gas station at 4910 N. First Ave. The clerk, Jennifer Dainty, said a man came to the counter with several items but left because another employee got too close to him. A few minutes later, the man returned when Dainty was alone and handed her a note saying he had a gun and was robbing the store.

"I don't have any money," Dainty told him.

Walsh didn't believe her.

"No, really, I don't," she said. "I can't get to it."

"This is bullshit!" Walsh said, stomping out of the store.

About half an hour later, Walsh returned to the Quik Mart store on East Prince Road, which he'd robbed twice previously. A third clerk was on duty. Walsh walked up to the counter and asked for a candy bar and pack of cigarettes. The clerk turned his back to reach for the smokes. When he turned around, Walsh had pulled up his shirt to reveal a gun.

"Dude, just give me the money or you're gone," Walsh said. The clerk gave him a little over $100 from the register and watched Walsh run away.

Four days later, police were called to the Quik Mart store at 1250 E. Fort Lowell Road, where a clerk said Walsh came up to the counter demanding, "Give me the money!" and pointing a gun at her. After getting the money, Walsh asked for a pack of Camels.

The next day, police were called to a Conoco gas station, 6500 S. 12th Ave., on Tucson's far South Side, regarding a carjacking. A woman said she had stopped at the gas station with her 11-year-old daughter. As she was finishing putting gas in the car, Walsh ran up and got into the driver's seat. The woman yelled at Walsh, who couldn't get the car started. She ran over to the passenger's side, where she was able to grab her daughter, but not before Walsh punched the girl in her arm.

Hours later, police were called to the C&T Oil gas station, 2710 N. First Ave., on the near North Side, where a clerk said Walsh approached the register and asked, "What's your policy if you get robbed?"

"I don't know," the clerk said.

"Well, you're gonna get robbed," Walsh said. "Would you put your life on the line for this money? It's not even yours. I'm sick. Just give me the money."

Walsh pulled out a folding knife and flashed it to the clerk.

"Come on, man!" Walsh yelled. "You don't want me to cut you."

The clerk handed Walsh the money in the register and watched him leave in the car he'd stolen at the Conoco station.

***

Walsh's next series of crimes didn't occur until late December. On Dec. 23, around 10:30 p.m., police were called to the Family Dollar discount store, 707 E. Fort Lowell Road, on the near North Side. The clerk said she was at the register when a man came up to her, acting as if he were going to pay for some merchandise. Then he put his right hand in his pocket.

"I'm going to rob you," Walsh said.

The clerk gave him $291. Walsh left.

On Christmas Eve, around 8:33 p.m., Walsh returned to the convenience store on East Prince Road wearing a nylon stocking on his head.

"I'm not going to hurt you," he told the clerk. "Give me the money."

"I only have $50," the clerk said. "It's not worth going to prison for, is it?"

"Just give me the money and a pack of Camels!" Walsh demanded.

After getting the cash and the Camels, Walsh left.

On Christmas Day, shortly before midnight, a clerk at the Quik Mart in the 1200 block of North Alvernon Way, back in the Midtown area, reported a robbery. Walsh, who again wore a stocking over his head, demanded money and Camels. He showed what looked to be the wooden butt of a gun in his pocket. The clerk gave him $15 and a carton of cigarettes.

The next day, around 9 p.m. the Prince Road store was robbed again. The clerk told police she recognized the robber from Christmas Eve.

"I'm back," Walsh said. "I'm sick, lady. I'm a heroin addict. I want all the money and everything that's under the drawer."

She complied, noticing as he was leaving that he used the sleeve of his jacket when he touched the door.

***

Over those few months, police connected Walsh to all of those robberies. They traced him to his mother in Patagonia. She called her son to confront him.

"I just want to die," Walsh told her. "Maybe sometime, the cops will get there and they'll shoot me. Then I can be with Dad."

***

On Dec. 28, a multiagency fugitive squad went to a house where Walsh was suspected of living to serve him with a warrant. They watched as Walsh got into a car and drove away. Members of the team trailed Walsh, but he quickly caught on that he was being followed and drove away from them at high speeds. Eventually, he crashed into a ravine, where he was arrested.

Walsh admitted committing the crimes and blamed his heroin addiction, which made him sick, though he couldn't kick it. After the first robbery, he thought, "I'm screwed now. I'm going back to prison." He continued the robberies, "just wanting to die," he said. He was hoping that a cop would shoot him because "death by cop" was the best thing for him. He said he had taken the cartridge out of the gun he used, so no one could have been hurt. Whatever he got from the robberies he used to buy more drugs. He felt bad because he "scared a few people" and wished he could have thought things out more clearly.

Walsh's arrest and crime spree brought big stories in the local papers. The news didn't escape the eye of Brad Schwartz, who was stewing in the Pima County Jail, accused of Brian Stidham's death. Here was a drug addict who was operating in the same neighborhood at the same time that Brian was killed, Schwartz realized. He asked his ex-wife, Joan, to send him a clipping of Dennis Walsh's arrest. Schwartz even discussed the possibility that Walsh might be Bran's true killer with his cellmate, Brandon West, who was in jail for child molestation, and other inmates. Before long, the Pima County Sheriff's Department knew about Schwartz's suspicions. Det. Jill Murphy obtained a search warrant for Brad's cell, which yielded an awkwardly written letter to Brad's attorney, Brick Storts, from Brad's cellmate:

Dear Mr. Storts,

My name is Branden West, and I have trying to get you information that I have about another crime. I want to make sure this info gets to the right people because I feel bad that someone murders a person and the murderer got away with it.

I was at a party before Thanksgiving and I meet someone who was selling drugs at this party, named Dennis Walsh. He is a scarey guy. He was bragging about stabbing a doctor near his office. He was gonna take the car to a chop shop near Bellevue Apartments but they wouldn't take it because there was blood in the car so he just left the car.

I feel real bad about this. I would have told the police sooner but I was scared of Walsh. He is very violent and likes using his knife. When I got here to jail, I heard that he got arrested so I wanted to set the record straight. Someone else got arrested for this crime. Can I tell the police or should I call the prosecutor? My lawer is Richard Parrish.

Thank you for your help.

Branden West

Attached to the letter was a rundown of information implicating Walsh in Stidham's murder:

Dennis (Duane) Walsh – about 5'9" tall, dark hair, dark eyes

Arrested around 12/29/04 Brooklyn accent (Italian)

– robbed 12 convenient stores near/around 1st and River Rd area between Oct. 3rd–Oct. 20

– Doctor stabbed outside his office on Oct 5th (at 1st + River) across the street from Circle K at 4810 N. 1st Ave.

– likes to use a knife – arrested for aggravated assault with a deadly weapon

– likes to car-jack, He took Stidham's 1992 white Lexus coupe + left it in parking spot at Bellvue apartments (near Speedway + Dodge) – right near "the compound" which is a known chopshop

Another inmate, Eduardo Aguirre-Nebrinksky, also alleged that Walsh was involved in stolen cars and had been shopping around a white Lexus. He recanted when confronted by detectives, saying Schwartz had put him up to it. Yet another inmate, Doug Morgula, said Walsh might have stolen his knife and used it in the carjackings. Carroll Carson Sanders, a convicted con man, told detectives about a new twist to the story. He claimed Schwartz offered him money if Sanders' son told detectives that Walsh had taken Brian's Lexus to a chop shop.

On June 21, 2005, an investigator interviewed Brandon West along with his attorney, Chiko Makanjoula, of the Pima County Public Defender's Office. West, who was then accused of molesting two boys in his neighborhood, said he met Brad when he was moved into the doctor's cell along with another inmate, Travis. Brad talked openly about his case and one day mentioned Dennis Walsh, who matched the description of Bruce Bigger. West told detectives that he told Brad he knew Walsh and had seen him trying to unload a stolen Lexus in October 2004 at a drug house. West said he assumed Walsh also had a knife, a folding knife about six inches long and another that was a bit longer with a straight blade, which West called a "CI-type" knife.

"Where was Walsh carrying the knives?" West was asked.

"In the blue-colored hospital scrubs he was wearing," West answered, adding the detail that the scrubs appeared to have the letters "UMC" on them. He had heard Brian's Lexus had been found near a chop shop that West and Walsh knew about.

"Did Walsh tell you the Lexus was stolen?"

"No."

"Why would Walsh show you the knives?"

"He was acting weird. I think he was trying to get rid of them."

"Did Walsh ever tell you he was involved with Dr. Schwartz?"

"No."

"Did you ever attend another party with Walsh?"

"No. I don't like to be around him. My friends told me he was a dangerous guy. He's committed armed robberies and purse-snatchings, and he's stolen some cars," West said.

"Did Travis hear you and Schwartz talking about Walsh?"

West said he did.

"Did Schwartz ask Travis to testify to anything on his behalf?"

"No."

"Did Schwartz offer you anything to testify on his behalf?"

"Yes, but he told me if I said anything it's because it's the right thing to do."

West later recanted his statement, saying Schwartz manipulated him into implicating Walsh.

The Pima County Sheriff's Department investigated and discounted Schwartz's interactions with the other inmates into West's alleged link to the case, but never investigated Walsh as a suspect in Brian Stidham's murder. Walsh is serving 16 life sentences, plus several hundred years, after he was convicted of some of the robberies and pleaded guilty to all of the remaining charges.

CHAPTER 16

Though witnesses in criminal trials swear to tell the truth, the whole truth and nothing but the truth, the trials themselves aren't about the whole truth. Before a jury is even sworn in, the scope of the trial already has been shaped by a series of hearings that whittle down the entirety of the evidence into a version of the truth that becomes the fodder from which jurors eventually decide which side, the state or the defense, prevails.

Pima County Superior Court Judge Nanette Warner consistently denied attempts to move both trials out of town. In a Dec. 1, 2005, ruling, she said, "The overwhelming percentage (84.3 percent) of the information in the media is factual in nature. Further, the majority of the articles which contain opinions of others were statements taken from Court documents or disclosure in criminal cases. With respect to information classified as inaccurate or outrageous, most of the inaccuracies involved significant matters such as the wrong trial date, the requested amount of the bond reduction and misstatement of names.

"For the most part, the outrageous or highly opinionated comments were found in the *Tucson Weekly*, the free newspaper distributed at various places throughout the city once a week with a circulation of 46,700 papers. Most of the information regarding this case in the *Tucson Weekly* appeared in a column known as 'The Skinny.' Furthermore, some of the publicity was generated by defendant Bigger or Schwartz' attorneys.

"Clearly," Warner wrote, "there has been extensive pretrial publicity in this case. ... The volume of the pretrial publicity has diminished significantly since the homicide. However, media attention persists, and most court filings are reported by the media as are court proceedings. Some of the newspaper articles and broadcasts contain information that will not be admitted at trial because it was not relevant or otherwise admissible."

Defense attorneys had not proven, Warner said, that the pretrial publicity was "so unfair, pervasive and prejudicial" that Brad and Bruce couldn't get a fair trial. The men were scheduled to be tried together until Bruce's defense attorney, Jill Thorpe, announced that his defense would be that Brad Schwartz actually killed Brian Stidham—something that even prosecutors never implied, but nevertheless qualified Bruce to have his own trial.

Her ruling wouldn't prevent defense attorneys for both men to continue to file motions asking that the trial be moved out of town, all of which Warner denied. For Bruce's trial, out of 450 prospective jurors questioned, 379 or 84 percent had read or seen some publicity. One juror who was excused for work-related issues told attorneys and Judge Warner that he'd only "faintly remembered" hearing about the case. Yet minutes later, he told a TV news crew that he immediately recognized Bigger when he walked into the courtroom. When the jury pool was whittled down to the 29 from which the jury and alternates were chosen, 24 or 83 percent knew something about the case, including the type of weapon used, details about Lourdes Lopez or Schwartz's trial outcome.

Idle chatter during breaks in the early part of Schwartz's trial often centered on what stars would be cast in the roles of what everyone thought was a tale prime for a made-for-TV movie. Prosecutor Sylvia Lafferty was incensed when a *Citizen* blog, which didn't attribute any of the suggested casting to anyone in particular, was published. "I thought whatever we talked about during breaks was protected!" Lafferty complained. "Now we won't be able to blow off steam." Regardless of Lafferty's disdain, most everyone had their own choices for casting suggestions:

Lafferty: Sigourney Weaver, Annette Bening, Sharon Stone (Lafferty said she'd rather not have Stone play her)

Platt, co-prosecutor: Ken Howard, Bill Pullman, Bill Paxton

Storts: Tommy Lee Jones, Gene Hackman, Harrison Ford, though Storts wants Jack Nicholson

Maria Davila, Storts's co-counsel: Winona Ryder, Christina Ricci

Ken Peasley, a disbarred prosecutor who was Storts's paralegal: Dennis Hopper

Warner: Catherine Crier of Court TV

Lourdes: Jennifer Lopez

Brad: Ed Norton

Bruce and Dennis Walsh: John Malkovich

Brian: Kevin Kline

Daphne: Kristen Davis

There was even circulated what became known as the "E! True Hollywood" version of the end of the movie. In that hypothetical ending, a Cadillac is driving down a dusty Texas road and stops in front of a diner. Daphne Stidham emerges from the Cadillac and enters the diner, headed toward a booth in the back. "I thought we had decided that it was too risky to meet anymore," she tells the woman seated there. Joan Schwartz sets aside a paper with the headline "Schwartz, Bigger convicted" and says, "We have one issue that still needs to be resolved." "Lourdes," the women chime.

***

Brick P. Storts III, Brad's court-appointed attorney, prepared for trial with the strategy that the state couldn't prove that Bruce had time to kill Brian on Oct. 5, 2004. And if Bruce didn't do it, then Brad is innocent. He was hamstrung by rulings Warner made before trial that prevented

Storts from telling the jury that Daphne was Suspect No. 1 and that Walsh was robbing stores and flashing a knife in the area near where Brian was killed around the same time he was killed—though most curiously, he wasn't accused of any robberies during the week Brian was stabbed to death. Warner said she would allow Storts to tell jurors that Walsh committed two carjackings—but one of them didn't happen anywhere near Brian's medical complex. If Storts attempted to bring in the Walsh evidence, prosecutors were ready to tell jurors that Brad tried deflecting attention to Walsh by coercing jail inmates to say they overheard Walsh confess to Brian's murder.

From the start, though, Storts made it clear that Brad would soon get to tell his side of the story.

"I can't try this case without having him testify," Storts told the *Tucson Citizen.*

Warner also gave prosecutors a step up when she ruled they would be allowed to present an expert witness, Tom Bevel, to testify about botched contract killings, blitz attacks and staged crimes, though he wouldn't be able to say whether he thought this murder applied to any of those.

Four hundred prospective jurors were summoned to the Pima County Courthouse on Jan. 25, 2006, to answer questionnaires prepared by prosecutors and the defense team. Voir dire, or direct questioning, of jurors began on Feb. 28. A panel of 12 jurors and four alternates were chosen on March 3, but minutes later, Warner was forced to send one of them home when he expressed misgivings about having been picked. Soon afterward, a frail juror was excused, though she wanted to stay on the panel.

On March 7, opening statements were delivered. In addition to the local press, media coverage included a live streaming feed to Court TV's website, producers from the CBS news show *48 Hours* and the NBC news show *Dateline.* Some witnesses expressed some trepidation over the TV exposure. Judge Warner ordered that attorneys ask each witness before testifying whether they wanted to be photographed. Warner signaled courthouse spokesman David S. Ricker before each witness took the stand as to whether it was OK for the TV and newspaper cameras to photograph them.

Brian's mother and sister attended the opening statements and most of the trial, as did many of Brian's colleagues and friends. In a rarity at Superior Court, spectators who weren't on a list for the defense, state or media, had to be issued passes to attend the trial. Once Brad's parents were finished with their testimony, they were allowed to sit in the gallery. Lois Schwartz brought homemade apple bread one day, hoping to be able to pass it along to her son and was chagrined when she was told he couldn't take it with him.

Pinal County Deputy Attorney Sylvia Lafferty told jurors that Brad was obsessed with the thought of getting revenge because of what Brian had done to him.

"The defendant was an angry man," Lafferty said. "And his anger turned into a grudge, and his grudge festered into an obsession that erupted into a toxic rage that led to a plan to conspire to murder Dr. David Brian Stidham."

After failing to recruit friends and lovers to damage Brian's reputation, Lafferty said, Brad recruited Lourdes' ex-husband, Danny Lopez, who was killed before the murder could be accomplished. Proof of that conspiracy was Brian's photo, which was found in Danny's wallet. So then Brad talked Bruce into killing Brian.

"Bruce Bigger suddenly, violently and brutally attacked Dr. Stidham, stabbing him 15 times in the chest and arms. Dr. Stidham tried to walk to the safety of his office, but within two minutes, Brian Stidham was dead."

DNA evidence from Brian's stolen Lexus will link Bruce Bigger to the crime, Lafferty told jurors. The morning after the murder, Brad took $10,000 in cash from his bank. Bruce Bigger, who couldn't afford to pay the cab fare to meet up with Brad on the night of the murder, soon treated two friends to a Las Vegas trip, jurors were told.

Storts used his opening statement to tell jurors that the state's version of events isn't the only one.

"The entire theory of the case of the state is that Mr. Bigger killed Dr. Stidham, and as a result of that, Dr. Schwartz is guilty because he hired Bruce Bigger. But if Bruce Bigger didn't commit the crime, Dr. Schwartz is innocent." Bruce would have had to stab Brian 15 times, find the keys to take the Lexus, dispose of blood-soaked clothes, drive the Lexus to the apartment complex more than six miles away, walk to a restaurant and use its phone all in a time span of 16 to 19 minutes, Storts said.

Storts promised to present testimony from a medical examiner who puts the time of death closer to the time when Brian's body was found, which would eliminate Brad and Bruce as suspects since they were in Lisa Goldberg's company at that time.

Storts admitted that Brad was upset when Brian left the practice. But by the time Brian died, Brad's practice was going so well that he was expanding and making about $250,000.

"Why then would he wait until his success was on the rise, and everything was going back into place for him to now go out and act on this man that he hated to find somebody to kill him?" Storts asked.

Shortly before the trial, Storts asked Henry and Lois Schwartz to hire another defense attorney, Maria Davila, to help him with some of the witnesses. Before any testimony began in the trial, though, Davila became the unwilling focus of attention because her cousin, Liliana Bibb, was scheduled to testify against Brad. The cousins had run into each other at a hair salon before the trial. Storts said he didn't think the accidental meeting or the cousins' chilly relationship would hurt the case. Storts said he'd ask for a mistrial if he couldn't have Davila helping him. Warner allowed Davila to stay on the defense so the trial could proceed.

***

Dr. Lisa Lane testified she and the other ophthalmology students chatted in the parking lot for a few minutes. She left around 7:15 p.m. and didn't notice anything suspicious. Though she had met Brian several times previously, she'd only met Brad once. "I don't think he would even remember me," she said.

Dr. Jason Lee testified that he told detectives in December 2004 that the man he saw in scrubs at the medical complex on the night of the murder wasn't Brad or Bruce. Lee, who got his medical degree from New York University, said the man in scrubs didn't speak with a New York accent.

Tom Bevel testified that Brian most likely was standing next to the driver's seat of his Lexus, with the door open, when he was attacked. Bevel said the lack of blood on the exterior driver's side door and blood drops on an armrest likely were cast off from the knife blade and suggest his position when he was first stabbed. His car would have been facing northwest as it was parked. A blood trail led to the back of the car and toward where his body was found, suggesting that he had been walking toward his office. Bevel said under direct questioning that the killer might not have had any blood on his or her clothing, but said in cross-examination that he also could have made contact with his killer, which would have left blood on the killer's clothes. Bevel said he knew of only one contract-killing investigation in which the killer got the money after the deed, though he'd only been involved with two professional "hits" and three nonprofessional.

Jennifer Dainty, the convenience store clerk, testified about a man in scrubs who came into her store on Oct. 5, 2004. Lafferty showed Dainty a light blue scrub top taken from Schwartz's apartment, which Dainty said looked similar to the scrub top the mystery man wore. Dainty told jurors she picked Bruce's photo out of a lineup as the man in scrubs. However, the complex workers who also saw a man in scrubs that afternoon testified that they didn't recognize Bruce's photo.

Tom Boager testified about picking up a man in his cab at the Bunny Ranch and driving him to Karuna's Restaurant, although he couldn't identify Bruce Bigger from a photo lineup as the man in the cab.

Lisa Goldberg had struck an immunity deal with prosecutors in exchange for her testimony to prevent any charges such as hindering prosecution from being filed against her. Schwartz watched her intently as she testified about their brief liaison, but she never glanced his way until Platt asked her to identify him.

***

Defense attorney Maria Davila asked for a mistrial after Stephanie Nagel testified, saying Lafferty repeatedly ignored Warner's ruling not to tell jurors about Schwartz's federal case. Lafferty suggested a fix: telling jurors that Schwartz was at the federal courthouse, where he met Nagel, for drug testing that they knew the medical board ordered. "Create a false story for the jury, that's interesting," Brick Storts grumbled. Warner denied the mistrial motion. Davila and Storts told Warner they didn't want to emphasize the federal court connection, so they didn't ask for any explanation to be given to the jury.

***

Carmen Fernandez, the LabCorp phlebotomist who had an affair with Schwartz, eventually came forward in January 2005 and told Det. Murphy the truth about her affair with

Schwartz and statements he made about Brian Stidham. However, she told Murphy that Brad didn't talk about wanting Stidham killed, but he was most angry about Brian "taking food off his table." She testified under cross-examination that even though Brad was jailed by the time Murphy first called her, she feared that he might be released and harm her or her family. She didn't report the threats he made initially, she testified, because she didn't take them seriously. Platt asked Carmen whether Schwartz made threats against any other doctor. She began to answer when Davila objected. After a bench conference, Warner told jurors to disregard the question and Carmen's response. It was the only time any other kind of threat had ever been raised. Carmen said she discussed Brad's threats with her co-worker, Carlos Ogas, and two of her criminal justice teachers at Pima Community College. The teachers urged her to call police, but she didn't.

Rosalia Humo testified that Brad was most interested in her former gang affiliations, which she acknowledged when he asked about her tattoos, when she came for an eye exam. Humo said Brad told her he had a "big problem" that he wanted her to try and get rid of: Dr. Stidham. Brad asked her to plant pornography or illegal drugs in Brian's office, Rosalia said. Then he asked if she could find someone to kill Brian, she said. "He said he wanted him fucking dead."

Rosalia was not the most credible witness. She had given three statements to police and each time, added more details about her talk with him in January 2004. Rosalia insisted that her memory solidified over time and that she wasn't adding details that she learned through the media reports. She also admitted inquiring about the reward money through the 88-CRIME tip line that she called initially after she spoke to Brad, but said she wasn't testifying to get reward money. She testified that she had been scared of Brad, even though he never threatened her or knew exactly where she lived.

Christopher Carney and Christopher Corley testified that they partied with Bruce Bigger in the days following Brian's murder. The men, who became known as "The Chrises" in the courtroom, said Bruce was "jittery" and "nervous" the last time they saw him, which happened to be during a night-long, drug-fueled party for which Bruce brought crack cocaine and a wad of money.

Dr. Mark Austein testified about his friendship with Brad Schwartz, saying he was willing to loan him tens of thousands of dollars because he knew Brad would pay it back somehow. Austein couldn't remember Brad ever talking about Brian, much less say anything bad about him.

Storts asked for a mistrial when Lafferty used a back-door method to bring information about Brian on Brad's Palm Pilot before the jury. The prosecutors never told the defense that they would use the Palm Pilot, which had information about Brian's car, at trial, Storts said. Warner denied the motion, but told jurors to disregard any information taken from the Palm Pilot.

***

The most anticipated witness was Lourdes Lopez. Before the trial, Warner ruled that jurors could not know that Schwartz was indicted in federal court on prescription drug charges. On the stand, though, Lourdes testified that she resigned from the Pima County Attorney's Office because she knew that she and Brad were going to be indicted in federal court. Platt had not told Lourdes about the ruling on the federal charges because, he said, it was hard getting to Lourdes because she had several attorneys representing her. Lourdes said she knew she wasn't supposed to say how her ex-husband died, but nothing about the federal case. Storts once again asked for a mistrial, which was denied.

Lourdes testified that Brad was angry when Brian left the practice. "He was upset because Dr. Stidham left him when he needed him the most. Brad had told me he wanted Dr. Stidham to die. He used an expletive, 'That guy is going to die.' Do you want me to say exactly what he said? Exactly what he said was that 'This fucking guy is going to die.'" But Lourdes also said she never took the threats seriously. "He is a doctor. He's been given a gift. He's supposed to preserve life. He took an oath to do that. He's a very good father. He had everything to live for. He would never throw everything away because of anger, no."

**

Rachel Atkinson testified that Brad asked her to say that he'd given her $2,500 if anyone asked, because he was missing money that she never received such money.

"It would have been nice to have $2,500, though," she said, laughing.

Lafferty asked if Rachel had gotten any money from Brad.

"Unfortunately not," she said. "I thought I was very lucky to get a pair of free contacts."

People in the gallery laughed at her remark, which prompted Warner to rebuke the spectators.

"I would ask the gallery to refrain from showing emotion," Warner said. "This is a serious matter."

She testified that when Brad was talking about selling the Camry, which supposedly was the reason he was "missing" $2,500, he mentioned an amount for $10,000.

Rachel testified that she was flattered a doctor wanted to date her and was satisfied being his girlfriend, but was not in love with him and didn't want to marry him.

Joan Schwartz paused to whisper "hi" to her ex-husband as she walked up to the witness stand. Joan didn't drop any bombshells about their marriage in her testimony, which centered on their divorce and financial arrangements. Joan asked for about $17,000 a month when they separated, but she settled for $11,000—$9,120 for alimony and $2,000 for child support—because she knew his practice wasn't in full gear at the time. That was lowered to $6,000 in alimony and $4,000 in child support, which helped her with taxes. Brad would give her an alimony check from his own account, she testified, but the child support came through a clearinghouse. In October 2004, she testified, Brad gave her $3,300 instead, saying he was short of cash because he got $3,000 less for the Camry that her mom crashed. Joan said Brad blamed Brian for filing reports that got him in trouble, but didn't say he was obsessed with hurting him. Joan smiled at Brad as she left the courtroom.

Det. William Knuth was called to the stand to identify Brad and Bruce as two men seen on security camera shots taken from the Sheraton hotel around 9:20 p.m. on Grant Road on Oct. 5, 2004. Bruce appeared to be wearing cargo-type shorts and possibly sandals.

Curtis Reinbold and Lorraine Heath, DNA analysts for the Arizona Department of Public Safety, brought Schwartz's trial to a screeching halt. Lafferty told jurors from the start that the case's DNA evidence was not rock solid. The core question was whether a small amount of DNA found on a console knob in Brian's Lexus was contributed by Bruce Bigger. Reinbold testified that 1 in 20 million whites have the same DNA type found on the console knob, which he used to show that Bruce Bigger was the source. Reinbold's figures would become the subject of much scrutiny during the defense portion of the trial and, in turn, greatly affect Bruce Bigger's upcoming trial.

Heath's testimony caused Storts to blurt out "Mistrial!" in front of jurors. Judge Warner had previously ruled that she couldn't combine her statistics over male DNA with Reinbold's. After Heath testified that male DNA found in Brian's Lexus matched some areas of Bruce Bigger's, Lafferty asked, "What opinion can you give about the likelihood that the DNA belongs to Ronald Bruce Bigger?" "Having looked at my own data and Curtis's—Mr. Reinbold's—I feel that it's very strong evidence ..." Storts objected at that point.

Later, after the jury was dismissed, Warner said she heard Heath finish her sentence and say Bruce's name. Warner scolded Storts for shouting "Mistrial!" in front of jurors, but she denied the motion. Warner later ruled that Heath didn't violate her ruling, but Lafferty was cautious about proceeding with Heath's testimony. "I'm scared to death to put her back on," Lafferty said. "I don't want to make a difficult situation worse. I think we all dodged a bullet." Storts also was leery of cross-examining Heath for the same reason. When Heath did take the stand again, she said she was confident the DNA on the knob was Bruce Bigger's.

Crime scene reconstructionist Tim Bright, who was hired to do a study by the defense, testified for the state that he could make the trip from Brian's medical complex to the apartment complex where his car was found in 13 minutes, strengthening the state's theory that Bruce could have killed Brian, driven the car across town, shown up at the Denny's and caught a cab in the proper timeframe.

Lois Schwartz was one of the first to testify in Brad's defense. She smiled at her son as she passed the defense table. Lois told how she fired Brian, at Brad's request, because he had been unethical to advertise his own practice while still working at Brad's. Lois said she heard no angry words exchanged between Brad and Brian at the time. "He told him what I told him, to please remove his things, please not touch the computer." Lafferty asked if Lois was sure it was a firing and not mutual parting of the ways. "Yeah," Lois said, "of course I'm sure because I did it."

Zhanna Chernobelskaya, who lives at the apartment complex where Brian's car was found and is assigned that space, caused a stir when she testified that she saw the Lexus in her space hours *before* Brian's death. Chernobelskaya insisted on the stand that she was sure of her observation, but later, outside of court, claimed she'd been misunderstood.

***

A third juror was dismissed shortly after the defense began. This juror admitted earlier to unwittingly bringing a newspaper into the jury room. She complained that she couldn't understand it and feared she would hinder deliberations. Warner was most reluctant to excuse the juror, saying three of 16 jurors chosen already had gone, leaving just one to be an alternate. Eventually, Warner dismissed the juror. "Let's keep our fingers crossed that there aren't more people come forward with that deer-in-the-headlights look," Warner said.

***

Kraig Marton, who represented Brad before the medical board, volunteered to testify on his behalf because he never heard Brad blame Brian for anything. Brad was glad to see Marton, beaming at him as he entered the courtroom. Marton returned the smile. As he passed Lois and Henry Schwartz, he patted Henry's shoulder and said, "I like your son!"

Marton said he had heard rumors that Brad was badmouthing Brian. "When I spoke to Dr. Schwartz about it … and asked if he was badmouthing him, he said he was not. I said, 'Well, if you are, don't do it anymore.' And he said, 'No, I won't.'"

Marton said he'd only heard Brad mention Brian's name about three times, none of which was in a bad context.

Lafferty's cross-examination brought another mistrial motion when she asked whether Northwest Hospital had a problem with Brad's privileges in the summer of 2004. "There was some kind of problem," Marton said. "But I don't know that I'm supposed to talk about that." Marton said outside the jury's presence that a state law prevented him from discussing the matter. Lafferty had no reason to ask the question, Storts argued, because Marton had said such in a pretrial interview.

"The jury is going to think we're hiding something," Storts complained. "This has got to stop." Warner denied the motion and asked Lafferty to rephrase the question. "It's not worth going into it," Lafferty said. "That's what's wrong with this," Storts said, meaning that the damage already had been done.

***

Storts called a DNA expert hired by the state, Robin Cotton of Selmar Laboratories, to testify about the blood in Brian's Lexus. Cotton said the blood came mostly from Brian, with some DNA found that was linked to Daphne Stidham. Bruce Bigger's DNA, she said, was excluded.

Then Brian Wraxall took the stand. Wraxall, a noted DNA expert, said Reinbold's figure that only 1 in 20 million whites had the same DNA found on the console knob, therefore Bruce Bigger was the contributor, was way off. Wraxall said it was actually more common at 1 in 1,363 whites and 1 in 1,632 in the overall population. "It's all about interpretations," Wraxall said. Bruce couldn't be excluded from contributing the DNA, Wraxall said, but the data Reinbold and Heath used to include him didn't consider any factor that could have excluded him. The DPS analysts, Wraxall said, were biased against Bruce Bigger when they interpreted the DNA data, pouncing on Heath's claim that she was "confident" Bruce's DNA was on the console knob.

There would be more twists and turns on the DNA evidence later in the trial that also would later affect Bruce Bigger's trial.

Dr. Philip Keen, who was then chief medical examiner for Maricopa County, testified that it would be "unusual" for Brian to have died before 9 p.m. that night, thus allowing for a solid alibi for both Brad and Bruce, who were driving around town with Lisa Goldberg around that time. And, Keen said, a cut on Bruce's finger seen when he was arrested Oct. 16, which prosecutors said could have been caused by wielding a knife, couldn't have been more than a couple of days old. Keen did allow on cross-examination that Brian could have been killed around 8 p.m., which was the time when Brad was dining with Lisa at Karuna's when Bruce joined them.

***

Storts called Winston back to the stand, and he stunned the courtroom when he said some of his previous testimony was incorrect. He had told Lafferty minutes before retaking the stand that he had erred, but Lafferty didn't pass the news along, prompting yet another mistrial motion. Storts had wanted Winston to clarify statements he made about how blood settled in Brian's body after he died, which can indicate time of death. Winston had testified that at the time of the autopsy, at 8:30 a.m. on Oct. 6, the settled blood indicated Stidham died within 12 hours. That would contradict the state's theory that Brian died just before 7:30 p.m. on Oct. 5. Now, Winston said he noticed the blood settlement around 4 a.m. Oct. 5, when he first saw Brian's body. Warner denied the mistrial motion and later told jurors to disregard his admission.

***

Two former medical students who attended Brian's lecture, Dr. Parham Morgan and Dr. Jason Lee, both testified. Morgan said he spoke to a man in scrubs that night but was never shown a photo lineup and couldn't say that it was Bruce. Lee testified that he didn't pick Bruce out of a photo lineup as the man he encountered, either.

***

The near-certainty that Brad would testify on his own behalf was dashed when Warner ruled that prosecutors could only bring in ex-jail inmates including Brandon West during the rebuttal phase if he did testify. If he did testify, prosecutors were free to ask him whether he goaded or bribed the men into blaming Dennis Duane Walsh for the murder. Later, it became known that while Storts very much wanted Brad to take the stand, another member of the defense team talked Schwartz out of testifying.

***

Dellene Moyer, the lab worker who saw a man with sandy blond hair lurking in the alleyway on the night Brian died, testified that she was shown a photo lineup in December 2004 that included Bruce's photo and didn't pick anyone out as the stranger she saw.

Det. Christopher Hogan testified that he never talked to the manager of the apartment complex where Brian's Lexus was found, even though two residents reported a car in the wrong space on Oct. 6. Hogan, who helped process the crime scene, also said he found one hair in Brian's hand—a hair that was not tested to see whose it was.

***

On April 19, 2006, Storts told Judge Warner that her rulings on limiting evidence about Walsh influenced Brad not to testify.

"I do want to point out for the record … that the defendant had close to 35 pages prepared in outline form and has spent a good deal of time preparing to testify," Storts said. "This is a decision that we are not making likely."

"I was prepared to testify," Brad confirmed. "Under advice of legal counsel, it's in my best interest not to testify."

After brief testimony from Joan Schwartz about the couple's finances, the defense rested.

***

In rebuttal, Lafferty brought in FBI scientist Dr. Bruce Budowle, who said Reinbold's math was wrong and Brian Wraxall's was closer to the truth. Reinbold did his calculation knowing Bruce had a particular DNA trait, but neglected to consider that the person who left the DNA could have two other traits. Budowle said Bruce and 1 in 13,000 whites could have contributed the DNA found on the console knob. Lafferty said she couldn't ethically send jurors into deliberations thinking Bruce and 1 in 20 million others shared the DNA traits, as Reinbold testified.

***

On April 20, 2006, Lafferty and Storts delivered their closing arguments. Lafferty said Brian was killed because of Brad's plummet from respect, as indicated by the letter he wrote to Piccarreta saying he'd have to leave town to practice medicine again. Lafferty reminded jurors about the women who said Brad threatened to have Brian killed and the evidence that indicated Danny Lopez had been hired to kill Brian. Brad's life wasn't rebounding at the time Brian was killed, Lafferty said. He was deeply in debt. When Bruce came into Brad's life, the men conspired to kill Brian, she said. No one saw them; no one heard them. Conspiracies are, by their very nature, secretive, she said.

"Isn't it interesting that Bruce Bigger seems to be at key locations at key times?" she said.

"This is all about the plummet," Lafferty said, as Brad slowly shook his head at the defense table. "It's all about the success that a physician enjoyed, and the status he had doing the thing he loved the most. This trial has shown you how far a soul can fall. The defendant descended into the lowest place a human being can occupy, a place where he's willing to conspire and plan and order the murder of another human being, David Brian Stidham, whose only known offense is putting out business cards in the defendant's waiting room."

Storts said the first question jurors should ask themselves is whether the state proved that Brian Stidham died between 7:26 and 8:46 p.m. on Oct. 5, 2004.

"If the state hasn't proven that to you beyond a reasonable doubt, then Dr. Schwartz is not guilty of either first-degree murder or conspiracy to commit first-degree murder. We can talk about a whole lot of things, but that's the real issue right there. If Dr. Stidham wasn't killed in that period of time, roughly 19 minutes and 23 seconds, by Mr. Bigger, this case is over."

Storts argued it would be close to impossible to stab Brian more than 15 times, drive from North First Avenue to River Road to North Dodge Boulevard and Speedway, dispose of the clothes and the murder weapon, and calmly enter a Denny's restaurant.

And, Storts pointed out, jurors might have gone to deliberate thinking the state had presented evidence that 1 in 20 million besides Bruce Bigger contributed the DNA found on the console knob, had the defense not presented evidence otherwise and the state later brought in another expert to correct the figures. Storts asked jurors to consider why the state never tested a hair found in the hand of a stabbing victim, why a witness saw Brian's car in her parking space hours before the murder and a waitress saw Bruce in the Denny's restaurant for about half an hour on the night of the slaying. The women who testified against Schwartz had little credibility. There was no evidence that Danny Lopez was hired to kill Brian. Brad Schwartz blamed himself for his professional downfall, Storts said, and was doing so well at the time of Brian's murder that he was expanding his practice to include plastic surgery.

Jurors deliberated for five days before announcing that they had reached their verdicts. When Judge Warner first saw the verdicts, her grim expression and command for the attorneys at her bench told court packed courtroom that something was amiss. Storts fumed when he saw the verdicts: guilty of conspiracy to commit first-degree murder, deadlocked on first-degree murder. Jurors had not been told what to do if they reached an impasse, Storts argued. He wanted a mistrial, as he had asked eight times previously in the 10-week-long trial. Judges often ask juries that are deadlocked to resume deliberations to try to reach a verdict, but Brad's jury later said nothing could have changed the minds of four jurors who couldn't declare him guilty of first-degree murder. Six jurors faced the media after the verdicts were announced, saying they felt they had to fill in a lot of holes to convict Brad.

"I was myself dumbfounded when the state rested its case because I wanted more," juror Susan Hilts Brown said.

"A lot was based on eyewitness testimony," juror Lavon Jean Brandon said.

At first, it seemed like a given that the state would see a retrial on the first-degree murder charge. Local defense attorneys said Brad would most likely be convicted on the second go-round, now that the state knew what its strengths and weaknesses were. But Lafferty soon announced that because the conspiracy conviction carries a life sentence—the only question would be whether Brad would have the chance of parole after 25 years—the state would only refile the murder charge if the conspiracy charge were overturned on appeal.

Daphne Stidham, who had not attended any of the trial, walked into the courtroom on May 30, 2006, for Brad's sentencing. She told Warner that she feared for her safety and that of her children. She was flanked by two attorneys, who were helping her in a civil suit against the county, LaWall, Skitzki and Lourdes Lopez, and spoke softly about how Brian was her "soulmate," her "whole life" and that she didn't know what happiness was before he came into her life.

"He was the most devoted husband and father," she said. With Brian gone, her children are "always scared, nervous and lost." Alexandre and Catherine Stidham will "never have the joy of sharing their lives with their father" and are "insecure," she said.

"I'm asking you to send him to prison forever," Daphne said of Brad.

Warner sentenced Brad Schwartz to life in prison, with the possibility of parole after 25 years. In Arizona, that's tantamount to a natural life sentence as the clemency board rarely recommends parole after the first application for parole for a convicted killer. To have a governor approve the parole is almost unthinkable. After sentencing, Warner acted on a request by the Arizona Medical Board to revoke Brad's license.

***

On Jan. 4, 2007, prosecutors announced a last-minute addition to their witness list for Bruce Bigger's trial, Dr. Ranajit Chakraborty, a top-ranked expert in the world of genetics. Despite subsequent arguments from the defense asking Warner to not allow Chakraborty to testify without allowing the defense to have a report on what he would say, the testimony was allowed.

Bruce's uncle, Dan, attended one week of the trial. Mary Sue attended every day after she was excused as a witness. She was often joined by her friend, Laverne Dunlap, Bruce's godmother. Shortly after Mary Sue landed in Tucson for the trial, she and Laverne took a sojourn to the historic San Xavier Mission, where Mary Sue prayed fervently for her son. As the trial wore on, Mary Sue was torn by emotional conflict. She believed in her son's innocence. But if he were guilty, he should pay for it.

After four days of deliberations, the jury returned with its verdicts: Guilty of first-degree murder, guilty of conspiracy to commit first-degree murder. Four jurors agreed to speak to the media, as the eight others remained silent in the back of the courtroom.

"Bruce Bigger was, in fact, a victim," Elizabeth Ann Freeman said. "But he made the wrong choice."

The jurors were clearly dazzled by testimony from Chakraborty.

"It was amazing to hear him talk," forewoman Hanna Raquel Gardner said. "Just to hear of all his accomplishments. It was a breath of fresh air to have someone of that stature speak during testimony that was very, very draining."

The jurors discussed the evidence that convinced them of Bruce's guilt: DNA evidence, the fact that Bigger had no money before the murder and lots of money to spend in Las Vegas, the timeline of events, eyewitness testimony that put Bigger near the murder scene and the fact that, in Lafferty's words, it was "too much bad luck" for Bigger to be so connected to the events.

After the press conference, the jurors regrouped at their favorite downtown restaurant, where they were joined by both prosecutors. Defense attorneys say they were not invited, despite a juror's claim that they were.

***

As with Schwartz, the only sentence possible for the conspiracy charge was life with parole possible after 25 years. However, Warner had to decide between life without parole or with parole possible after 25 years for the murder charge. Bruce's attorneys argued for the possibility of parole, maintaining that Bruce continued to claim he was innocent of all charges. A psychological report by Dr. Judith Becker noted that Bruce had a personality disorder with narcissistic features and antisocial features, though she said he did not have antipersonality disorder. Bruce's disorders, Becker said, made him susceptible to manipulation. That seemed to fit hand in glove with what jurors said following the verdicts, though it also seemed to fly in the face of Bruce's claims of innocence and his own defense's attempts to paint Brad as the real killer.

In a motion asking for a new trial, Bruce's defense attorney Harold Higgins brought up the issue of presenting third-party culpability evidence regarding Daphne Stidham and Dallas Henry, the husband of one of Schwartz's paramours. Warner's decision to exclude the testimony "was dramatized by the comments of the jury both to counsel and to the press after the verdict was returned. … Of particular note was the fact that the jury had originally been split on the case, six to six. In addition, the jurors noted that in a circumstantial case such as this, they were able to agree on a verdict only after dismissing all circumstances that did not match the state's theories. Defendant strongly believes that had the jury been presented with the Daphne Stidham and Dallas Henry scenarios, they would have seen the difficulty that other circumstantial sets of facts present, and been unable to eliminate those other sets of possibilities."

Higgins also noted that despite requests for disclosure of any exculpatory information that the state might have, especially regarding DNA evidence, it wasn't until after the jury's verdicts in Bruce's trial that the defense learned about materials questioning the integrity of the DNA lab and Curtis Reinbold's work.

In arguing against a new trial, Platt said Warner was correct to rule out the third-party defense strategies—Daphne in Brad's trial, Henry in Bruce's. Platt maintained the state did disclose the DNA lab reports in 2006, and the defense could have obtained further documentation on their own. Warner agreed with the state and denied a new trial.

CHAPTER 17

Pima County prosecutors had offered Brandon West a plea deal under which he would serve no more than seven and half years, far fewer than the 120 years he could face if convicted of molesting two boys. The plea was offered before West claimed Schwartz sought out jail inmates to frame Dennis Duane Walsh in Stidham's murder.

On Feb. 24, 2006, West's attorney, Natalie Prince, filed a motion to disqualify the Pima County Attorney's Office from prosecuting him. Prince said the case had theoretically bounced back and forth between Pima County and the Pinal County Attorney's Office. When Prince was first assigned to the case, after Richard Parrish had to withdraw because of his involvement early on in the Schwartz case, she was told that Pinal County was handing the case. Deputy Pinal County Attorney Sylvia Lafferty told Prince in July 2005 that the case had never been sent over. Deputy Pima County Attorney Angela Woolridge told Prince she knew nothing about the case being transferred, either. David Berkman, the chief criminal Deputy County Attorney with Pima County, didn't return Prince's calls until later that month. He told her the case wouldn't be transferred because there was no conflict. However, Prince said, Berkman indicated that he would consider any recommendation from Pinal County regarding a plea that was offered to West in March 2005 before he became a witness in the Schwartz/Bigger case. Berkman advised Prince to talk to Lafferty and her colleague, Richard Platt.

On Aug. 16, 2005, Prince drove to Florence and met with Lafferty and Platt. Over the course of two hours, Prince filled them in on the background of the case and modifying the plea. Prince called the Pinal County Attorney's Office numerous times in November and December to urge them to call Berkman but got no response, she said.

During a Jan. 9, 2006, hearing, Woolridge said in court that Berkman realized any recommendation Pinal County made would create a conflict of interest, so he would not consider any such recommendation for West if he cooperated with the Schwartz case. The judge told Woolridge and Prince to resolve any potential conflict issue. Prince called Berkman numerous times between Jan. 9 and Feb. 4 with no response. Woolridge told Prince that Berkman was handling the matter and she couldn't help her. On Feb. 6, Berkman left a message on Prince's answering machine:

"Natalie, this is David Berkman. I finally got ahold of Sylvia Lafferty, and I'm prepared to talk to you, if you want. I'm not giving up that case, and if you want us to conflict it out, you'll have to file a motion. I will tell you, however, that I do not believe that Pinal County will take the case, so that if there is a conflict, it will be conflicted somewhere else. If you have any questions, give me a call."

Lafferty told Prince on Feb. 13 that she never told Berkman Pinal County wouldn't take West's case.

Prince said West had been kept in protective custody for 23 hours a day because he feared retaliation for agreeing to testify against Brad Schwartz. Prince obtained a transcript of the free talk, that is an interview with law enforcement with the agreement that the prosecutors would consider the defendant's cooperation with another prosecution in exchange for the evidence depending on the value of the evidence, along with eight transcripts of phone calls West made at the jail, which the Pima County Attorney's Office had made yet never disclosed. After this, Prince filed a complaint with the State Bar of Arizona alleging Berkman committed ethical violations.

Prince also was seeking any information that Brad Roach or Nicki DiCampli had of West's molestation case when they were in the special victims unit of the Pima County Attorney's Office. "Those prosecutors may have had access to information regarding defendant Brandon West, and could potentially provide such evidence to the defense team for Dr. Schwartz," Prince wrote in her motion. "Ken Peasley, a disbarred attorney, is the paralegal for Brick Storts, counsel for Bradley Schwartz. David Berkman and Ken Peasley worked together for many years in the Pima County Attorney's Office. Lourdes Lopez, another former Pima County Deputy Attorney, also worked in the sex crimes unit and is alleged to have friendships with Brad Roach, Nicki DiCampli, Paul Skitzky and Janet Altschuler, all employed by the Pima County prosecutors office during November and December 2004, the time period that the West matter was being considered and was taken to grand jury."

In her argument for prosecutorial misconduct, Prince cited the Alex Hughes case, which was prosecuted by the Pima County Attorney's Office. In that case, the Arizona Supreme Court held "that the cumulative effect of the prosecutor's misconduct deprived (Hughes) of a fair trial." In another Pima County case, the Supreme Court said, "We have routinely noted that a prosecutor has an obligation not only to prosecute, but to seek justice."

Berkman made all the decisions in the West case, Prince noted and was aware of all conflicts. That was obvious when the county recused itself in the Schwartz/Bigger case. Berkman, Prince said, told her things and then reversed himself. Woolridge even noted the potential conflicts; yet Berkman maintained there were none. Berkman lied when he said Pinal County wouldn't take the West case, Prince said. He also gave misleading statements to the court, she said. The fact that Prince was filing a Bar complaint against Berkman was, in itself, a conflict.

The Pima County Attorney's Office, in response, gave the case to senior prosecutor Rick Unklesbay, who in turn declared there was no conflict to send the case out of the county. Unklesbay called the Bar complaint offensive and "unprofessional" and said it doesn't pose a conflict either.

"The motion is not well taken," Unklesbay fired back in a motion, "is void of any facts constituting a conflict, at best contains speculation and, at worst, is an unprofessional accusation of fictional wrongdoing." Unklesbay said Roach and DiCampli had nothing to do with West's case and said she threw in Peasley and Lopez as if they somehow made the conflict "clear and valid."

"(Prince) states that the conflict in her client's case is the same as the conflict that existed in the Schwartz case," Unklesbay wrote. "It is not. The Pima County Attorney conflicted the Schwartz case because members of that office became witnesses in that case."

Prince argued that West was being treated differently than other defendants who gave evidence in other cases. Other defendants, she said, got probation-eligible plea deals for their evidence.

"This is standard operating procedure which is not being implemented in the case of Brandon West because of the person against whom he has information, namely Bradley Schwartz," Prince wrote in a motion. "It is not fair that because Pima County cannot prosecute Bradley Schwartz, they cannot confer consideration or act in the interest of justice in the prosecution of Brandon West." If Unklesbay believes Prince's Bar complaint is "offensive" and "unprofessional," he could file his own complaint against her, she volleyed.

"Furthermore," Prince wrote, "the fact that now a third prosecutor with the Pima County Attorney's Office has now become involved in his prosecution, is demonstration that a conflict exists with the persons involved thus far."

After hearing from both sides, Pima County Superior Court Judge Charles Sabalos issued his ruling.

"Whether there is an actual conflict of interest requiring the state to be disqualified from this prosecution is a close question," Sabalos said. "The manner in which counsel for the parties have conferred and apparently been unable to agree that this case should be prosecuted by an office other than the Pima County Attorney's Office does not lead this Court to conclude that the attorneys involved in these discussions have willfully violated any of the provisions of the Rules of Professional Conduct. The Court does not believe that the filing of a Bar complaint in a particular case, in and of itself, mandates that the complained-against lawyer should be withdrawn as counsel of record, and this case is no exception.

"However, the Pima County Attorney's Office has conflicted out of its representation in State v. Schwartz and may be, because of that conflict, constrained from comprehensively evaluating Defendant West's offer to cooperate in the Schwartz case for the purposes of making plea concessions and a sentencing recommendation in the West case. Under these circumstances, the Pima County Attorney's Office's possible inability to confer the same consideration to Defendant West's case that it might confer in any other case appears to deprive Defendant West and the public from procedural justice and a fair and impartial prosecution. For this reason, Defendant's Motion to Disqualify the Pima County Attorney's Office is granted."

West, who didn't testify in either Brad's or Bruce's trial, was sentenced to two years and six months in prison for sexual conduct with a minor. Because of the time he had served in jail, he spent only a month in prison and was released in April 2007.

In early November, 2006, a hearing officer for the Arizona Supreme Court's Disciplinary Commission held hearings about Lourdes Lopez's dealings with Brad and whether she should be sanctioned after the State Bar filed a complaint against her.

The hearing officer concluded after nine witnesses, including Lopez, that she had violated standards and recommended a one-year suspension. Lopez, he concluded, acted "within the context of a personal, emotional, and ill-fated relationship with Bradley Schwartz, and not when she was engaged in the practice of law. It is within the circumstances of this relationship that (her) actions must be viewed."

Six members of the Disciplinary Commission, however, wanted Lopez disbarred. Three demurred, saying she should be given a less-severe sanction. It would be up to the state Supreme Court to decide whether to uphold the disbarment or impose another punishment. Before it did, Lopez's attorneys had one shot at asking for a lesser sanction.

Lopez's attorneys argued that disbarment was excessive and that other attorneys had done much more and yet received lesser punishment. They stressed that Lourdes was under the influence of Brad Schwartz when she agreed to help him obtain the Vicodin.

"Unknown to Ms. Lopez," they wrote, "Dr. Schwartz was a sociopathic liar and was adept at exploiting and manipulating other people." When he asked her to get the Vicodin, they said, "She not only felt compassion for the man she loved, she empathized with his plight, having herself battled severed migraine headaches. ... Desperate to help her boyfriend alleviate his pain, her judgment clouded by her intimate relationship with him, and legitimately intending to use some of the medication herself, Ms. Lopez agreed."

When Lopez was first approached by the DEA, she "lied to those investigators in a foolish and misguided effort to protect her boyfriend." Once Schwartz spoke to the DEA and admitted his own guilt, Lopez was "free from her worry that she would incriminate Dr. Schwartz" and told the truth (though it took her two months to confess). Lopez did tell Judge Velasco that she had complied with all of her pretrial conditions in securing the plea deal, simply forgetting that she had continued to see Brad despite the no-contact order, her lawyers said. That was because she was going through a "very stressful" time and "turned to Dr. Schwartz for emotional and financial support."

The Supreme Court could do one of two things: Accept review of Lopez's disbarment case and possibly allow oral arguments to decide for themselves or decline to review the case and thereby let the Disciplinary Commission's disbarment recommendation stand.

On Nov. 29, 2007, the justices declined to review Lopez's case and let her disbarment stand. Lopez found work in another defense attorney's office as a paralegal and can still practice law on the Pascua Yaqui Indian Reservation.

***

Though Daphne Stidham told detectives on the night Brian died that Brad Schwartz had threatened her husband, by the following March—the same month she filed a $20 million claim against the county, County Attorney Barbara LaWall and former prosecutors Paul Skitzki and Lourdes Lopez—Daphne couldn't recall if Brad ever threatened Brian.

"Did Brian receive any threats from Brad?" Murphy asked.

"I don't know," Daphne said. "He just said that, in the middle of the night, shortly after he opened his practice, someone would ring on his cell phone and then hang up, and the only one that had his cell phone number was his family and Brad, so he was assuming it was Brad. And it was in the middle, it used to wake us up, sometimes one, two in the morning, and it wouldn't be his mother or sister doing that, but it went on for several days, and then sporadically after that. So he assumed it was Brad."

The two surgeons did cross paths on occasion after Brian was fired, Daphne said, but each kept their distance.

"(Brian) said Brad kind of just kept a low profile," Daphne said.

"Did he ever mention any worries to you that he thought Brad would do something to him?" Murphy asked.

"No," Daphne said. "A couple of times (I) even asked him if I should approach his ex-wife just to talk and see how things were, and he said, 'Nah, it'll go away. Just try to stay out of his way.'"

Daphne did say that Brian heard from other doctors, staff members and patients that Brad was asking questions about Brian's practice, how long patients had to wait, etc. She said because her husband was so well liked and Brad wasn't, that when Brad would send roses to an office to curry favor and get referrals, the office would refer patients to Brian instead. Brad's prescription drug case became a standing joke among the medical community, she said.

"My husband's theory and my theory was if there's nothing else going on in Tucson, it was such a big thing having a surgeon indicted on drug charges, it was sort of entertaining to talk about it and sort of perpetuated itself," she said.

"Do you know of anybody that ever warned Brian that Brad was gonna hurt him or could have done?" Murphy asked.

"No," Daphne replied.

Daphne told Det. Jill Murphy in March that Brad was ready to give up the pediatric practice to Brian because it was too draining on him to do everything. Joan Schwartz had complained that Brad wasn't home enough with the kids, Daphne said.

Daphne Stidham's claim, which accused the defendants of indirectly causing Brian's death because no one took action to warn him and police about Brad Schwartz's threats, became a wrongful death lawsuit. In the fall of 2007, two weeks before a trial was set to begin, the Pima County Board of Supervisors approved a $2.9 million settlement on Paul Skitzki's behalf, with the accusations against the county, LaWall and Lopez dropped in exchange. Daphne Stidham previously settled for an undisclosed amount with the Altschulers for having unsafe conditions in the parking lot of the medical plaza.

Daphne and her children moved to Texas shortly after Brian's death, settling down in the Dallas/Fort Worth area.

In 2007, when this book was about to be published by another company, Daphne asked to see the manuscript, offering to share a photo of Brian and the children in exchange. When her offer was refused, she hired several attorneys from a prestigious Tucson law firm to set up a telephonic meeting requesting to see the manuscript. In that call, the attorneys expressed their client's hope that the book wouldn't contain anything about the medication she was taking at the time of the murder or that she was the first suspect. When they were told the information would be in the book, they threatened to stop its publication, an empty threat that no court would ever consider but was enough to scare the publisher about the cost of fighting her attorneys in court.

Stephanie Nagel, the woman who'd met Brad Schwartz at the federal courthouse, testified in his trial about statements he'd made about wanting someone taken out. She admitted that she didn't go to the police at first, not until she was facing three to five years in prison—with no probation available— on a local charge. Nagel eventually was given a year and a half in prison with seven years on intensive probation.

Carmen Fernandez, the phlebotomist who met Brad Schwartz when he gave urine samples for drug testing at LabCorp, never paid back the $2,000 she borrowed from him. At the time she testified against him, Carmen was working for another doctor. The piece of paper that Brad allegedly gave Carmen with Brian Stidham's picture and personal information was thrown away. Carmen was vague about when she threw it away, either right before Det. Murphy called her or sometime later.

By the time of Brad Schwartz's trial, Liliana Bibb was a medical assistant in an orthopedic office and a real estate agent recently married to a man in the U.S. Air Force special operations. She was not a willing witness and had been difficult to interview by both the prosecution and defense in the months leading up to the trial. On July 13, 2005, Liliana called 88-CRIME and inquired about the reward for Dr. Stidham's killer, since she'd had her little sister call in the day after the murder.

Rachel Atkinson testified against Brad Schwartz in his trial. In the spring of 2007, she also consented to an interview to the ABC news show *20/20* allegedly on the condition that they also educate the public about the ailment that brought her son to Brad Schwartz. The segment aired, but didn't include anything about her son's condition. Atkinson moved to another state, fearing for her safety.

Wendell Hunt was fired by the Tucson Police Department for sexual harassment and his involvement in the Schwartz/Bigger case. Hunt appealed to the county's merit system commission, which upheld the firing regarding the sexual harassment issue only. Nevertheless, Hunt didn't lose his law enforcement license and his ability to work in the field, including being a town marshal somewhere in rural Arizona.

None of the former prosecutors linked to Lourdes Lopez and Schwartz were called to testify in either trial. Judge Warner refused to allow Paul Skitzki (and a DEA agent) to take the stand to impeach Lopez's credibility, which was one prong of Schwartz's appeal. It didn't look like his testimony was needed, however. Neither jury found Lopez to have much credibility. Skitzki was hired by the Pima County Public Defender's Office. Nicki DiCampli and Brad Roach each started their own separate practices. Janet Altschuler also opened her own practice with another former prosecutor. They set up an office in the complex owned by Altschuler's parents, the same complex where Stidham died. Skitzki and DiCampli, who had a baby together, live together on the Northwest Side of Tucson. Roach continues his annual fund-raising Halloween party, moving it from his house so he could open it to the public.

No one has determined who stole the Mitsubishi pickup truck parked behind Brian Stidham's office.

Despite flubbing the DNA testimony in Schwartz's case and that trial's split verdict, Sylvia Lafferty and Richard Platt were named felony prosecutors of the year by the Arizona Prosecuting Attorneys' Advisory Council in 2006 and given "Home Run Hitter" awards by the National District Attorneys Association in December 2007. LaWall, who had been forced to move the case out of the county because some of her own prosecutors were linked to Schwartz, nominated the pair for the national award.

CHAPTER 18

Brad Schwartz hasn't spoken in depth to anyone outside his circle of family, friends and attorneys about Brian Stidham's murder case. Mike Piccarreta, the attorney who represented Brad in the federal drug case, has always said that the sheriff's department made a big mistake by not taking Schwartz up on his offer to talk to them about Stidham's death before arresting him. Unlike Bruce, who gave a TV interview shortly after his arrest, Brad hasn't granted an interview to any reporter. It's safe to say that it wasn't for lack of any reporter in Tucson (and producers from network TV shows) of trying. Myself included. The first time I approached Brick Storts, Brad's trial attorney, about talking to him, the only thing Storts would agree to would be to consider any written questions and pass them along to Brad, who had yet to be tried. Knowing that Storts wouldn't allow Brad to answer any questions about the case before the trial, I asked questions about his background, to get a better understanding of who he was. Brad wouldn't have anything to do with that, however.

After Brad's trial, when he was already driven up to the main Arizona State Prison Complex in Florence, I wrote to him again. I offered to help him tell his side of the story to the readers of the *Tucson Citizen*. Thus began an exchange of letters between Brad and me. It began tenuously, with Schwartz expressing much doubt whether anything that a reporter could do would help someone in his situation. I wasn't sure he would ever write again, but he did. Sometimes several times a week. Throughout our correspondence, Schwartz's letters centered on his proclamation of innocence and that he had been unfairly tried.

"I am not quite sure why you have written me," Schwartz wrote in his first letter, on July 25, 2006. "Is Tucson news getting boring now that I am no longer the topic of conversation?"

Schwartz's first letter took on an angry tone, lashing out at the media for reporting what he saw as the lies of the prosecution and unfair rulings of the judge.

"Don't worry about me," he wrote. "I'll be out in about 1 year after I win a new trial. ... Anyone who was in that courtroom & has half a brain knows I should have walked out of there. That jury found me guilty of conspiracy with 'the women' not Bruce Bigger according to juror statements after trial. Neither he nor I had anything to do with this. But then again, you don't care, just so long as you get to write some trashy article about me, Lourdes Lopez or any other of the 'Cast of Characters.' "

The "Cast of Characters" referred to the headline of a pretrial story that included a list of key witnesses expected to testify in his trial.

"Are you happy that you have contributed to keeping my children from their father, an innocent man?" Schwartz asked. "Well, with you (and other reporters) writing all that garbage, how could I ever get a fair trial in Tucson? ... You contributed to the circus atmosphere. So—thank you for your so called help. How else can you possibly help me?"

He signed the letter "Bradley Schwartz, M.D."

Then he included a postscript: "Maybe if Lafferty lowers the threshold enough your DNA will come up on the knob LX39. ha ha!"

And another postscript: "Send a copy of this to Brick. See what he says. So tell me—how can you help me? I'm curious. You have me listening (or reading I should say)."

I wrote back, explaining that certain points he mentioned in his first letter were reported in a blog that I wrote throughout his trial. Schwartz's next letter wondered why they weren't included in newspaper articles.

"Were you ordered by your superiors to avoid *anything* that would show me in a favorable light?" he asked in an Aug. 16, 2006, letter.

Truth is, very little of what is made part of the public record before a trial favors the defendant. Over the months, I tried to explain to Brad that a reporter's capabilities to see everything in any particular case are limited. I explained that people would like to learn his side of the story told in his words.

"Personally, I have nothing to gain by that," Schwartz wrote. "The trial's over. I'd just as soon allow things to subside. ... I am reluctant at this point in time to even be quoted (as you asked me), but that is subject to change. I need to think about it. First off, if I profess my innocence & scream it from the rooftops—who would believe me? So, what would it benefit me? You? Anyone? Who really cares at this point?"

But he agreed to be open to a list of questions that Storts also would be able to see.

"We can continue 'chatting' like this," he wrote. "Keep in touch.

"P.S. Sorry my letter sounded harsh, but, as you heard in the trial, I am not too shy about stating my opinions."

In September, Brad shared a glimpse of what prison life was like for him.

"I hope this letter finds you well," he wrote. "Sorry I didn't write back sooner. I guess I can't use the old excuse about 'how busy I've been.' (He drew a smiley face.)

"Overall, I guess I am holding up well. The toughest part is not actually sitting in here, but the knowledge that I'm here for something I had nothing to do with."

When the list of questions was sent, neither Storts nor Schwartz thought it was a good idea to respond to them.

"I have read over your letter that includes your questions and I have given quite a bit of thought to this," he wrote on Dec. 1, 2006. "After great cogitation, I have come to the conclusion that there is absolutely no way I can answer your questions and hope to get any type of fair portrayal & representation in your newspaper. Your editors have basically spelled that out. Plus, from what I have seen up till this point in time, I would be brain dead if I thought otherwise. Your editors 'won't allow personal slams against ...' yet, this is all they have done to me for over 2 years (as well as you ...) On top of all this, you don't even offer us the opportunity to confirm that your article will be even handed prior to its printing."

As he would say in many of his letters, Schwartz maintained that his was a trial in which prosecutors sought "a conviction at any expense."

"Basically, there has never been a level playing field," Brad wrote, "nor can I hope to have one. No one wants to hear me say I'm innocent, because no one wants to think that as a possibility. Everyone feels safer thinking that JFK was killed in some big conspiracy rather than a lone gunman. There is safety in thinking that bad events may be 'rationalized' rather than random acts of violence. If the latter is true, then no one is really safe. It's a lot easier to think that Dr. Schwartz pre-arranged the murder of sweet, poor little Dr. Stidham rather than something random. Randomness is scarey."

Brad said he understood that I was just doing my job as a reporter and that I shouldn't take it personally that he wouldn't answer my questions.

"People who are innocent don't look for that attention," he wrote. "I will never get a fair shake in Tucson because of what the 2 newspapers have done. I don't owe anybody anything in Tucson, especially the press."

He ended the letter: "Take care, A.J. Write back to me if you wish. Brad S."

Over the next few months, the letters became an exchange of minor information about the case. Brad did reveal some things that I had never heard before that occasionally led to a document or fact that was helpful in understanding the case. I, in turn, complied with his occasional request to send a copy of a certain newspaper article or explain what was going on with Bruce's case.

But Brad didn't want to be quoted. I agreed to withhold his discussions of the case until his appeal had been heard. Storts agreed to represent Brad in his appeal. At the same time, Daphne Stidham's lawsuit was progressing. Brad often wrote letters stressing certain points that came up during his trial or were in defense documents that weren't allowed at trial that pointed the finger at other people as Brian Stidham's killer.

"I don't want to force any of this on you," he wrote in February 2007. "I am not a ranting, raving lunatic despite the way I have been portrayed."

In that letter, he explained the physical ailments he faced that led him to drug addiction—including herniated disks in his neck, two spinal fusions and two torn rotator cuffs—that he had conquered long before Stidham died.

"I had (shoulder) surgery about 2 weeks before Stidham was killed and I was in a sling for 2 weeks," he wrote. "I'm not saying what I did was right (self-medicating), but I had significant pain issues and tried to treat myself so I could continue to function. (I also had 9 root canals & assorted dental procedures, but I'm not even gonna get into that.) That DEA stuff was way before Stidham came to Tucson, but they tried to say I was angry at Brian for that. He had nothing to do with it."

His letters showed that, without the tasks of preparing for the trial and sitting through it, Brad replayed segments of the testimony over and over in his mind. For instance, one of Stidham's employees, Ruby Gonzales, handled his car keys on Oct. 5, 2004, to fetch the surgeon's wallet so he could pay for pizzas for the medical students. Yet Gonzales's DNA wasn't on the keys. Bruce's wasn't. Daphne's was. If the killer drove the car to the apartment complex, and the killer were Bigger, there would be a good chance his DNA would be there. Why was Daphne's DNA there? How could Lafferty dismiss that evidence by saying, "What wife wouldn't handle her husband's car keys?" Daphne had her own vehicle, which had the safety seats for the children. She'd have no reason to have Brian's keys, right?

Brad was eager for inside information on Bruce's trial. When prosecutors presented DNA testimony that seemed to shore up their case against Bruce as the killer, Brad wrote several letters explaining in detail how the numbers still didn't add up to the state's theory. He wondered why Judge Warner turned down his defense's request to present another DNA expert because it would "confuse the jury," yet prosecutors were able to present an entirely different DNA presentation than his trial, without FBI expert Bruce Budowle, who was hired to help the state and ended up helping the defense more.

After the DNA testimony in Bruce's trial, Det. Murphy, the lead investigator, took me aside and said, "You still don't believe that Schwartz had nothing to do with this, do you?"

"I'm not saying that, but I'd feel a lot better if I knew certain things such as why Daphne Stidham, the first suspect, was eliminated," I said.

"Who said she was the first suspect?" Murphy said.

"Every deputy who stepped into her house that night, who saw the estate papers, who heard her ask how Brian died before they told her he died."

"If you knew Daphne," Murphy said, "you'd know she wasn't capable of doing this."

Brad didn't need to be told that the sheriff's department never investigated Daphne Stidham once she uttered his name. Though the deputies suspected her and a detective asked what clothes she wore, nobody checked her car for any evidence. Nobody checked the laundry or the trashcans for evidence.

Likewise, Brad also knew that Walsh was never investigated as the killer. As Storts would outline in his appeal, Brad prodded me to see the pattern of Walsh's crime spree in which he appeared to rob stores on a regular basis in order to get his heroin fix—except for the week that Stidham was killed.

Several months after Brad's trial, I had an extensive interview with several of his jurors. For the better part of two hours, I asked them how they had made their decisions and what they thought of the trial. Then I told them what they hadn't heard. How Daphne Stidham acted on the night of the murder. How Walsh had flashed knives, robbed stores and committed a carjacking during the time Brian was killed and in a close radius of the medical plaza. The jurors were shocked. One juror said had she known those facts, she might not have convicted Brad of anything. Others who had said they were sure Brad was guilty, but that there wasn't enough proof to stick a first-degree murder conviction on him, also expressed doubt after hearing the alternate theories.

One letter in the spring of 2007 showed a glimpse of what Brad would have been able to do had he taken the stand in his own defense. It came during Lisa Goldberg's testimony in Bruce's trial in which she revealed that Bruce, a Catholic, had said a "Hail Mary" prayer when they were driving around the night of the murder, presumably to show how guilty he felt about murdering someone, and that Brad had remarked to her that Bigger had a big knife strapped to his bicycle.

Goldberg, Brad said, was extremely tired that night and kept dozing off in the Escalade.

"She misread some of Bigger's sarcastic remarks," Schwartz wrote, "like the 'Hail Mary' stuff. He was making fun of my driving. She also misrepresented what I was pointing out on that bike. He had a barbecue tool set on the bike—strapped to the center bar. You know—a spatula, tongs & the big fork—all things that one would use with their BBQ. I thought it was funny looking riding around on a bike with a BBQ set! Have BBQ will travel! (He drew a smiley face.) That's exactly what I said."

It was enough to wonder how Brad could have turned the whole case around by taking the stand. He had the smarts to counter whatever Lafferty could have thrown at him, but would he be able to control his temper before the jury if Lafferty pushed his buttons? Would Schwartz have been able to answer what no one has been able to? Could an extremely intelligent man (Phi Beta Kappa, summa cum laude, one of a few specialists in the states) who was two months away from having his full medical privileges restored and on his way back to making millions of dollars a year hire a near-stranger with no violent criminal history to go to Brian's office, wait for him to leave, stab him to death, drive to an apartment complex miles away, walk to a pay phone to meet up with him and a date, then drive him around town and buy him a hotel room with his own credit card? What about the man in scrubs? Was it Bruce? According to witnesses, Brad said Brian worked late and the complex was dark. But Brad would have known that Brian, like himself, *wasn't* prone to working late. Except on that one night. How would Brad and Bruce have known that the night of Oct. 5, 2004, marked the first night Stidham would lecture medical students, so he would be leaving the office late, when no one else was around? If they didn't know, then was the plan really for Bruce to hang out in the parking lot, being so careless as to interact with people, so they would see his face, and ambush Brian before dark as other complex workers were leaving while there was plenty of rush-hour traffic on First Avenue? Witnesses gave a variety of descriptions of the mysterious man in scrubs, but none of them noticed Bruce's most prominent feature: His broken nose. And what amateur hit man would choose a knife over a gun?

It got to the point that the nickname for the case around the newsroom, played off the hit comedy "Dumb and Dumber" was "Bigger and Dumber," because a man of Brad's stature would have to be extremely dumb to ask his hit man to dinner and pay for a hotel room with a credit card. Even Brad could see the dark humor.

"If it weren't me who were in here," he wrote in July 2007, "it would be comical and I would laugh it off."

"I am innocent!" Schwartz claims.

Two juries said otherwise.

CHAPTER 19

From the start, this was a murder case filled with twists and turns—and the ensuing years since the trials took place have had their share, too. With both defendants still maintaining their innocence, their appeals are still being played out in the Arizona court system.

Schwartz and Bigger both appealed their convictions to the Arizona Court of Appeals, which affirmed them. Neither case was accepted by the Arizona Supreme Court for review. The next step for their attorneys—Brad still being represented by Storts and, after a time trying to appeal on his own, Bruce's defense landed in the Pima County Public Defender's Office. In the meantime, both men suffered head injuries while in prison. In May 2011, Jeffrey Allan Wood, already a convicted murderer, was convicted of aggravated assault, after attacking Brad. Brad testified that he was standing in line at a water fountain when Wood called him a "dirty Jew," hit him up to 30 times and kicked him at least twice. Brad suffered numerous injuries including fractures in his eye sockets and an optic nerve, resulting in double vision and loss of his sense of smell due to nerve damage. Brad's injuries were included in a lawsuit against the Arizona Department of Corrections over poor health care management. Recently, Bruce alluded to having "suffered serious head trauma resulting in surgery," in a letter to a judge in his appeal. Bruce's attorney, David Euchner, said he couldn't discuss the injury.

Brad's first appeal to Pima County Superior Court, called a request for post-conviction relief (PCR), centered on DNA evidence introduced in Bruce's trial, framed as "newly discovered evidence" that was related to the "motive and possible culpability of Daphne Stidham." The PCR was dismissed and an appeal to the Court of Appeals was denied.

Bruce's first PCR landed back in Pima County Superior Court and was working its way through the court in 2018, as this book was updated. Bruce submitted hundreds of hand-written documents acting as his own "pro se" attorney, to supplement Euchner's motion for a new trial. In a Feb. 9, 2018, letter to Judge Christopher Browning, Bruce wrote that he believed he received ineffective assistance of counsel by Thorpe:

"... a conflict I was not aware of but, hindsight and statements by trial counsel proved after conviction I had no defense prepared by Ms. Thorpe.

"I'd thank you to please consider this request and forgive the excited nature of my writings ... every word is true."

In Bruce's motion, he points the finger at Dallas Henry or the person who stole the Mitsubishi pickup truck as suspects that were too quickly dismissed by investigators. He also complains that Judge Warner showed bias at his sentencing, delaying proceedings until the crew from the CBS show *48 Hours* arrived, presenting a prepared statement and crying. Bruce also claims that Thorpe lied to him and talked him out of testifying.

Other claims include:

•–Warner unfairly denied a change of venue,

•–Warner failed to preclude testimony offering probability analysis of DNA evidence,

•–Warner should have allowed evidence of third-party culpability

•–Warner should have recused herself because she worked for Brian's family's law firm 20 years previously, had personal interest in seeing Bruce convicted since the jury hung on the murder charge in Schwartz's case, "cooked the books" in Brad's trial

•–Thorpe's presented theory that Brian was killed in a carjacking gone wrong or that Brad was the actual killer hurt his defense and instead, should have argued that Brad hired someone to kill Stidham, but not Bruce (the state's response says if she had done that, prosecutors would have seized on it to emphasize that Bruce was the hit man),

•–Thorpe hurt his case by agreeing to allow hearsay evidence in statements, including those Lisa Goldberg testified to (regarding how the "scrubs worked out" and referring to a "knife" on Bruce's bike).

•–Thorpe was wrong to not present character witnesses, so it looked to the jury that there was no evidence of good character for Bruce regarding being nonviolent (the state points out that Thorpe had intended to present such witnesses but withdrew them after seeing state's evidence of charges Bruce once faced that included some violence),

•–Jennifer Dainty's testimony identifying him was tainted by investigators and too unreliable to be used as evidence against him.

***

It's Schwartz's newest request for a new trial that contains the most explosive claims. In his second PCR, Storts argues that there's newly discovered evidence that shows in the months leading up to Stidham's death, Lourdes Lopez was trying to hire a hit man to kill Brad. If true and if Brad's team had known about this evidence at the time of the trial, Storts could have used it to impeach Lourdes's testimony in March 2006 that was crucial to prosecutors' case of conspiracy to commit murder, the one count that jurors reached a verdict for.

"The very crux of the 'conspiracy' charge was provided by the testimony of Lourdes Lopez," Storts says in the PCR.

In the PCR, which was filed in March 2018, Storts says an inmate being held in the same prison as Brad, Guillermo Urquidez, claims Lourdes asked him to kill Brad. Urquidez was arrested and brought to Pima County Juvenile Court on charges of aggravated assault and misconduct involving weapons for a Jan. 18, 2004, incident. Lourdes was appointed to represent him in June 2004. Keep in mind that Lourdes and Brad had become engaged in January 2004 and had broken up in May, just one month before Lourdes met Urquidez. By July, Brad was already dating Liliana Bibb and by September, he was seeing Lisa Goldberg.

Urquidez says Lourdes told him about her personal issues involving "the Doc" over several visits to the Pima County Jail between June and October 2004, before Brad's arrest. Lourdes told him about her part in the Vicodin scheme with Brad and how she was forced to resign from the Pima County Attorney's Office and fired as Pascua Yaqui prosecutor because of it. She allegedly said Brad physically abused her, bruising her arms, neck and legs in domestic violence incidents.

Urquidez says Lourdes was "intrigued" by him and his gang affiliation, which was an issue in his case. He says he told her that he could "order a hit outside of the jail" if she wanted. "There was no doubt in Mr. Urquidez's mind," Storts wrote, "that Ms. Lopez wanted to have Dr. Schwartz killed and in effect requested him to carry out that desire."

Lourdes said she "wanted to end her relationship" with Brad, that "the Doc has money and (she) will take care of you and your friend," Urquidez told an investigator.

Once Brad was arrested, according to the Urquidez, Lourdes said he "sealed his fate and that the matter discussed was dead." No outside meeting took place between Urquidez and another person.

***

Brad's second PCR and Bruce's first were awaiting hearings in Pima County Superior Court in mid-2018.

For More News About A.J. Flick,
Signup For Our Newsletter:

http://wbp.bz/newsletter

Word-of-mouth is critical to an author's long-term success. If you appreciated this book please leave a review on the Amazon sales page:

http://wbp.bz/toxicragea

BETTER OFF DEAD by MICHAEL FLEEMAN

http://wbp.bz/boda

Read A Sample Next

1.

An hour before sunset, Shaun Ware swung his white work truck right off Goodrick Drive into the Summit Industrial Park, a complex of metal buildings with tall garage doors. It was Sunday, Aug. 17, 2014, a warm summer evening in the high desert. Shadows enveloped the Tehachapi Pass, the mighty turbines in the windmill farm standing still in the light western breeze. Traffic roared by on Highway 58, cars and trucks shuttling between Bakersfield and the Mojave Desert. Every half hour, a long freight train from Burlington Northern Santa Fe Railway would rumble behind the complex.

Arriving for his overnight shift, Shaun pulled his truck up to a space with "BNSF" stenciled on the concrete parking block and immediately felt something was wrong. The metal door to the work area was closed. The day-shift responder, Robert Limon, would have kept it open to ventilate the stuffy garage during the 89-degree afternoon. Robert would have told him if he were out on a service call or making a food run.

Shaun raised the door with a remote opener. Robert's BNSF utility truck was parked next to his personal car, a silver Honda. Shaun walked into the garage along the right side of the truck. He nearly stepped on broken glass that appeared to have come from one of the fluorescent fixtures hanging from the 18-foot ceiling.

To his right, the door to the small office was wide open. That was wrong, too. The office door always stayed closed. The office appeared to have been ransacked. File drawers had been yanked open and papers strewn across the floor. A BNSF-issued Toshiba laptop was missing.

Shaun walked around the front of the work truck, which pointed toward the kitchenette against the back wall. The door of the small refrigerator was flung open. So was the door to the bathroom.

That's when he saw him.

Robert Limon was on the floor, his back slumped against the driver's side tire of the truck.

Shaun kneeled.

"Rob, what happened?" Shaun said. "Wake up, buddy."

Robert had a vacant look on his face, one eye closed, the other half opened. Blood had pooled beneath him. He didn't respond.

Panic gripped Shaun. He called 911 on his cell phone. He told the operator that he had found his coworker on the ground around a lot of blood and that he wasn't moving.

The operator asked if Shaun was willing to try CPR. He said yes. Following the operator's instructions, Shaun pulled Robert down flat on his back. He put his face close to Robert's. There was no breath. The operator asked Shaun to push his hands against Robert's chest to begin compressions.

One push and blood oozed out of Robert's mouth.

The operator told Shaun to get out of the building, now. He did, in a daze. The cell phone still to his ear with the 911 operator on the line, he wandered out to the asphalt parking area.

A man approached—somebody who worked in a neighboring unit—and asked Shaun what was going on.

"I think Rob's dead," Shaun told him.

Then it hit him. Shaun dropped to his knees and his body convulsed. He felt tears coming.

How long he was like this, he couldn't remember. The next thing he knew, he heard cars approaching. Sirens. Lights. He looked up and saw a woman in a sheriff's uniform.

Shaun pointed to the garage and said, "He has two kids."

2.

Two deputies from the Kern County Sheriff's Office fielded the 911 call at 6:46 p.m. for a "male found bleeding and not breathing" at 1582 Goodrick Drive, Tehachapi, Calif. They arrived in separate one-deputy patrol cars. Both had often seen the facility from the 58, but had never been on call there.

Goodrick Drive took them to a cul-de-sac with a driveway leading into the five buildings of the complex. Since it was a Sunday night, all of the garage doors were shut—save for one—and the place empty, except for the man crouched on the pavement.

Kern County Senior Deputy Marcus Moncur got there first. The 10-year veteran cop approached the man, who was shaking but saying nothing. A second, deputy, Anna Alvarez, a rookie patrol officer, arrived in her patrol car. Moncur asked her to stay with the man and talk to him while he checked out the garage 50 yards away.

There, the deputy saw the silver Honda and the white Chevy work pickup with the utility bed. On the ground next to the driver's side door, he spotted a man flat on his back. He was a big, strong man, about 6 feet tall, with a shaved head and tuft of beard on his chin. He wore an orange safety shirt, black tank undershirt, gray pants and black shoes.

Moncur could see that the man had a lump on his eye and blood around his mouth and right cheek. A large pool of blood congealed beneath his head and upper body. His right arm extended from his body as if hailing a cab. The body showed signs of lividity, the purple discoloration caused by blood pooling under gravity at low points in the body after the heart stops. Just behind the man, red spots were splattered on an open refrigerator door. A sign on the wall read: "A culture of commitment to safety to each other."

Moncur radioed for a paramedic and walked carefully out of the garage so as not to step on any evidence. He asked Alvarez to cordon off the area as a crime scene.

Within minutes, an ambulance and a paramedic truck raced into the complex. Two emergency medical technicians took the man's vital signs and ran a field EKG reading. No signs of life. The EMTs called a physician at the Kern Medical Center in Bakersfield, recited their findings.

At 7:06 p.m., the man was officially declared dead. Over the next half hour, phone calls went out to supervisors and investigators, plus crime scene technicians and the coroner. Moncur started a crime-scene log to keep track of what would be a small invasion of law enforcement personnel overnight.

He then waited an hour and a half.

Covering more than 8,000 square miles, Kern County is just smaller than the entire state of New Jersey. But with 880,000 people, it has only a tenth of its population. Kern County is vast and in most places, empty. The rectangular-shaped county is made up of sprawling farmland, rugged mountains and wide swaths of desert.

The closest detective was more than an hour's drive away in the county seat of Bakersfield. Randall Meyer of the robbery homicide division got the call at home from the Kern County Sheriff's Office Communication Center at about 7:30 p.m. A former patrol deputy, training supervisor and investigator in the sex crimes unit, Meyer had been transferred to robbery-homicide six months earlier. He put on a suit and tie and headed east for Tehachapi.

He got to the top of the pass at 8:30 p.m. Pulling off Highway 58, he made his way on side streets to Goodrick Drive to the industrial complex. He flashed his ID, got logged in and was directed to the crime scene through two checkpoints, one at the outer perimeter near the entrance to the facility, the second the taped-off inner perimeter closest to the garage.

Darkness had come to the high desert. At an elevation of more than 4,000 feet, even on this summer night the temperature would plunge more than 40 degrees to the mid-50s. The complex was ablaze with emergency lights and full of cops.

Meyer received a briefing from another Kern County detective, Mitchell Adams, who was in charge of processing the crime scene. Adams had phoned another detective with instructions to seek a search warrant from a night-duty judge. In the meantime, Adams had an evidence tech videotape the exterior of the garage. He walked around to the back of the building, looking for any signs of evidence. Behind the garage, in the hard-parked dirt, he spotted what looked like footprints near the back door. He had the tech photograph those. About 15 feet west of the corner while waking southeast, he found another shoe track, also photographed.

After 90 minutes, Adams had a search warrant and for the first time entered the garage. Adams told Meyer that he followed the same path as Shaun Ware along the right side of the truck, stepping over the glass shattered into a powder. The fixture above was missing one of its two fluorescent bulbs and Adams could see some damage to the metal frame.

On the ground, directly below the fixture, he spotted a bullet. It was mangled from apparently hitting the light fixture. It appeared to be a larger caliber, .44 or .45, from a big, powerful gun.

To his right, through the office door, he could see a television, sofa, desk and office chair, exercise machine, photocopy machine, whiteboard, calendar and two desks against the wall. The bottom desk drawers were open and items, including file folders, had been removed and thrown on the floor. Behind the bookcase on the northwest wall were several binders on the ground that Adams believed had been hastily removed from their previous location. Two cell phones sat on the desk.

Walking around the front of truck, Adams saw the body for the first time, the blood on the face and a bump on the back of the head. Behind the man, red dots from blood spatter were on the doors of the refrigerator.

An evidence technician photographed the interior of the office, the bullet fragment on the ground, the tiny blood spatter on the interior of the refrigerator door, the door of the truck—everything Adams pointed out.

That was the extent of the physical evidence. Beside the footprints, Adams found nothing that a killer or killers would have left behind. An evidence tech dusted for fingerprints, but analysis would take days.

"I immediately started thinking that it was possibly a staged scene," Adams later said in court, repeating what he told Meyer. "In numerous investigations, with burglary and robberies and such, I've never seen items placed as those were and the amount of items."

How the victim died would remain a question mark. The bullet on the ground and the blood on and around the body suggested he was shot. The bump on the head could have come from a blow. An autopsy would sort that out.

No gun or other weapon was found. Nor did they find spent brass ammunition shells, suggesting the shooter used a revolver or picked up the ejected shells from a semi-automatic.

Meyer was led to the "reporting party," Shaun Ware. A burly man with a shaved head, Shaun could have been the victim's brother. Shaun explained that the garage was leased by Burlington Northern Santa Fe Railway as a repair shop.

He and the victim, whom he identified, worked as "rapid responders," going into the field when trains break down, which they had a habit of doing on the Tehachapi Pass.

From the flat San Joaquin Valley, the trains strain up the grade, so steep in one spot that the tracks form a circle, like a spiral staircase, that takes the trains up 77 feet in a mile. Train buffs flock from around the world to see the famed Tehachapi Loop. YouTube is full of scenes of the loop.

Some 20 trains a day labor up the pass, making it one of the busiest stretches of single track in the country and one of the hardest on engines. Metal cracks, hoses blow, wires short circuit. That's when the phone rings in the BNSF garage in Tehachapi. A rapid responder jumps in a truck and races out to the scene of the breakdown, diagnosing the problem and making repairs.

Shaun told the detective the Tehachapi responders work 12-hour shifts. They always work alone. The 7 p.m. to 7 a.m. shift the night before belonged to Shaun, that day's 7 to 7 to Robert Limon.

The last time he'd spoken to Robert was that morning during the 7 a.m. shift change. They talked about Robert's iPad, which was not working. Shaun slept all day before his overnight shift and had no idea what Robert had done during the day shift.

Meyer asked Shaun how well he knew Robert. He said he'd worked with him off and on for about two years. "He was a very friendly guy, very outgoing," Shaun later said in court, repeating what he told Meyer.

Robert was married with two kids and lived in a community called Silver Lakes, in the town of Helendale, in San Bernardino County, about an hour-and-half drive away toward Barstow. Shaun had never known Robert to use drugs or have been involved in any illegal activities. He couldn't think of anybody who'd had an argument with Robert, much less want to harm him.

Then Shaun said something that Meyer found particularly intriguing. Robert did not usually work in Tehachapi. He was based far across the Mojave Desert to the east at Barstow Yard, BNSF's sprawling rail classification yard where rolling stock is changed between engines along a labyrinth of tracks. According to Shaun, Robert was filling in that Sunday for the regular responder, who was either out sick or taking vacation time. Shaun didn't know which employee was out but he knew that Robert had taken the shift at the last minute.

Shaun told him something else: the BNSF work truck in the garage, like all trucks, was equipped with a forward facing camera that activates during accidents. It may have captured something.

When the processing of the scene was complete, the body was released to the coroner's investigator, who put bags over the hands to preserve evidence and pulled the wallet from the victim's back pocket. The driver's license confirmed what Shaun Ware had said. The victim was Robert Limon, age 38, with a home address on Strawberry Lane in Helendale.

The coroner investigator and two other body removal assistants placed the corpse into a blue body bag and sealed it with a tag. Robert Limon—husband, father and railroad worker—was now coroner number C01615-14.

One of the cell phones in the office belonged to Robert. It had several missed phone calls and text messages. The last text came at 8:30 p.m.: "Babe I'm worried about you. Call me. Leanna wants to say goodnight."

Det. Randall Meyer would find out that the text had come from Robert's wife, now widow.

It was never returned.

http://wbp.bz/boda

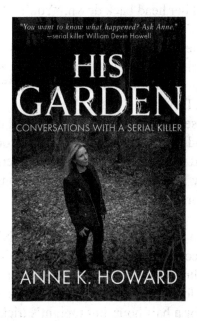
1.

July 25, 2003

The monster stirred inside him. Most times, he could tame it. Keep it hidden. Silence its screams. But tonight, the beast demanded release.

She lifted her head up. "You're taking too long. I'm done."

He pressed her head back down. "You're done when I say you're done …"

She wriggled beneath the firmness of his grip. "No!" she protested, forcing herself up from his lap. She stared him straight in the eyes—defiant and unafraid. "That's all I'm doing for you, Devin."

His calloused fingertips nervously tapped the upholstered backbench and his spine tingled with an odd mixture of excitement and fear. The beast was rising. There was no going back. Not now. Not ever. "Rape her," the monster instructed. "Rape the whore!"

*

It had been a long night of hustling for Nilsa Arizmendi and Angel "Ace" Sanchez. Maybe it was the hot weather, but the regular johns were being especially cheap and irritable, and Nilsa was forced to negotiate smaller fees. Ordinarily, she charged $30 for a half hour, but tonight's tricks were turning a maximum of only $20 and some demanded blowjobs for a measly 10 bucks. Like shrewd customers at a turn-of-the-century street market, the johns knew that the vendor in question was desperate for cash.

Ace loitered around the corners of New Britain Avenue, where his girlfriend worked. He stared glumly at the filthy surroundings, trying not to think about Nilsa's activities. He did not like their lifestyle. In fact, he despised it. But how else could he and Nilsa score drugs? The couple's shared habit was not cheap. In July 2003, they were each smoking about 20 to 30 pieces of crack per day and shooting up a bundle-and-a-half of heroin, which translated to about 10 to 15 bags on the streets. Sometimes, Nilsa used up to three bundles of heroin a day, depending on the amount of crack she smoked. It was a nasty cycle. The crack got Nilsa and Ace ramped up and wired and the heroin brought them down. They needed both to survive.

Without the drugs, sickness set in. Being drug sick was terrible—worse than having the flu. In the darkness of their motel room, the childhood sweethearts huddled together in sweat-soaked sheets, shivering with nausea and chills. Every joint and bone ached as invisible bugs furiously crawled beneath the surface of their skin. In between fits of vomiting, their bowels loosened and the bed became soiled. Nilsa kept the curtains drawn and placed the Do Not Disturb sign on the outside door handle for days at a time. The room was a mess. Their lives were a mess. Besides the incessant and all-consuming craving for heroin, she felt shame.

"This shit has to stop," Ace thought as he watched Nilsa emerge from the back seat of an old man's car. She walked toward him, tucked her tie-dyed T-shirt into her dungaree shorts and offered a faint smile. Normally 140 pounds, the 5'2", dark-haired woman was now only skin and bones. "I'm tired," she said. "Let's go home."

On the walk back, Nilsa briefly disappeared and scored a blast of crack at Goodwin Park in Hartford. She returned to Ace and attempted to take his hand. He pulled away. "I'm done with this shit. You gotta go to rehab, Nilsa. We both gotta go."

She acted like she did not hear him. It was usually the best way to avoid a fight.

But tonight, Ace would not let up. "I'm done with the fucking drugs," he mumbled, running his hand through his greasy dark hair. Normally, he kept it long, but a few days before, he had cut it short. "Done with the hustling. Fuck. Fuck this shit."

Their shadowy figures forged into the night, softly illuminated by the neon lights of outdated motels. Rolling hills of forest stood far in the distance, strangely comforting and yet somehow sinister. When Nilsa's high wore down, they started to quarrel. This time, Ace would not take no for an answer. They both had to go to rehab in the morning.

Nilsa was reluctant. She had been in and out of rehab for years and it never did her any good. Still, she loved her four children and desperately wanted to be done with the drugs and get clean forever and for good. Overhead, the night sky opened and a warm drizzle began to fall. The blue rock watch on Nilsa's frail wrist ticked into the early morning hours. They walked southbound along the pike, past Cedar Hill Cemetery containing the corpses of Connecticut's affluent class, including legendary actress Katharine Hepburn, and then a smaller cemetery containing the remains of lesser-known citizens.

Ace gently elbowed Nilsa. "You gonna start singing?"

She sometimes sang Christian hymns that she learned in childhood as they walked along the pike. It passed the time and gave them both a sense of comfort in the midst of all the pain. She smiled beneath the foggy moonlight. "You want me to?"

"You know I like your voice," he replied.

Her smooth, clear voice chimed like a bell into the darkness of the night:

O Lord my God, When I in awesome wonder,
Consider all the worlds Thy Hands have made;
I see the stars, I hear the rolling thunder,
Thy power throughout the universe displayed.

By the time they reached the parking lot of the Stop & Shop in Wethersfield, Ace had persuaded Nilsa to agree to the plan. Nilsa was worthy of a long and healthy life. After all, Ace needed her. Her mother needed her. *Her children needed her.* She vowed to never turn another trick again or inject poison into her veins. The party was over and fuck her if it had not been the party from Hell.

Nilsa eyed a lone vehicle parked in the far corner of the store's lot. "That's Devin's van."

"Let's get back to the motel," Ace said.

"I'm just gonna say hi."

Nilsa walked across the lot to the beat-up blue van owned by their mutual acquaintance, Devin Howell. They had met Howell a few months before. At the time, he was pumping gas at the Exxon gas station on the corner of Broad Street and New Britain Avenue. The rain was heavy and Ace and Nilsa were soaking wet as they approached Howell's van and asked for a ride to their motel room on the Berlin Turnpike in Wethersfield. "We'll give you five bucks," Ace said.

Howell had to go to Lowe's to price out some supplies for an upcoming job. He was driving in that direction anyway, so it was not a problem to assist two near-strangers who appeared down on their luck. "Yeah, sure. The door's unlocked."

Nilsa and Ace squeezed into the bucket seat on the passenger side. Nilsa used her street name, Maria, when she introduced herself to Howell. As they drove to The Almar Motel, Howell told the couple in his mild Southern drawl that he had a lawn-care business. Ace glanced over his shoulder at the back of the van. The space was large, with a long bench sofa littered with lawn service tools and clothing. The stench of body odor pervaded the vehicle's interior.

When they arrived at the motel, Ace and Nilsa invited Howell into their room to hang out. Howell brought some beer and marijuana. Nilsa and Ace offered to share a little crack, but Howell refused. He was a weed and booze guy. Together, the three got high on their poisons of choice. Howell told them that he was living in his van and he often parked it at the Stop & Shop parking lot in Wethersfield. He left the motel less than an hour later. As he drove back to the Stop & Shop lot to bed down for the night, he glanced at the open ashtray and saw that a $20 bill rolled up inside of it was gone. "No fucking good deed goes unpunished," he cynically thought. Ace and Nilsa had ripped him off.

In the months that followed, the occasional contact with Howell proved beneficial to Nilsa and Ace. The couple had lived on the Berlin Turnpike for the last 18 months or so, first at The Elm Motel and then at The Almar. Their daily routine involved walking from the motel on the pike to the familiar section of New Britain Avenue in Hartford where Nilsa turned tricks, about 1½ miles from The Almar. Ace had not worked a job for seven or eight months and he no longer had a vehicle of his own. Especially in the cold weather, Nilsa and Ace relied on acquaintances to spot them walking along the busy roadway and offer a lift. Occasionally, they had money for a cab, but that meant less money for drugs.

Howell also proved useful in assisting Nilsa and Ace to cop drugs. He did not mind driving them to local dealers living 15 to 20 minutes away. He would not get high with them when they scored. He seemed content to do them a favor by giving them a ride in exchange for a few dollars. All told, Howell served as the couple's makeshift Uber driver on about five occasions over the course of one month.

At approximately 2:45 a.m. on July 25, 2003, Ace watched Nilsa's skeletal form traipse across the empty parking lot. It was hard for him to believe that this was the same woman whose weight had sky-rocketed to 180 pounds when she was last released from federal prison—all beefed up by the cheap, starchy food. Nilsa stopped at the van and appeared to talk to Howell, who sat in the driver's seat. Then she walked around the van and got into the passenger side. Howell turned on the engine and slowly drove away. It was the last time Ace would see Nilsa alive.

*

When Christ shall come, with shout of acclamation,
And take me home, what joy shall fill my heart.
Then I shall bow, in humble adoration,
And then proclaim: "My God, how great Thou art!"

Nilsa "Coco" Arizmendi, Jan. 29, 1970–July 25, 2003
Rest In Peace

2.

It's a strange thing, writing letters to an alleged serial killer. Stranger still is reading the letters that he writes back.

When I first contacted William Devin Howell in July 2015, he was serving a 15-year sentence for the murder of Nilsa Arizmendi. Howell had yet to be charged with the murders of six other victims whose bones were found in the same wooded area behind the strip mall in New Britain. Nonetheless, the tone of his first letter to me indicated that he knew that the remaining charges were about to slam down upon him with the force of a sledgehammer.

Two months earlier, Howell's image had been smeared across local and national news channels when Chief State's Attorney Kevin Kane named him as the main suspect in the New Britain serial killings. Kane's announcement was a long time coming. Howell told me that two years earlier, he refused to speak with police officers about the accusations without a lawyer present. His refusal to speak resulted in Howell being stripped of his industry job in prison as a kind of punishment by the Department of Corrections (D.O.C.).

While not a big deal to a prison outsider, for an inmate who lives for a few extra dollars a week to purchase better quality soap or tinned spicy tuna at the prison commissary, it was a grave loss for Howell. He took pride in having an industry job. It paid a whopping $1 an hour compared to typical prison jobs that pay 75 cents a day. Howell explained to me that he had worked all his life, whether in lawn care or a pizza parlor or a 7-Eleven in Florida. No job was beneath him and it discouraged him to be sitting in isolation doing nothing.

In April 2015, after speaking with one of Howell's former cellmates, Jonathan Mills, who told investigators that Howell confessed many details of the crimes to him, police obtained a search warrant for Howell's cell at Garner Correctional Institution in Newtown, Conn., where he was being held at the time. The search warrant detailed items taken from the inmate's cell: a newspaper article about the death penalty in Florida; a notebook with handwritten entries that referenced darkvomit.com, a website that sold memorabilia associated with serial killers and other notorious murderers; and a cell phone bill from July 2003 with words written by Howell, "This just shows the day after I killed."

The newspaper article about the death penalty in Florida prompted authorities to look into whether Howell was behind the unsolved murder of April Marie Stone, 21, who went missing on Jan. 14, 1991, after she was seen walking along a state highway in South Apopka, Fla. Her body was found two days later beside a dirt road in nearby Sanford. She had been stabbed to death and wrapped in a blanket. At the time of the killing, Howell was living about 15 miles away in a trailer in Casselberry with his girlfriend, Mandy, and their infant son. A few months after police found Stone, Howell was charged with soliciting prostitution in Altamonte Springs, the next town over from Casselberry. He had approached the undercover officer in a blue Ford pickup truck and offered her $15 for oral sex, according to the arrest report. He entered a plea of guilty and avoided jail time by paying a fine. It was not until 2015, after Howell was charged with murdering six more victims found behind the strip mall in New Britain, that law enforcement looked into the possibility that he may have been behind Stone's murder in Florida, years before. Investigators in Florida looked into the matter, but did not find any evidence linking Howell to Stone's murder.

I never thought that Howell was behind the slaying of April Stone. She was not part of what appeared to be his target group—prostitutes, many with substance abuse issues—and her body, though wrapped in a blanket, was not buried. Additionally, although Howell had been accused of grisly atrocities—including slicing the fingertips of one of his victims and dismantling her jaw, death by stabbing did not conform to his apparent modus operandi.

I took a deep breath before writing my first letter to Howell, fully aware that I was about to step aboard Ozzy's proverbial Crazy Train with no hope of escape in the years ahead. Here is my letter of introduction:

July 19, 2015
RE: Correspondence and Visitation
Dear Mr. Howell:

I am doing some research and writing about the unsolved murders in New Britain. Since you are the main suspect, I would very much like to correspond with you and meet with you to discuss the allegations. Juliana Holcomb, the daughter of your ex-girlfriend Dorothy, describes you as a "kind-hearted giant." In personal photos, you appear to be a friendly individual who would not harm a fly. I would like to hear your side of the story in this matter.

Please write to me and let me know if I can get on your visitation list. I am a practicing attorney. However, I have no desire to become involved in any of the legal aspects of your incarceration. In my capacity as a journalist, I simply want to hear your side of the story.

Sincerely:
Anne K. Howard
Attorney at Law

And so began my relationship with a man that I believed would one day take the title of Connecticut's most prolific serial killer.

http://wbp.bz/hisgardena

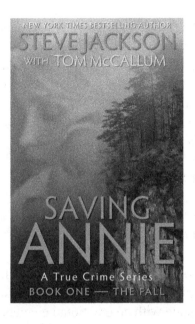

SAVING ANNIE: A TRUE STORY by STEVE JACKSON

http://wbp.bz/savingannie1

Read A Sample Next

CHAPTER ONE-*The 911 Call*

March 16, 2009
Hood River County, Oregon
6:09 p.m.

When the 911 call came into the Hood River Sheriff's Office, it wasn't so much what the caller said, but how he said it. His voice neither rose nor fell as he phlegmatically relayed the information.

911 OPERATOR: *"911, where is your emergency?*
CALLER: *"Hello. I need help. I'm at, uh, Eagle Creek."*
911 OPERATOR: *"Okay, and what's going on there?"*
CALLER: *"My girlfriend fell off the cliff. I hiked back. And I'm in my car."*
911 OPERATOR: *"Okay. You're at the Eagle Creek Trailhead right now?"*
CALLER: *"Yeah."*
911 OPERATOR: *"Okay, and where on the trail did she fall?"*
CALLER: *"I don't know. I think about a mile up."*
911 OPERATOR: *"Okay."*

The 911 operator thought it was odd. That he was odd. Normally people calling 911 to report a traumatic event are in an agitated state with an emotional element in their speech ranging from weeping to a rapid-fire data dump to shouting or screaming. This guy might as well have been reading a manual on how to change a sparkplug.

CALLER: *"I hiked down and got her, uh, and I'm in my car now, and I don't know if I ...* (unintelligible)"
911 OPERATOR: *"Okay."*
CALLER: *"... suffering from hypothermia. I don't think it's that cold but ..."*
911 OPERATOR: *"Okay, so she fell off the trail down a cliff, and then you went down the cliff and pulled her, brought her back up onto the trail?"*
CALLER: *"No she's dead."*

There was a stunned pause as the operator absorbed his last statement; 911 callers in emergency situations tend to get to the point right away and gush with information. But this was more worried about telling her in his flat, monotone voice that he was cold than that his girlfriend had just died. And every time the operator tried to get more details about the victim, he turned the conversation back to his needs.

CALLER: *"I went down to get her. I went to the bottom. Then in the river (unintelligible) took me about an hour to get to her. I finally go over to her, then I was startin' to shake. I got too cold, so I'm, uh, now, I just got to my car, and I need someone to come and help me ... Please send someone I'm at, uh ..."*

911 OPERATOR: *"Okay, hang on just a minute ..."*

CALLER: *"... Eagle Creek."*

911 OPERATOR: *"... one second."*

CALLER: *"Okay."*

911 OPERATOR: *"And what's, what's your name, sir?"*

CALLER: *"Steve."*

911 OPERATOR: *"Okay Steve, what is, um ..."*

CALLER: *"I'm freezing. Will you please send someone?"*

911 OPERATOR: *"Um, hang on just one second for me, okay?"*

CALLER: *"All right."*

911 OPERATOR: *"Steve, what is your last name?"*

CALLER: *"Nichols."*

911 OPERATOR: *"And what's her name, Steve?"*

CALLER: *"Rhonda."*

911 OPERATOR: *"Rhonda's last name?"*

CALLER: *"Casto."*

911 OPERATOR: *"Could you spell that for me please?"*

CALLER: *"R-H-O-N-D-A ... C-A-S-T-O."*

911 OPERATOR: *"Do you need an ambulance? Do you feel like you might need medical attention?"*

CALLER: *"I don't know if I'm shaking from, I don't know ... I'm really cold."*

911 OPERATOR: *"Okay, okay, Steve."*

CALLER: *"I'm just really cold."*

911 OPERATOR: *"Are you able to start the car and get warm?"*

CALLER: *"Yeah, the ..."*

911 OPERATOR: *"Blankets?"*

CALLER: *"... car is running."*

911 OPERATOR: *"And now Steve, I know this is a difficult question for you to answer for me, but what makes you think she was deceased?"*

CALLER: *"I don't know it for sure. I stayed with her for about an hour and a half, and I gave her mouth-to-mouth, and I tried covering up her leg. There was blood coming out of her leg, and I just sat and helped her, and then I started shaking uncontrollably, so ... (unintelligible)"*

911 OPERATOR: *"Okay."*

CALLER: *"Had to go back, and ..."*

911 OPERATOR: *"Was she breathing when you left her?"*

CALLER: *"No."*

911 OPERATOR: *"Do you know if she had a pulse?"*

CALLER: *"Uh, no, I don't think so."*

911 OPERATOR: *"Okay, Steve, we have an officer who's on his way."*

CALLER: *"All right. How long ... how long will it take an ambulance to get here?"*

911 OPERATOR: *"It'll take just a minute. Would you like an ambulance for you?"*

CALLER: *"Uh, uh ..."*

911 OPERATOR: *"If there's a question, I can send them, and, um, then you can decide not to go with them if that's what you choose to do."*

CALLER: *"Just so cold. That's the thing, I'm cold. ... How long will it take to the police car to get here?"*

911 OPERATOR: *"They're on their way, okay? Hang on just a second. How far down the trail, how far over the cliff is she?"*

CALLER: *"Uh, I don't know, like a hundred feet ..."*

911 OPERATOR: *"A hundred feet, okay."*

CALLER: *"I don't know."*

911 OPERATOR: *"Steve, how old are you?"*

CALLER: *"Uh, 34."*

911 OPERATOR: *"I'm going to send the ambulance for you, okay?"*

CALLER: *"All right."*

911 OPERATOR: *"Hang on just a second for me. You're going to hear some silence, okay?"*

CALLER: *"Okay."*

The caller waited patiently and quietly for the 911 operator to get back on the line. When she did, she assured him that the ambulance was on its way and she would stay on the line with him until somebody got there.

CALLER: *" 'kay."*

911 OPERATOR: *"And we have an officer on his way from Hood River."*

CALLER: *"Where's that?"*

911 OPERATOR: *"Hood River? Um, it's about twenty minutes away, but he's on his way, about seven minutes ago, okay, and we have an officer coming from Corbett. Do you know where that's at?"*

CALLER: *"No I don't."*

911 OPERATOR: *"He's a little closer so he'll be there shortly."*

CALLER: *"Okay."*

911 OPERATOR: *"So I'm going to stay on the phone with you. Are you getting any warmer in the vehicle with the heat on, Steve?"*

CALLER: *"No but I have it on full so that should heat up."*

911 OPERATOR: *"Are you in wet clothes at all?"*

CALLER: *"Tried to ... (unintelligible) ... up river. Uh, was too strong, so ..."*

911 OPERATOR: *"Are you able to get your wet clothes off and put something else warmer on?"*

CALLER: *"Yeah ... (unintelligible) ... shirt off."*

911 OPERATOR: *"You what? You have warmer clothes to put on or dry clothes at least?*

The caller was silent.

911 CALLER: *"Steve?*

Still no answer.

911 OPERATOR: *"... Steve? ... Steve?"*

CALLER: *"Yeah, that helps. ... How far away is he?"*

911 OPERATOR: *"He said just a few minutes."*

CALLER: *"Okay."*

911 OPERATOR: *"Are you there?"*

CALLER: *"Yeah."*

911 OPERATOR: *"Hang on just a second for me, okay?"*

There were several more pauses over the next couple of minutes as the operator checked with law enforcement and the ambulance crew. Again, the caller patiently waited for her return and would then inquire as to when someone would be there to help him. He never once said anything about his girlfriend without being asked a direct question.

CALLER: *"What time is it?"*

911 OPERATOR: *"It's 6:18. They're going to be there in a few minutes, okay?"*

CALLER: *"Okay."*

911 OPERATOR: *"So Steve, how far up the trail did you say she is?"*

CALLER: *"I don't know. I think a mile."*

911 OPERATOR: *"Okay. What was she wearing?"*

CALLER: *"Uh, jeans. ... I don't know the top. ... She put on my shirt, but I think she put one over ..."*

911 OPERATOR: *"Okay. They're on their way, okay?"*

CALLER: *"Yeah."*

911 OPERATOR: *"Hang on one second for me, Steve, okay?"*

CALLER: *"Mm hmm."*

The 911 OPERATOR spoke to one of the responding officers: *"Brandon ... (unintelligible) ... responding? I have a hypothermic guy sitting in his car."*

The 911 OPERATOR then addressed the caller. *"They're on their way, okay."*

THE CALLER: *"Uh huh."*

911 OPERATOR: *"They're on their way. They said less than five minutes, okay? He'll be there in just a couple of minutes."*

THE CALLER: *"All right."*

The operator asked a few more perfunctory questions, such as date of birth for both the caller, January 4, 1975, and his girlfriend, July 2, 1985. The operator then attempted to gather more details about the "accident."

911 OPERATOR: *"Do you know what made her fall, Steve? Did she lose her footing, or did she get hurt? ... Do you know why she fell?"*

CALLER: *"I think she's high on something."*

911 OPERATOR: *"Have you done any drugs or alcohol today?"*

CALLER: *"No."*

911 OPERATOR: *"What do you think she's high on?"*

CALLER: *"I don't know. She always hides that stuff from me."*

911 OPERATOR: *"Okay. Are you doing okay?"*

CALLER: *"Yeah, I'm warming up a little."*

911 OPERATOR: *"Oh, you're ..."*

CALLER: *"Shaking. ... I can't stop shaking."*

911 OPERATOR: *"The ambulance is on its way. It will be there in a few minutes."*

CALLER: *"Uh huh."*

Again the 911 OPERATOR broke to speak to the responding officers: *"Are you guys aware of what's going on?"* After speaking to them, she returned to the CALLER: *"Did you leave anything on the trail showing where she went down over the cliff? ... Did you leave a backpack or anything there?"*

CALLER: *"No, I left my backpack ...* (unintelligible) *... farther down, so I could go down. But then when I made my way back up, I got it. ... Only thing I left was my sweatshirt."*

911 OPERATOR: *"You left your sweatshirt there on the trail?"*

CALLER: *"No that was down by the river. ... It's close to where she is, but that's where I went in the river. ... The policeman's here."*

911 OPERATOR: *"Okay. I'll go ahead and let you go."*

CALLER: *"Okay."*

911 OPERATOR: *"Okay."*

CALLER: *"Thank you very much."*

911 OPERATOR: *"You're welcome."*

CALLER: *"Bye."*

911 OPERATOR: *"Bye bye."*

With that exchange of pleasantries, the call ended. A young mother was dead. But the important thing, at least according to the 911 call, was that her boyfriend was cold.

CHAPTER TWO—*First Responders*

Eagle Creek Trailhead
6:28 p.m.

When Hood River Sheriff's Office Deputy Marc A. Smith heard the 911 operator's radio dispatch that a woman had fallen from the Eagle Creek Trail and that her boyfriend was possibly suffering from exposure, it came as no great surprise. Every year deputies from the sheriffs' offices in Hood River and Multnomah, the two counties responsible for law enforcement in that part of the Columbia River Gorge Scenic Area, participated in about thirty search and rescue missions to assist injured, lost, or simply ill-equipped hikers.

Sometimes people died on the trails through falls, loose rocks, heart attacks, or one of the biggest threats in that climate, hypothermia, a potentially fatal drop in body temperature due to exposure. The Eagle Creek trail had its share of fatalities due to its natural splendor, easy access, and proximity to a city.

The trailhead was located about forty miles east of Portland and a half-mile off Interstate 84, the east-west corridor that parallels the Columbia River. It's one of the most beautiful hikes in Oregon, climbing through a primordial Pacific Northwest rainforest along a 24-mile path that leads to a half-dozen waterfalls, bridges a spectacular gorge, and even burrows through 120-feet of rock behind thundering Tunnel Falls.

The trail starts off along Eagle Creek, which is a typical stream for the area—vigorous, boulder-strewn and littered with logs and debris—cutting noisily through a steep-sided gorge on its way to the Columbia. But the stream and trail soon part as the path begins to climb along a slope populated by moss-draped cedars, Douglas Fir, and a variety of hardwood trees that provide a thick and brooding canopy over maidenhair ferns and impenetrable undergrowth.

It's not a tough hike. The first four miles up to Punchbowl Falls is rated by online trail guides as an "easy to moderate" climb, gaining 500 feet in elevation, with footing that ranges from a smooth, gently-sloping forest path to broken chunks of rock that hikers must pick through to avoid a turned ankle.

This initial portion of the trail is generally safe, traveled without incident by numerous families and hikers of all ages and abilities, but there is one area that deserves caution. Slightly less than a mile from the parking lot, the trail grows suddenly steeper and narrows as it traverses a cliff 300 feet above the gorge floor. There's even a hand rail of cable and pipe fastened to the rock face on one side for those intimidated by the precipice on the other. It's with this spot in mind that the trail guides warn that children and dogs should be supervised.

If the caller, who'd identified himself as Stephen Nichols, was right, it was in that area where his girlfriend, Rhonda Casto, had fallen.

A 10-year veteran with sheriff's Office, Smith had been driving back to Hood River from the state capital of Salem and was near the town of Corbett when he heard the call come over the radio. He knew that sheriff's investigator Matt English was on his way, but realizing he was closer than his colleague, Smith had radioed that he would respond as well. Pulling into the trailhead parking lot, Smith noted there were two cars: an unoccupied, maroon-colored mini-van with Washington plates; and the blue Mazda the caller had identified. Getting out of his own car, the deputy saw a male sitting in the driver's seat of the Mazda, his head on the steering wheel. The occupant didn't have a shirt on and was covering his upper body with a blanket.

The man didn't appear to notice him when Smith walked up, so the deputy knocked on the driver's side window. Even then the occupant was slow to respond, but he at last rolled the window down partway. He was still on his cellphone with the 911 operator: "The policeman's here. … Thank you very much. … Bye bye."

Smith introduced himself and ascertained that the man's name was Stephen Nichols. The deputy could see that

Nichols' hair and pants were wet. He wasn't wearing any shoes or socks either. The deputy cautioned Nichols to stay warm and offered his fleece coat.

"When will the medics get here?" Nichols asked.

"They're on their way and will be here in a few minutes," Smith replied. He indicated the front passenger seat. "Mind if I sit down while we talk?" Nichols leaned over and unlocked the passenger side door.

Entering the car, Smith removed a wet t-shirt from the seat and place it on the floorboard. Nichols explained that it was wet because he tried to swim upstream to reach his girlfriend, Rhonda Casto. "There's probably some blood on it from me giving her mouth-to-mouth resuscitation," he added.

"How far up the trail did she fall?" the deputy asked.

"About a mile," Nichols said before describing how he'd then run back down the trail one-half to three-quarters of a mile before he could find a spot to scramble down to the creek. He then tried walking back along the bank, he said, but it was too rough. So he got in the stream and attempted to "swim." This, too, proved difficult and he climbed back out to walk.

Nichols also repeated his story about trying to give her mouth-to-mouth resuscitation. "But she was dead."

At one point during their conversation, Nichols' cellphone rang. He looked at the Caller ID but didn't answer. He told Smith that the caller was Rhonda's mother, Julia Simmons, who was watching the couple's nine-month-old daughter, Annie.

"I don't know how to tell her or Rhonda's sister, Melanie, that Rhonda's dead," Nichols said.

Smith assured him that either he or some other law enforcement official would inform Rhonda's family. "You don't need to talk to them right now."

While questioning Nichols, the deputy noted that the young man seemed withdrawn and didn't readily offer any information, but rather had to be drawn out with questions. He also alternated between a somber expression and sobbing.

An ambulance from the Cascade Locks Fire and EMS arrived. Nichols got out of the car and headed for the medical team. In the ambulance, paramedic Wayne Overcash took five tympanic (ear) temperature measurements between 6:34 p.m. and 6:52 p.m., all of them either 36 degrees or 37 degrees Celsius.

Normal tympanic body temperature is 35.5 to 37.5 degrees Celsius. Readings of 32 to 35 degrees is considered "mild hypothermia" with symptoms being shivering and slurred speech, but alert;" 28 to 32 is considered "moderate" and symptoms of "sleepiness" but no shivering; and 20-28 is severe. The body temperature of Nichols, who Overcash noted was "verbal and alert," was normal.

When Nichols exited the Mazda to go to the ambulance, Smith got out as well and looked at the back seat. He saw a pair of wet hiking boots and a woman's purse on the floorboard in the back; a backpack that also appeared to be wet was sitting on the seat.

Soon after Nichols got in the ambulance, Deputy Matt English arrived. He spoke briefly with Smith and got Nichols' account of the "accident." Then, while Smith joined Nichols in the ambulance to continue the questioning, English talked to Cascade Locks Fire Chief Jeff Pritcher, who was preparing to hike up the Eagle Creek trail with a Cascade Locks Fire department volunteer, Zach Pardue, to locate the victim.

Both men were also members of the Hood River Crag Rats, the oldest volunteer search and rescue organization in the United State, and especially trained for technical rock-climbing and avalanche rescues. With twilight fading and night falling, the pair left the parking lot at 6:38 p.m.

Back in the ambulance, Smith asked Nichols what his girlfriend had been wearing. He was given a brief description of "jeans" and that she had blond hair. The deputy then asked what happened to cause her to fall.

"She must have been high on something," Nichols said. "She was just flying around."

Rhonda had been about fifty feet in front of him, Nichols explained, and heading down the trail. He said he was trying to catch up to her when she suddenly plunged off the cliff. He said that when he reached that spot he looked over the edge and saw her "lying in the water" and screamed. That's when he ran down the trail to find a place where he could get to the stream.

Nichols also gave a rough description of the spot where his girlfriend fell, saying it was between two sets of cables attached to the rock face along the trail. He said she fell about 3 p.m.

After providing his and Rhonda's personal information, and stating that they lived together, Nichols was asked if he knew what made her "high." He said he didn't know but that she'd had a drug problem in the past.

Detective Sergeant Gerry Tiffany, the senior detective on the small Hood River Sheriff's Office staff, arrived. After obtaining Nichols' consent, he and Deputy English began to search the car while Smith continued his interrogation.

Nichols told him that he'd known his girlfriend for about four and a half years, living together for four of it. He also said that he and Rhonda had hiked the trail before, and that she had been on it "frequently" prior to knowing him. "She used to come up here to drink vodka and take pills," he asserted.

At that point, the ambulance crew said they'd be taking Nichols to the hospital for further evaluation. Nichols asked if he could retrieve his cellphone from his car, but Smith told him that he'd bring it and his wallet to him at the hospital. The ambulance then departed at 7:03 for the twenty-minute ride.

Smith then returned to Nichols' car where the other officers were searching the contents. They gave him a bottle for a prescription made out to Rhonda Casto that had been located in her purse. They'd also located a checkbook belonging to Nichols, noting he'd recently written a check to the Oregon Department of Revenue for more than $20,000, and that was another check $1600 check for "child support." The searchers also found a small card from a jewelry store with various diamond cuts and sizes on it.

Taking the prescription bottle, as well as Nichols' wallet and cellphone, Smith was about to leave for the hospital when Tiffany told him to question Nichols again about his relationship with his girlfriend.

Arriving at the hospital, Smith was met by emergency room doctor Phil Chadwick, who asked about weather conditions at Eagle Creek and Nichols' physical behavior when he was being questioned. The deputy reported that Nichols shivered, though not all of the time, and that he switched back and forth between an oddly flat demeanor and voice, and sudden sobbing.

Smith showed Chadwick the prescription bottle for *Gabapentin* and was told it was an anti-seizure/anti-depressant medication. The deputy then asked to speak with Nichols.

When Smith entered the examining room, he handed over the cellphone. Nichols looked at it and told the deputy that Rhonda's mother, Julia Simmons, had tried to call several times and had texted once asking where they were. He again expressed concern about her being told of her daughter's death.

Smith asked for Simmons's address so she could be notified. But Nichols said he didn't know it, though he could personally find her house in Hillsboro, Oregon.

The deputy then asked Nichols to again go over the events leading to Rhonda's fall. Nichols said that they'd arrived at the trailhead about 2 p.m. "We're trying to lose some weight by hiking," he said.

They got as far as Punchbowl Falls before turning around and heading back down the trail. On the way back, he said, Rhonda started acting like "Super Girl," running down the trail, forcing him to hurry to catch up. Then when he reached her, she'd take off again. He repeated his assertion that she was "high" on something and that she'd run ahead fifty feet when she slipped and went over the edge at a narrow place on the trail.

Again, he recounted how he'd looked over the edge and saw her lying "in the water," not moving. After scrambling down to the stream, he said he got in and attempted to "swim" upstream for several minutes but that the current was too strong. He claimed that he then got up on the bank and made his way to her body where he gave her mouth-to-mouth resuscitation. But he soon realized she was dead and returned to the trailhead where he had cell service and called 911.

"What were the weather conditions like?" Smith asked.

Raining at times with some hail, Nichols replied. There was even snow on the sides of the trail, which he described as "wet and slippery." However, he noted, they both were wearing hiking shoes that were good for the conditions.

When Smith asked about his hiking activities, Nichols said he didn't do much. It was his fourth time on that trail but only the second time with Rhonda. He repeated his story that she'd been there frequently to drink vodka and take pills.

"How did you know she was high?" Smith asked.

Nichols said that he'd known her to do "everything under the sun," but she hadn't done drugs to his knowledge since the birth of their child. He wouldn't elaborate on the types of drugs she'd allegedly used.

"What about today specifically?"

Nichols shrugged. He hadn't seen her take, drink or smoke anything. However, he said, whenever she acted as she had prior to her fall, she was "usually on something."

Smith asked if Nichols knew if Rhonda was taking any prescription drugs. At first, Nichols denied it, but a few minutes later said she was taking something for post-partum depression. When the deputy showed him the anti-seizure medication bottle, he said he didn't know anything about it.

Moving on, Smith asked about his relationship with Rhonda. Nichols replied that the relationship was a good one. They'd had their arguments like any couple, he said, but denied they'd been fighting lately. He also said he'd never been physically abusive to her.

The deputy wanted to know if Rhonda had any injuries before her fall. "She was clumsy," Nichols answered. "Just this week she fell down for no reason in the bedroom. Two weeks ago she fell down the stairs and hit her head hard. ... She was always tripping and falling."

Other than the issue with post-partum depression, Rhonda was in good health, Nichols said. She'd seen her doctor a week earlier, but Nichols didn't recognize the doctor's name on the prescription bottle.

The interview ended with Smith asking what the couple did for a living. Nichols said he was a day trader; Rhonda mostly stayed home and took care of Annie.

About this time, Deputy English arrived, and Smith asked him to question Nichols again while he listened from another room. Nichols repeated his answers without deviating, except for one item.

When Nichols noted that Julia Simmons had continued trying to contact him, Smith told him that law enforcement had not been able to find her at the location he'd given them. Now, however, Nichols suddenly remembered that she was staying at his house watching Annie.

"Did she know you and Rhonda were going hiking?" English asked.

"She just knew we were going out for a few hours," Nichols replied, adding that Simmons didn't know they were going to hike on the Eagle Creek Trail.

Both Smith and English would note in their subsequent reports that throughout the questioning that Nichols had remained withdrawn and somber. He'd answered their questions unemotionally and without volunteering any information unless they asked a direct question.

After English finished questioning him, Nichols asked if he could make a call from his cellphone. He was told he could make any call he pleased.

Nichols said he wanted called his father, Stephen P. Nichols Sr., who lived in Bend, Oregon, a mid-sized city in Central Oregon about a three-and-a-half hour drive from Hood River. Nichols placed his call and reached some unknown person with whom he made some small talk as the deputies listened. He then told the person on the other end that he needed to talk to his father because Rhonda had died. The call was brief, as was Nichols' crying during it.

After he hung up, he asked if Rhonda's mother had been notified of her death. And if he was free to go.

About 8:30 p.m., Dr. Chadwick said Nichols could go. His body temperature readings had all been normal, and other than a small bruise on the palm of his left hand, he had no other injuries despite "scrambling" down a steep incline, attempting to swim a vigorous, debris-filled stream, and then working his way through brush, fallen trees and rocks to reach his girlfriend.

English and Nichols left the hospital to return the latter to his car at the trailhead. On the way, the detective called the Washington County Sheriff's Office and requested that they contact Simmons at Nichol's house.

During the drive, Nichols said he wanted to drive home. English replied that the deputies were concerned with him operating a motor vehicle after all he had been through. But Nichols assured him that although he was "sad like when my mom died" and depressed, he was fine to drive. He said he just wanted to go meet his father so that he could help him with Annie.

Upon arriving back at the trailhead, English and Nichols found Sheriff Jerry Wampler waiting. He was there to check on the search and recovery effort.

Wampler and English reiterated the concern with Nichols driving. However, when he insisted, the sheriff said that English would follow him as far as Cascade Locks to observe how he did on the road.

"I want you to wait for me there until we hear from Washington County that Rhonda's mother has been notified," English added.

When they reached Cascade Locks, Nichols parked near the deputy who could see him making phone calls. English called the Washington County Sheriff's Office and spoke to Corporal Scott Mikkelson, who told him that there'd been a holdup contacting the family because they couldn't locate a chaplain in case the family needed spiritual help. Mikkelson told him that Rhonda's family had filed a missing person report.

After waiting several more minutes, Nichols asked if he could leave. English said yes on the condition that he not go into his apartment until Rhonda's family had been notified. He promised to wait outside if he arrived before then.

English returned to the Hood River Sheriff's Office where he was contacted by Mikkelson a short time later. The other deputy told him that Rhonda's mother, Julia Simmons, had been notified "and things are not going well."

Without having been told any details beyond that she'd fallen from a cliff while hiking with Nichols, Rhonda's family believed that he was responsible for her death. "Apparently, he took a million-dollar life insurance policy out on her recently," Mikkelson said. "And they're saying that she told some of them that if something happened to her, or she died, he was responsible."

Hanging up with Mikkelson, English then asked dispatch to call Nichols and tell him the family had been notified. He then called Tiffany and Wampler to tell them about the insurance policy and the family's accusations.

Just three hours after Nichols called to report an "accident" that claimed the life of his child's mother, it was appeared that there might be an entirely different theory about what happened that afternoon on the Eagle Creek trail.

http://wbp.bz/savingannie1